EXPAND YOUR VOCABULARY

THE DYNAMIC IN-CONTEXT WAY

A Practical 40-Day Introduction to New Words
Plus
A Day-By-Day Commentary on
"Language Uses and Abuses"

Ray Nadeau

University Press of America, Inc.
Lanham • New York • London

Copyright © 1996 by
University Press of America,® Inc.
4720 Boston Way
Lanham, Maryland 20706

3 Henrietta Street
London, WC2E 8LU England

Library of Congress Cataloging-in-Publication Data

Nadeau, Ray E.
Expand your vocabulary : the dynamic in-context way : a practical 40-day introduction to new words plus a day-by-day commentary on "language uses and abuses: / Ray Nadeau.
    p.   cm.
Includes bibliographical references and index.
1. Vocabulary. 2. English language--Usage. I. Title.
PE1449.N33   1996   428.1 --dc20   96-31236 CIP

ISBN 0-7618-0462-5 (pbk: alk. ppr.)

Acknowledgment

My thanks to Julie LeBlanc, daughter and AT&T Systems Engineer, for providing her expertise on technical detail, for making suggestions on format, and for detecting errors in copy. She was ever available to discuss problems in those and other areas and to help find solutions for them. R.E.N.

CONTENTS I

Listed below are the context-passages from which the new words for this study have been selected. A complete citation for each passage appears with it at the beginning of study for a given Day.

Context-Passages

CONTENTS II—LANGUAGE USES AND ABUSES

This supplementary table of contents is a listing of the topics covered in the second part of the discussion for a given Day.

COMMUNICATING MORE EFFECTIVELY

In this age of information and high-tech, communicating effectively is not only a key to holding a job, but it's a key to advancement as well. On the job or looking for a job, you know that making the best impression possible is crucial to your future. And as you move up the job ladder, skills in both speaking and writing become increasingly important. Adding words to your vocabulary is basic to those skills; it enables you to interact more clearly and more vividly with subordinates, with co-workers, with superiors, and with small or large groups.

It's also a fact of life that the larger vocabulary of the successful person comes *before* his or her success, not after it. Although a wide vocabulary may not be *the* element of success, it is a vital one. That's why it's sound planning to get ready now for the next opportunities as they come along.

Why This Book?

This book is different from current vocabulary-building programs in two significant ways:

1. You become acquainted with new words in dynamic, real-action paragraph-length quotations rather than in static, separate, and unrelated sentences. As you read the context-paragraphs, all of them chosen for varied and interesting content, some of the words selected for study (those underlined) will be new to you, some you will be unsure about, and some you will already know. You will find, however, that most of the words classified as new will make valued additions to your vocabulary, either because you had not encountered them before or because you were uncertain about how to take advantage of them. If one or more of the words not underlined are also new to you, take advantage of the nearest dictionary to look them up and add them to your list of newly acquired word-choices.

2. You not only see those and other words in action but you also have the opportunity, through Day-by-Day sections on "Language Uses and Abuses," to check and improve the language patterns in which they will appear.

New Word-Choices

You will be gaining new word-choices...

First, through your becoming familiar with a selected list of quoted-in-context words. For just one example of the importance of context in determining meaning, *overture* means one thing on a concert program and something else as an offer of conciliation or friendship.

Secondly, through your using the origins of words as an aid to remembering meanings. For example, the word astronaut is based on the Greek *astron* for "star" and the Latin *nauta* for "sailor" Its meaning, then, is "star sailor" or "one who sails among the stars."

You'll shortly be doing some "sailing" of your own, this time among words; that experience could make you a fully qualified "word sailor" or verbonaut, based on the Latin *verbum* for "word" and, again, *nauta* for "sailor" (The frequency in this book of words of Latin or Greek origin reflects the fact that 55% of our vocabulary comes to us directly or indirectly through Latin and another 10% through Greek. For more information on the origins of our language, please see Appendix B.)

Thirdly, by your becoming acquainted with synonyms of a word, those words having the same or essentially the same meaning. You will already know some or all of the synonyms listed for a word; your knowing them will help you better understand the meaning of the word itself. Recognizing them will also make for variety in your word choices; once you've used a word in a paragraph, a synonym gives you another option for emphasizing the same idea.

Fourth, by your becoming acquainted with antonyms of a word, those words having meanings opposite to that of the word under study. Again, if you know some of the antonyms of a word, you have added keys to its meaning. And if you are discussing both "pros" and "cons" of an issue, antonyms can be essential.

Fifth, by your making a definite point of using at least one new word per day in conversation, or in speaking to a group, or in writing a personal or business letter. Using a new word is a sure way to make it a part of your working vocabulary.

Study Plan

Word analysis

The selection of a word for study is indicated by its being underlined in a given paragraph and then listed below it. These details follow:

Pronunciation. If a word has one accented syllable, that syllable appears in caps (e.g., dih-SWAYD for *dissuade*). If a longer word has one or more minor accents, each is underlined (e.g., res-to-RAY-shun for *restoration*). This pronunciation system features a simple, sounds-of-speech approach; it requires no pronunciation key.

Definition. To keep definitions both clear and brief, plural nouns and adjectives are listed as singulars; verbs are listed in their simplest forms. The primary meaning given for a word—and sometimes the only one—is that for the word as used in the passage.

Sources. Among the other-language sources of a word, you will often see Latin present participles (for which the abbreviation is prp.). Active in voice, these participles end in *ans* or *ens*; for example, *volans*, flying, and *audiens*, listening. Latin past participles (abbreviation pp.) are mostly passive and end in *us* as in *monitus*, advised, and *captus*, seized. However, your main concern will be to see how a particular verb form affects meaning and, with the information provided for each word, you can do that very nicely without being an expert on participles.

From same base. If there are other words closely related to the one under study, they appear under the "same base" heading. The definition and derivation of a word like *ethnic*, for instance, is followed immediately by "From same base: ethnical, ethnically, ethnicity."

Synonyms, listed next, exist for almost all words.

Antonyms, if there are any, are listed last.

Related terms

As you work through the analysis of a word, you will often encounter these terms:

Prefix.   A prefix is a syllable or group of syllables added to the beginning of a word to modify or alter its meaning. For example, the verb *heat* means to make warmer; *preheat* (with prefix *pre*, before) means to heat or make warmer beforehand.   The word prefix itself means a particle of some kind "fixed" to the beginning of a word.

Combining form.   A combining form is an independently existing root word which, when combined with another independently existing root word, forms a new word. *Astronaut* as "star sailor" is a good example, and so is the word for "fear of strangers," *xenophobia* (*xeno*, stranger or foreigner, + *phobia*, fear).

If combining forms are involved in the comment on sources of a word, those forms are listed within parentheses. For example, the origin of the word *photograph* would appear as follows: From Greek *phos* (photo), light, + *graphia* (graph), writing or imprinting. Photo and graph are, of course, the combining forms. (In the Word Index to this book, combining forms are indicated by the abbreviation c\form.)

Suffix.   A suffix is a standard syllable or set of syllables added to the end of a word, primarily to help us recognize the part of speech to which the word belongs.   Typical noun endings are fief*dom*, ill*ness*, intern*ship*, invoca*tion*, equal*ity*, and infer*ence*.   Among adjective endings: ami*able*, use*less*, wonder*ful*, cred*ible*, and existenti*al*. Among verb endings: fratern*ize*, exempl*ify*, cogit*ate*, and soft*en*.   The common adverb ending is -*ly*. There is little emphasis on suffixes in this book.   The aim is to focus your attention on deciding what a new word means in a particular context, and that decision can normally be reached by determining how the pre-suffix part of the word should be interpreted.

Language Uses and Abuses

In this second section for a given Day, you will find either a short analysis of how some words are formed or comments on ways to check and, if need be, improve your language usages.

"I agree," you say, "that anyone can use a wider range of word choices to improve his or her communication. But no one has been critical of the way I use words or my language patterns, so why should I be concerned about them now?" The reason to be concerned is that no one of us is entirely free of questionable language usages, including a few outright mistakes. Friends do overlook a lack of finesse in certain aspects of one's language. But workplace associates, superiors, supervisors, employers, clients, and others are not so understanding. If, for example, you repeatedly add the unnecessary "you know," "I mean," "and so on," or any other constantly repeated phrase as a kind of vocal filler before or after every second or third phrase or sentence, you're not making an outright mistake, but you have a language habit which many people consider undesirable. Your business or professional image suffers accordingly.

Quick Checks on Comprehension

A particular Day's activity closes with brief comprehension checks of your understanding of the words you've covered. In addition to the words under direct study, you will come across other unfamiliar words here. Again, if you have the time, looking them up in a dictionary will give your growing "word treasury" a fine daily bonus.

Look, Listen, and List

To supplement study along the lines suggested above, you may want to work some of your daily reading and listening into the plan. One way to do that is to jot down and look up any new words you see in your newspaper or hear on TV and radio news-programs. You'll also find poor word-choices and inappropriate language in all media. Becoming conscious of those errors is another step toward eliminating them in your own speaking and writing.

Magazine articles, novels, and non-fiction books offer another route toward reaching your word and language goals. You're not going to stop in the middle of reading to consult a dictionary, but reading with a note pad at hand makes it easy to record a new word or phrase for later checking.

This book has been written in the hope that working with it will increase the overall numbers of words in your vocabulary, add to the variety of words available to you as choices in a given situation, sharpen your overall communication skills, and enhance your chances for advancement.

Happy sailing!

DAY 1

New Word-Choices
From Jeff Davidson, speech on "World Population and Your Life,"
Vital Speeches of the Day, 61 (June 15, 1995) 17, p. 518. f.

It took from the beginning of time until 1850 for the world population to reach one billion,...and by the middle of this decade [less than 150 years later] it will exceed six billion. Nothing has prepared us for such <u>explosive</u> population growth. Some of the early <u>economists</u> already predicted this would happen, and <u>prophesied</u> that we'd get to the point where population began to <u>outstrip</u> <u>planetary</u> resources. However, nobody wants to deal with the issue.

The biggest <u>detriment</u> to population planning is narrow-minded name-calling. Anytime someone comments about the need for population planning, he or she is labeled with <u>epithets</u>: <u>geneticist</u>, racist, God-player. If we don't plan for population, there will come a time when Nature takes care of things in a coldly efficient way; the population will crash. We need to realize that we've got a <u>finite</u> amount of space to manage on the earth.

explosive (ik-SPLOH-siv), having the nature of a sudden bursting forth. From Latin *explosus*, pp. of *explodere*, to drive off (an actor) by loud clapping, the Roman version of hissing.
<u>From same base</u>: explosively, explosiveness.
<u>Synonyms</u>: eruptive, loud, clangorous, deafening, resounding, stunning, glamorous, thunderous.
<u>Antonyms</u>: low-pitched, subdued, gentle, faint, inaudible, muffled, silent, quiet, hushed, noiseless.

economist (ih-KON-uh-mist), a specialist in the science of the production, distribution, and consumption of wealth. From Greek *oikonomia*, management of a household (*oikos*).
From same base: economy, economical, economically, economics, economize, economizing, economized.

prophesy (PROF-ih-sy), to predict a future event. From New Testament Greek, *propheteia*, the gift of speaking "as a prophet."
From same base: prophesying, prophesied, prophet, prophecy, prophetical, prophetically.
Synonyms: predict, presage, foretell, forecast, anticipate, envision.
Antonyms: disappoint, balk, frustrate, disillusion, disenchant.

outstrip (owt-STRIP), to exceed, surpass. From Old English *ut* up, away, + *strepen*, to strip away.
From same base: outstripping, outstripped.
Synonyms: outrun, outpace, outstride, outdistance, override, eclipse, surmount, surpass.
Antonyms: revert, relapse, reverse, backslide, recede, retreat, retire.

planetary (PLAN-ih-tehr-ee), having to do with one or more of the planets; in this instance, the planet Earth. From French *planetaire* with same meaning and, in turn, from Greek *planetes*, pl. of *planes*, a wanderer.
From same base: planet.

detriment (DEH-truh-ment), obstacle, drawback. From Latin *detrimentum*, loss, damage, injury.
From same base: detrimental, detrimentally .
Synonyms: loss, harm, hurt, obstacle, drawback, injury, damage, deterioration, disadvantage, impairment.
Antonyms: advantage, gain, profit, benefit, help, assistance, utility.

epithet (EP-ih-thet), a disparaging or abusive name. From Greek *epitheton*, that which is added in the form of an unflattering name.
From same base: epithetical.
Synonyms: insult, nickname, vituperation, invective, attack, denunciation, revilement.
Antonyms: approval, acceptance, endorsement, appreciation, commendation, praise, admiration.

geneticist (juh-NET-uh-sist), someone using genetic engineering in the effort to change inherited characteristics of mankind; an expert in the science of heredity. From Greek *genesis*, the way in which something comes into being.

<u>From same base</u>: genesis, genetic, genetical, genetically.

finite (FY-<u>nyt</u>), having definite bounds or limits. From Latin *finitus*, pp. of *finire*, to enclose within limits.

<u>From same base</u>: finitely, finiteness.

<u>Synonyms</u>: limited, bound, circumscribed, confined, delimited, definite, fixed, defined.

<u>Antonyms</u>: endless, unlimited, unconfined, indefinite, boundless, ceaseless, incessant.

Language Uses and Abuses

Like as a preposition and as a verb

A high school student's complaint: "The one thing that bothers me about my parents is that they don't respect some of my friends. It's *like* they don't *like* a part of me."

Although *like*, as in its first use above, may be creeping into the language as a conjunction, it is still better form to use *as* or *as if* for that purpose. The student quoted could have said, "It's *as if* they don't *like* a part of me." Another correct example: "The natives of the upper Amazon are living now *as* [instead of *like*] they have for centuries past."

Standard, correct uses of *like* as a preposition: "He looked *like* a professional wrestler." " She sings *like* an angel." And of *like* as a verb: "…they don't *like* a part of me." "We *like* spinach."

Quick Checks on Comprehension

In each line below, highlight or check off the word or phrase that best matches the meaning of the word to the left.

explosive   impressive, collective, resounding, expounding
prophesy   purify, exemplify, testify, forecast
outstrip   surmount, suggest, suspend, liquefy

detriment   inspiration, drawback, implement, pretense
epithet   respite, invective, integrity, solvency
finite   frivolous, lamentable, fixed, repressive

In each line below, highlight or check off the two synonyms.

flattering, bound, confined, exonerated
insult, neglect, fallacy, attack
acquittal, damage, espousal, injury
renew, disperse, eclipse, surpass
envision, provide, predict, suspect
preventing, eruptive, stunning, invasive

In each line below, highlight or check off the two antonyms.

hushed, rushed, hearkening, deafening
impel, foretell, disappoint, ameliorate
outdistance, outweigh, retreat, repeat
turbulence, origin, obstacle, advantage,
denunciation, evaluation, commendation, nomination
spirited, limited, useless, boundless

If unsure about your comprehension choices, please see Appendix A.

Help make your day—try a new word today!

DAY 2

New Word-Choices
From Norman F. Bates, letter to the editor,
<u>The Atlantic Monthly</u>, 275 (February, 1995) 2, p. 10.

[Peter F. Drucker's <u>intriguing</u> essay,] "The Age of Social <u>Transformation</u>," with its <u>montages</u> of illustrations, is <u>apocalyptic</u> in its attempts to convey a historically <u>unprecedented</u> change in national social conditions in the twentieth century, with emphasis on the industrialized countries. I would have thought that an essay on social transformation in the twentieth century would at least discuss the change in the United States from an <u>ethnically</u> <u>segregated</u> society to an <u>integrated</u> society.

intriguing (in-TREEG-ing), exciting interest, curiosity, fascination.
   From French *intriguer*, to plot, scheme.
<u>From same base</u>: intrigue, intrigued, intriguingly.
<u>Synonyms</u>: attracting, enchanting, captivating, charming, alluring, enticing, inviting, fascinating.
<u>Antonyms</u>: dreary, uninteresting, boring, tedious, tiresome, wearisome, fatiguing, irksome, dull, monotonous.

transformation (<u>trans</u>-for-MAY-shun), the process of changing the form, appearance, condition, or function of a person or thing. From Late Latin *transformatio* with same meaning.
<u>Synonyms</u>: conversion, modification, evolution, alteration, change, variation, development.

montage (mahn-TAZH or mohn-TAZH), a rapid sequence of associated illustrations or ideas; the putting together of a number of photos or parts of photos into a composite piece of art, or doing the same with a number of paintings, drawings, or posters. From French *monter*, to mount, to set together.

apocalyptic (uh-<u>pok</u>-uh-LIP-tic), depicting or disclosing the symbolic triumph of good over evil in final and violent struggle. For example, with helicopters hovering overhead and fighter planes screaming by, "The sky is full of apocalyptic sound." From Greek *apokalyptein*, to uncover, reveal, disclose.
<u>From same base</u>: apocalypse, apocalyptically.
<u>Synonyms</u>: violent, earth-shattering, cataclysmic, savage, fierce, calamitous.

unprecedented (un-PRES-ih-<u>den</u>-tid), unheard of, novel, without precedent. From prefix *un*, not + Latin *praecedens*, prp. of *praecedere*, to precede, come before in time.
<u>From same base</u>: precedent, precedence.
<u>Synonyms</u>: novel, remarkable, singular, exceptional, unique, unheard of, unusual, uncommon, phenomenal, extraordinary.

ethnically (ETH-nih-cal-ly), racially, nationally (designating any body of people with the same background and customs). Adverb from Greek adjective *ethnikos* with same meaning.
<u>From same base</u>: ethnic, ethnical, ethnically.

segregated (SEG-rih-<u>gayt</u>-ed), referring to a system that separates one group from another; used mainly in references to racial groups. From Latin *segregatus*, pp. of *segregare*, to set apart.
<u>From same base</u>: segregate, segregating.
<u>Synonyms</u>: separated, divided, parted, disunited, disjoined.
<u>Antonyms</u>: integrated, unified, united, consolidated, blended, allied, related.

integrated (IN-te-<u>grayt</u>-ed), made whole, complete, united. From Latin *integratus*, pp. of *integrare*, to make whole.
<u>From same base</u>: integrate, integrating.
<u>Synonyms</u>: unified, united, merged, desegregated, blended, consolidated, allied, related.
<u>Antonyms</u>: segregated, separated, parted, disunited, divided, disjoined.

Language Uses and Abuses

How *not* to make a good impression

Conversation (shortened) between a teenage gang member and a reporter. Source: Edna Buchanan, <u>Suitable for Framing</u> (New York, NY: Hyperion, 1995), p. 44.

Teenager: "I got your message."

"I'm glad you called."

"The information was inseminated that you wished to discuss a matter with me."

"You mean disseminated?"

"Whatever. What is the nature of your requisition?"

"Let's get together and talk."

"We are conversing at the present time. How may I assist you?"

"We have to meet. Do you have a car?"

"No, but I can acquire the necessary transportation."

The use of out-of-place words to make an impression never works, and using them incorrectly compounds the problem. The passage above is an example of what is inappropriate in conversation or in writing.

Quick Checks on Comprehension

In each line below, highlight or check off the word or phrase that best matches the meaning of the word to the left.

intriguing	fascinating, tricking, dodging, conspiring
transformation	insinuation, altercation, modification, unification
montage	artful photo, fine painting, illustration, a composite of photos
apocalyptic	rare, cataclysmic, unusual, unsuitable
unprecedented	following, subsequent, extraordinary, last
ethnically	ethereally, racially, eventually, generally
segregated	separated, associated, unsettled, devious
integrated	suffused, rankled, belated, unified

In each line below, highlight or check off the two synonyms.

captivating, motivating, energizing, enchanting

revealing, calamitous, acrylic, violent

remarkable, unbelievable, exceptional, unimaginable
procession, conversion, change, propulsion
set apart, emaciated, extroverted, divided
merged, satiated, united, asphyxiated

In each line below, highlight or check off the two antonyms.

uninteresting, subliminal, uneventful, attracting
parted, synthetic, consolidated, zealous
reticent, separated, contentious, desegregated

If unsure about your comprehension choices, please see Appendix A.

Pave the way—use a new word today!

DAY 3

New Word-Choices
From Paul H. Robinson, "Moral Credibility and Crime,"
The Atlantic Monthly, 275 (March, 1975) 3, p. 72.

[By the mid-1970s]...deterrence became popular as an alternative
to rehabilitation. Potential offenders would be dissuaded from
committing offenses by the threat of serious penalties. The longer the
prison term, the greater the disincentive. The high cost of
imprisonment would normally put a natural limit on the severity of the
deterrent threat, but the threat could be made dramatic without
courting fiscal crisis if longer sentences than would actually be served
were publicly imposed.

deterrence (dih-TUR-ense), the act of keeping or discouraging
  someone from doing something by inciting anxiety or fear. In line 6
  above, the adjective **deterrent** (dih-TUR-ent) means hindering or
  discouraging. Both words from Latin *deterrens,* prp. of *deterrere*, to
  frighten from anything.
Synonyms: dissuasion, discouragement, prevention, restraint,
containment, control, suppression, repression, constraint.
Antonyms: persuasion, encouragement, inducement, incitement,
conversion, conviction.

alternative (awl-TUR-na-tiv), a choice between two things or courses
  of action. From Latin *alternus*, one after the other, by turns.
From same base: alternatively, alternately.
Synonyms: preference, option, choice, selection, election.
Antonyms: necessity, constraint, restraint, obligation, requirement.

rehabilitation (<u>ree</u>-huh-<u>bil</u>-i-TAY-shun), the act of restoring to mental or physical health; putting back in good condition. From Middle Latin *rehabilitatus*, pp. of Latin *rehabilitare*, to restore.
<u>From same base</u>: rehabilitate, rehabilitating, rehabilitated.
<u>Synonyms</u>: restoration, replacement, reconstruction, reproduction, renovation, reparation, renewal, revival, correction.
<u>Antonyms</u>: destruction, ruination, demolition, breakdown, dissolution, overthrow, disintegration, extinction.

potential (poh-TEN-shul), that which can come into being but has not yet done so. From Latin *potens*, prp. of *posse*, to be able, capable.
<u>From same base</u>: potent, potency, potentiality, potentate.
<u>Synonyms</u>: possible, undeveloped, unrealized, eventual, conceivable, imaginable, likely, latent, dormant.
<u>Antonyms</u>: active, actual, real, in being, concrete, material.

dissuade (di-SWAYD), to advise or persuade against. From Latin negative prefix *dis*, not, + *suadere*, to persuade, advise.
<u>From same base</u>: dissuading, dissuaded.
<u>Synonyms</u>: curb, discourage, dishearten, deter, hinder, admonish.
<u>Antonyms</u>: coax, entice, convince, impel, induce, influence, exhort.

disincentive (<u>dis</u>-in-SEN-tiv), a deterrent; something that keeps someone from doing something. From Latin negative prefix *dis* + Late Latin *incentivus*, pp. of *incinere*, to encourage, motivate.
<u>Synonyms</u>: discouragement, warning, restraint, admonition.
<u>Antonyms</u>: encouragement, inducement, motivation, stimulation.

severity (seh-VEHR-ih-tee), harshness, strictness. From Latin *severitas* with the same meaning.
<u>Synonyms</u>: austerity, gravity, seriousness, sternness.
<u>Antonyms</u>: leniency, gentleness, compassion, tolerance.

dramatic (druh-MAT-ik), vivid, striking; filled with action, emotion, excitement. From Greek *dramatikos*, having the characteristics of drama, plays.
<u>From same base</u>: dramatics.
<u>Synonyms</u>: vivid, exciting, striking, colorful, lively, spritely, brilliant, bright, vibrant, theatrical, stellar.
<u>Antonyms</u>: dull, boring, uninteresting, lifeless, dismal, tedious.

fiscal (FIS-kul), financial, having to do with financial affairs; most often used in reference to annual budgets. From Latin *fiscus*, originally a basket, then a purse.
<u>From same base</u>: fiscally (as in "fiscally sound").

Language Uses and Abuses

Two handy Latin phrases

A conversation between a potential informant and a detective. From Ed Dee, <u>14 Peck Slip</u> (New York, NY: Warner Books, 1994), p.94 f.

"You know what I'm talking about. It's ancient history. Once you get an arrest number, you're *persona non grata*."
"But you have information, Sid, and we need it to pursue the case."
"You're some interrogator, you know that? Are you from the Phil Donohue school? Ever hear of *quid pro quo*?"
"It's a homicide, Sid. A cop, your partner."
"Yeah, he's dead and I'm alive. So what are you going to do for me?"

So these two Latin phrases do sometimes "come in handy":

persona non grata (per-SOHN-ah non GRAHT-ah), an unwelcome person or, in the Latin word order, a person not welcome.
quid pro quo (kwid pro kwoh), a fair exchange of one thing (*quid*) for (*pro*) another (*quo*). The detective above wants information and the informant wants to know "What's in it for me?"

Quick Checks on Comprehension

In each line below, highlight or check off the word or phrase that best matches the meaning of the word to the left.

deterrence	restraint, competence, deference, choice
alternative	constraint, urgency, option, prevention
rehabilitation	renewal, import, repression, assumption
potential	developed, eager, tolerant, possible
dissuade	disappoint, oppose, motivate, tolerate
disincentive	perspective, indulgence, restorative, warning
severity	austerity, asperity, polity, boredom
dramatic	ascetic, exciting, acerbic, casual

dramatic   ascetic, exciting, acerbic, casual
fiscal   responsible, hostile, servile, financial

In each line below, highlight or check off the two synonyms.

dissuasion, incision, prevention, omission
constraint, reference, selection, preference
delegation, survival, revival, renovation
undeveloped, impossible, tolerant, unrealized
superimpose, hinder, imagine, deter
perspective, dissuasion, restorative, admonition
gravity, austerity, leniency, restraint
ascetic, exciting, acerbic, vivid

In each line below, highlight or check off the two antonyms.

inducement, separation, orientation, discouragement
recompense, constraint, imposition, choice
restoration, preparation, demolition, memorization
latent, dull, soporific, actual
exhort, postpone, dishearten, preserve
discouragement, inducement, settlement, enlightenment
sternness, stress, selfishness, gentleness
zealous, contentious, uninteresting, striking

If unsure about your comprehension choices, please see Appendix A.

With new words galore, you'll smile far more.

New Word-Choices
From Stephen Bertman, commencement address on
"Cultural Amnesia,"
<u>Vital Speeches of the Day</u>, 61 (July 15, 1995) 19, p. 604 f.

In 1992, a Department of Education survey tested the <u>literacy</u> of 26,000 adult Americans. <u>Extrapolating</u> from its findings, the Department concluded that half of all American citizens—some 90 million of us—lack the basic skills required to <u>compose</u> and comprehend written English: the ability to write a simple business letter, for example, or to understand written instructions.

Historically and with few exceptions, the <u>emergence</u> of civilization has been associated with the invention of writing and the development of a vocabulary whose accuracy is matched to society's own <u>complexity</u>. The birth of civilizationhas also been associated with the creation of a <u>literature</u> in which those words, and the wisdom they contain, are enshrined. In <u>inverse</u> fashion, as a civilization declines, its people lose touch with those instruments and their meaning. Thus illiteracy ultimately becomes <u>expatriation</u>.

literacy (LIT-ur-uh-see), the ability to read and write. From Latin
   litera, letter of the alphabet.
<u>From same base</u>: literal, literally, literalism.

extrapolate (ek-STRAP-uh-<u>layt</u>), to infer from facts that are known.
   From Latin prefix *extra*, outside, + *polire*, to polish, finish.
<u>From same base</u>: extrapolating, extrapolated.
<u>Synonyms</u>: infer, deduce, conclude, judge, presume, reason, decide.

compose (kum-POHZ), to fashion or create. From prefix *com*, (originally Latin *cum*) with, together, + Old French *poser*, to place, arrange, form.
From same base: composing, composed.
Synonyms: form, make, fashion, formulate, write, arrange, construct.
Antonyms: break, scatter, destroy, ruin, disarrange, disperse.

emergence (ih-MUR-jense), a coming out of or rising from. From Latin *emergens*, prp. of *emergere*, to come forth, rise up.
From same base: emergency.
Synonyms: egress, emanation, exit, issue, outbreak, eruption, discharge, appearance, outlet.
Antonyms: ingress, entrance, entry, admission, incoming, influx.

complexity (kum-PLEK-sih-tee), the state of being involved, intricate, complicated. From Latin *complexus*, pp. of *complecti*, to encircle, embrace.
From same base: complex.
Synonyms: involvement, entanglement, intricacy, composition, constitution, structure, organization.

literature (LIT-ur-uh-chur), written works of enduring importance. From Latin *litteratura*, a writing composed of letters.

inverse (in-VURS), reversed or opposite in order or effect. From Latin *inversus*, pp. of *invertere*, to turn about, transpose.
From same base: inversing, inversed, inversely.
Synonyms: reversed, opposite, inverted, overturned, reverted, turned back, regressive, recessive.
Antonyms: continuous, unbroken, uninterrupted, constant, persisting.

expatriation (eks-pay-tree-AY-shun), the state of leaving or of being banished from one's homeland. From Latin prefix *ex*, from, out of, + *patria*, fatherland.
From same base: expatriate.
Synonyms: dismissal, banishment, removal, ejection, exile, rejection, expulsion, ouster, suspension, eviction, deportation.
Antonyms: acceptance, reception, admission, adoption, approval.

Language Uses and Abuses

Too much of a good thing

Unique (yoo-NEEK from the Latin *unus*, one) is an adjective meaning "the only one of its kind." Yet, you sometimes hear *very* used with it as in "I had a very unique experience yesterday." If something or some act is unique, the *very* is in error as well as being unnecessary.

Anyone is an indefinite singular pronoun, but you may still hear a sentence like this: "Anyone with a ticket is free to take their place in the line." That sentence should read, "Anyone with a ticket is free to take his or her place in the line." Or if only males are involved, "Anyone is free to take his place in the line." If only females, "Anyone is free to take her place in the line."

Everyone, is also an indefinite singular pronoun but, again, some assume that it is plural. For example: "Everyone should take their places on the stage." That sentence should read, "Everyone should take his or her place on the stage." Or if only males are involved, "Everyone should take his place on the stage." If only females, "Everyone should take her place on the stage."

Everybody is another indefinite singular pronoun. It is in error, for instance, to say, "Before the play began, everybody took their seats." That sentence should be, "Before the play began, everybody took his or her seat." Or if all males, "Before the play began, everybody took his seat." If all females, "Before the play began, everybody took her seat."

Every, on the other hand, is a singular adjective used to modify singular nouns. A network commentator on professional baseball should not be saying, "Every player has their own idea of sportsmanship." He should be saying, "Every player has his own idea of sportsmanship."

Quick Checks on Comprehension

In each line below, highlight or check off the word or phrase that best matches the meaning of the word to the left.

extrapolate   deduce, seduce, produce, reduce

compose	oppose, repose, order, write
emergence	pressure, issue, lapse, image
complexity	intricacy, perplexity, surety, supremacy
inverse	opposite, requisite, perverse, dominant
expatriation	promotion, elation, insurgent, banishment

In each line below, highlight or check off the two synonyms.

dismissal, remission, referral, expulsion
bonded, overturned, reverted, denigrated
impoverish, cherish, endanger, treasure
involvement, installment, entanglement, enlightenment
permission, rescue, outbreak, eruption
promise, form, reform, fashion
conclude, delude, deride, decide

In each line below, highlight or check off the two antonyms.

batter, arrange, scatter, arrogate
management, exit, inscription, influx
inquire, furbish, treasure, abhor
reversed, persisting, insisting, immersed
projection, rejection, consolidation, approval

If unsure about your comprehension choices, please see Appendix A.

With a new word each day, you're well on the way!

New Word-Choices
From jacket description of Neil Postman's The End of Education:
Redefining the Value of School
(New York, NY: Alfred A. Knopf, 1995)

In this brilliantly challenging response to the education crisis, Neil Postman, author of *Teaching as a Subversive Activity*, returns to the subject that established his reputation as one of our most insightful social critics. Starting from his belief that schooling is now too often a trivial pursuit, a mechanical exercise, he argues with stunning clarity that we have lost sight of the inherent value and substance of learning, and sets out to restore it for our time.

brilliantly (BRIL-yunt-lee), showing great intellect, talent; glowing with light. Adverbial form from French *brilliant*, prp. of *briller*, to sparkle, glitter, and, in turn from Italian *brillare*, with same meaning..
From same base: brilliant, brilliance, brilliancy
Synonyms: glowingly, brightly, dazzlingly, sparklingly, intelligently.

challenging (CHAL-en-jing), arousing interest, excitement; making demands on. From Old French *chalenge*, a demand, claim.
From same base: challenge, challenged, challenger, challengeable.
Synonyms: demanding, exacting, appealing, stipulating, requiring.

subversive (sub-VUR-siv), tending to overthrow or destroy (a government, institution, belief, etc.). From Latin *subversus*, pp. of *subvertere*, to overturn, overthow.
From same base: subvert, subverting, subverted, subversively, subversion, subversiveness.

Synonyms: rebellious, seditious, disruptive, revolutionary, insurgent, dissident, perfidious, treasonous, unruly, supportive.
Antonyms: uplifting, elevating, heightening, organizing, establishing, instituting, upholding, conserving, preserving.

insightful (in-SITE-ful), having the ability to see and understand clearly. From Middle English *insiht* (i.e.,in + sight), a looking in.
From same base: insight.
Synonyms: perceptive, perspicacious, judicious, intuitive, discerning, clear-sighted.
Antonyms: shallow, bewildered, incapable, unenlightened, perplexed, confused, doubtful.

critic (KRIT-ik), a person who forms and expresses judgments of people or things according to certain standards or values. From Greek *kritikos*, able to discern
From same base: criticize, criticizing, criticized, critical, critically, criticism, critique.
Synonyms: judge, commentator, analyst, analyzer, reviewer.

trivial (TRIV-ee-ul), of little value or importance, commonplace. From Latin *trivialis* (*tri*, three, + *via*, road), of the crossroads and, therefore, of no consequence.
From same base: trivialize, trivializing, trivialiized, trivia, trivially, triviality, trivialism.
Synonyms: trifling, insignificant, inconsequential, unimportant, irrelevant, immaterial, frivolous, nonessential.
Antonyms: important, significant, relevant, essential, grave.

stunning (STUN-ing), impressive, astonishing. From Vulgar Latin *extonare* (intensive *ex* + *tonare*, to thunder), to daze, overwhelm.
From same base: stun, stunned, stunningly.
Synonyms: impressive, astonishing, astounding, staggering, remarkable, striking.

inherent (in-HEER-ent), characteristic, basic. From Latin *inhaerens*, prp. of *inhaerere*, to cling to, cleave to.
From same base: inherence.
Synonyms: basic, characteristic, inborn, innate, natural, inseparable, native, intrinsic, ingrained, congenital, inbred, indispensable.

<u>Antonyms</u>: superfluous, superficial, extrinsic, incidental, superimposed, fortuitous, casual, external, accidental.

substance (SUB-stense), the real or essential part of anything. From Latin *substantia* (*sub*, under, + *stare*, to stand), substance, essence.
<u>From same base</u>: substantial, substantially.
<u>Synonyms</u>: essence, element, matter, material.

Language Uses and Abuses

Some troublesome pairs

podium, lectern. "The speaker hurried to the podium." A podium, from the Greek *podos* (*foot*, as in our word, *podiatrist*), is a low platform on which one stands. You see it in use by orchestra conductors and sometimes by singers. A speaker, on the other hand, typically speaks not from a podium but from a lectern (from Latin *legere*, to read). The lectern is a kind of upright desk; it is wide enough to hold manuscripts or notes, and it can also serve as a mount for microphones. In cut-down form, it rests on a table; the speaker of the moment stands behind the lectern. In other words, a speaker makes his or her presentation from a lectern, seldom from a podium.

fame, notoriety. Sportscaster: "She first achieved notoriety when she won the gold medal in the last Olympics." The common meaning of notoriety is *unfavorable notice*. The only way to achieve it in the Olympics is to get caught taking drugs or doing something equally objectionable. On the other hand, someone who becomes known for high achievement in any worthwhile field has achieved fame, not notoriety. Similarly, to be notorious is the opposite of being famous.

fewer, less. Fewer refers to separate things or beings. "I have fewer appointments today than I had yesterday." "The older he gets, the fewer acquaintances he has." Less refers to amounts. "Due to all the delays, we have less time to get there." "Meet your responsibilities and you'll feel less pain."

farther, further. Farther refers to distances, real or symbolic. "I live farther down the road than my parents do." "He went farther into detail than I wanted to go." Further refers to abstract or theoretical matters. "We'll discuss this further when we have more time." "This issue is important enough to require further debate."

Quick Checks on Comprehension

In each line below, highlight or check off the word or phrase which best matches the word to the left.

brilliantly	literally, ideally, intelligently, socially
challenging	interesting, demanding, arresting, suspending
subversive	dissident, relevant, expectant, transient
insightful	learning, respectful, hopeful, discerning
critic	analyst, specialist, realist, socialist
trivial	decorous, omnivorous, frivolous, riotous
stunning	remarkable, amicable, laughable, capable
inherent	monastic, characteristic, acerbic, synthetic
substance	presence, essence, deviance, flamboyance

In each line below, highlight or check off the two synonyms.

indispensable, irritable, lamentable, inseparable
repressive, impressive, astounding, abounding
nonessential, quintessential, pilfering, trifling
spectator, interviewer, commentator, reviewer
introspective, perceptive, prescriptive, intuitive
seditious, perfidious, permissive, spontaneous
remanding, protracting, requiring, exacting
protractedly, glowingly, arrestingly, brightly

In each line below, highlight or check off the two antonyms.

disruptive, inventive, supportive, indicative
concerned, impetuous, judicious, bewildered
relevant, special, immaterial, undulant

If unsure about your comprehension choices, please see Appendix A.

Keep your rivals at bay—use a new word today!

New Word-Choices
From George Will, "Balancing the National Budget,"
in his column for February 13, 1995.

Balancing the national budget would not be <u>intellectually</u> hard work—there are many paths to balance. It would involve <u>acrimonious</u> arguments about <u>priorities</u>, but political arguments are presumably not unpleasant to legislators, who were not herded into Washington at bayonet point. However, it would be a <u>daunting</u> task if the aim were to do it without derailing the <u>careerism</u> of people hoping to make Congress a permanent home.

Hence the <u>undiminished</u> <u>salience</u> of the case for term limits. Those who say the <u>churning</u> of Congress in recent elections disproves the need for term limits are misunderstanding the primary reason for limits. The primary reason is not to dislodge entrenched <u>incumbents</u> who use the resources of the modern state as entrenching tools. The primary reason is to remove one motive—careerism—for entering, and for making decisions while in, Congress.

intellectually (<u>in</u>-tel-EK-choo-uh-lee), pertaining to use of the mind.
Adverb from Late Latin adjective, *intellectualis* with same meaning.
<u>From same base</u>: intellectual, intellectualism.
<u>Synonyms</u>: mentally, inventively, reflectively, thoughtfully, studiously, deliberatively, keenly.
<u>Antonyms</u>: dully, thoughtlessly, inanely, foolishly, flightily, irrationally.

acrimonious (<u>ak</u>-rih-MO-nee-us), pertaining to bitterness or sharpness in temper, manner, or speech. From Middle Latin *acrimoniosus* with same meaning.

Fom same base: acrimony, acrimoniously.
Synonyms: acerbic, tart, harsh, sharp, bitter, irascible, severe, caustic.
Antonyms: amiable, gentle, kind, tender, courteous, polite.

priority (pry-OR-ih-tee), a first right based on need or emergency; a
   right to being first in doing something or having something done.
   From Latin comparative form, *prior*, higher, sooner, of the adjective
   primus, first.
From same base: prior
Synonyms: precedence, first right, antecedence, previousness.

daunting (DAWNT-ing), disheartening, intimidating.   From Old
   French *danter*, to discourage, make afraid.
From same base: dauntless, dauntlessly, dauntlessness.
Synonyms: intimidating, discouraging, disheartening, frightening,
scaring, dismaying, terrifying.
Antonyms: encouraging, assisting, aiding, helping, urging,
stimulating, inciting, comforting.

careerism (ka-REER-iz-um), a primary interest in achieving one's
   own ambitions to the neglect of all else. From French *carrière*, road,
   one's journey through life.
From same base: career, careerist.

undiminished (un-dih-MIN-isht), not made smaller or less in size or
   degree. Negative of diminish from Latin *diminuere*, to lessen, make
   smaller.
Synonyms: increased, enlarged, extended, lengthened, prolonged.
Antonyms: lessened, reduced, contracted, compressed, curtailed,
retrenched, decreased, shortened, trimmed, abridged, cut off

salience (SAYL-ee-ense), strength in standing out, in being
   noticeable, conspicuous, prominent. From Latin *saliens*, prp. of
   salire, to leap forward.
From same base: salient, saliently.
Synonyms: visibility, prominence, impressiveness, noticeability,
conspicuousness, emergence.
Antonyms: invisibility, inconspicuousness, concealment.

incumbent (in-CUMB-ent), one holding office. From Latin *incumbens*, prp. of *incubare*, to lie on or dwell in. (As an adjective, **incumbent** means obligatory or necessary; for example, "It was incumbent on her to fulfill her campaign promises.")
From same base: incumbency.

Language Uses and Abuses

Similar-sounding pairs

appraise, to place a value on. A house appraiser, for example, is a professional who appraises houses.
apprise, to inform or notify. "He apprised me of my rights."

complement, the amount, number, or thing added or required to complete the whole. "Her scarf was the ideal complement to a striking costume."
compliment, as we know, means something said in praise, admiration, or flattery. "She received compliments on her good taste."

likely carries the idea of probability. "Harry is likely to be the next president of our club." "Rain was a likely cause of the loss, and the builder may be liable for the damages."
liable, as in the second clause of the preceding sentence, means responsible, obligated, or legally bound. It also means exposed to or subject to something unpleasant. "She is liable to heart attacks."

forte (fort), as a *one-syllable* word, means something that a person does especially well. "As a pianist, his forte is the music of Mozart."
forte (FOR-tay), as a *two-syllable* word, is a musical notation directing a musician or musicians to "play it loud."

Quick Checks on Comprehension

In each line below, highlight or check off the word or phrase that best matches the meaning of the word to the left.

intellectually   presumably, thoughtfully, artfully, skillfully
acrimonious   kind, solicitous, tacit, bitter

priority	precedence, enmity, authority, austerity
daunting	holding fast, neglecting, scaring, forcing
undiminished	extended, suspended, intended, entitled
salience	essence, sense, presence, prominence

In each line below, highlight or check off the two synonyms.

reflectively, unintentionally, prematurely, deliberatively
acoustic, acerbic, severe, passionate
antecedence, reclusiveness, solidarity, precedence
upbraiding, hurrying, dismaying, intimidating
increased, prolonged, churned, exasperated
existence, noticeability, composure, emergence

In each line below, highlight or check off the two antonyms.

visibility, eccentricity, concealment, procurement
lengthened, entrenched, unaided, shortened
surrendering, assisting, frightening, apprehending
social, zealous, sharp, civil
ardently, studiously, inanely, perfunctorily

If unsure about your comprehension choices, please see Appendix A.

Hey, hey, don't delay—try a new word today!

New Word-Choices
From Amory B. Lovin and L. Hunter Davis,
"Reinventing the Wheels,"
The Atlantic Monthly, 275 (January, 1995) 2, p. 75.

   With more skill than vision, the Big Three auto makers have been painstakingly pursuing incremental refinements on the way to an America where foreign cars fueled with foreign oil cross crumbling bridges. Modern cars are an extraordinarily sophisticated engineering achievement—the highest expression of the Iron Age. But they are obsolete, and the time for incrementalism is over. Striking innovations have occurred in advanced materials, software, motors, power electronics, and a host of other advances. Artfully integrated, they can yield safe, affordable, and otherwise superior family cars getting hundreds of miles per gallon.

incremental (in-kree-MEN-tl), increasing steadily. From Latin
   incrementus, pp. of *increscere*, to increase.
From same base: increment, incrementalism.
Synonyms: augmenting, extending, enlarging, expanding, enhancing,
magnifying, growing, developing.
Antonyms: diminishing, lessening, contracting, shrinking, dwindling,
decreasing, reducing, eroding.

sophisticated (suh-FIS-tih-kayt-ed), complicated in design; or, in
   reference to individuals, having refined tastes, cultured. From Greek
   sophidzomai, to devise cleverly or skilfully.
From same base; sophisticate, sophisticating, sophistical, sophistically,
sophistication.
Synonyms: polished, knowledgeable, worldly, urbane, refined.

Antonyms: naive, artless, simple, ingenuous, plain, common.

expression (ex-PRESH-un), an outward indication, sign; cast of features that indicates state of mind; word or phrase used in communication. From Latin *expressio*, a describing or expressing in words.
From same base: expressionism, expressionless.
Synonyms: declaration, utterance, communication, representation, designation, statement, demonstration.
Antonyms: retention, repression, restraint, containment, deterrence, suppression, repression, constraint.

incrementalism (in-kree-MEN-tl-ism), state of increasing rapidly. Noun form as distinguished from adjective incremental above.

obsolete (ob-suh-LEET), out of date, out of fashion; no longer used or practiced. From Latin *obsoletus*, pp. of *obsolescere*, to go out of use.
From same base: obsoletely.
Synonyms: disused, old-fashioned, archaic, antique, ancient, antiquated, rare, old, primitive, time-worn.
Antonyms: new, novel, recent, modern, up-to-date, late.

innovation (in-uh-VAY-shun), something newly introduced as a method, idea, etc.; change in the way of doing things. From Late Latin *innovatio* with same meaning.
From same base: innovational.

Language Uses and Abuses

Being direct and to the point

What do you suppose is the "clear meaning"of this sentence from the speech of a candidate for public office?

It is absolutely essential to our hope for peace, stability, democracy, and better foreign policy to have a world that is growing and expanding with a tide that is rising, upon which all boats can rise, as opposed to this zero-sum, fiercely divisive Darwinian struggle in which nations are locked into mercantilistic practices and protectionistic policies that drive people apart, as opposed to bringing people together in a liberal democratic fashion as I think America was founded upon two hundred years ago.

In contrast, here's an example of a clear, easy-to-understand speaking style from a 1987 speech on leadership by Edward L. Flom, at the time Chairman of the Board and CEO of Florida Steel Corporation.

> If I had to choose the one talent that is most beneficial in a leadership role, my first choice would be insight. But then insight is a given rather than a learned talent. Probably the second best talent to have is patience. Lord Chesterfield explained it perfectly when he said, "Patience is a most necessary quality for business; many a man would rather you hear his story than grant his request." Our company has always had an open policy. Most people refer to policies like this as open door policy. We go one step farther. Not only can anyone make an appointment to see anyone in Florida Steel, but anyone can telephone any person without having to identify himself. Whenever possible, which is most of the time, we all answer our telephones. No one is allowed to ask, "May I say who's calling?" Lord Chesterfield was right; most people would rather talk to you than get their way.

In the Flom approach, you have no lengthy sentences, no burdensome formality. He uses the kind of language that would fit almost any listeners. So our suggestion for the Day is to be direct and to the point. When you or I or anyone else speaks or writes in long and complicated sentences (like the political candidate on the preceding page), the listener gets lost. It's good practice, as you see Mr. Flom doing, not only to speak and write in "listener language" but also to speak and write in fairly short sentences. Note, too, that it's difficult to be excessively formal when your messages are sprinkled with "we" and other personal pronouns.

Quick Checks on Comprehension

In each line below, highlight or check off the word or phrase that best matches the meaning of the word to the left.

incremental	growing, sensing, protecting, expressing
sophisticated	habituated, cogent, worldly, satiated
expression	impatience, declaration, knowledge, art
obsolete	discreet, elementary, naive, antique

In each line below, highlight or check off the two synonyms.

time-worn, aggressive, disused, infringed
introduction, communication, designation, irritation
polished, serrated, castigated, urbane
originating, developing, resolving, enhancing

In each line below, highlight or check off the two antonyms.

artless, respected, excited, refined
obliging, extending, eroding, jamming
participation, frustration, repression, utterance
elitist, primitive, up-to-date, depressed

If unsure about your comprehension choices, please see Appendix A.

Trying a new word each day will help you on your upward way!

DAY 8

New Word-Choices
From John Pearson, The Serpent and the Stag
(New York, NY: Holt, Rinehart and Winston, 1983), p. 34.

But Bess was not a gentleman. As a woman she was free from the extravagant male chauvinism and the elaborate code of honour and display that could prove such a crippling luxury for the Elizabethan aristocrat. Indeed, no mere Elizabethan male could have risen from such humble origins as swiftly and securely as she. For in this society, dominated by men, where women were not supposed to indulge in the male prerogatives of independence, moneymaking, knowledge of the law, and cool ambition, Bess had a great advantage as a woman. As Countess of Shrewesbury she could act the part of the great lady while never for an instant losing the bourgeois-puritan qualities of thrift, of love of profit, and the ever-open eye for a shrewd financial deal.

extravagant (ek-STRAV-uh-ghent), overly lavish, wasteful; immoderate, unrestrained. From Latin *extravagans*, prp. of *extravagare*, to wander beyond.
From same base: extravagantly, extravagance.
Synonyms: lavish, wasteful, liberal, excessive, extreme.
Antonyms: miserly, beggarly, niggardly, mean, avaricious, stingy, close-fisted.

chauvinism (SHOW-vih-niz-um), an unreasoning or fanatical attachment to or support for one's sex, race, ethnic background, nation, etc. Derived from Nicholas Chauvin's overzealous support of Napoleon Bonaparte.
From same base: chauvinist.

aristocrat (uh-RIS-tuh-<u>krat</u>), a nobleman or member of a privileged class; a person with the manners, beliefs and tastes of the that class. From Greek *aristos* (aristo), best, + *kratos* (crat), rule, power.
<u>From same base</u>: aristocratic, aristocratically, aristocracy.
<u>Synonyms</u>: patrician, noble, blue blood, socialite.

dominated (DOM-ih-<u>nayt</u>-ed), controlled, governed.   From Latin *dominatus*, pp. of *dominari*, to rule, master. (House or home was *domus*, and master of the household, *dominus*.)
<u>From same base</u>: dominate, dominating.
<u>Synonyms</u>: tamed, controlled, governed, ruled, mastered, directed, supervised, commanded, subjugated.
<u>Antonyms</u>: free, untamed, spirited, independent, unrestricted, unconfined, self-reliant, self-sufficient.

indulge (in-DULJ), to gratify or yield to one's own desires or whims or to the desires or whims of someone else. From Latin *indulgere*, to yield to.
<u>From same base</u>: indulging, indulged.
<u>Synonyms</u>: foster, cherish, gratify, please, humor, favor, placate, satisfy, satiate, nurture, sustain.
<u>Antonyms</u>: torment, harry, annoy, molest, bother, harass, sadden, distress, afflict, thwart, worry, vex.

prerogative (pree-ROG-uh-tiv), an unquestionable right belonging to a person or persons. From Latin *praerogatus,* pp. of *praerogare*, to ask (for an opinion, vote, etc.) before asking others.

bourgeois-puritan (boor-ZHWAH + PYUUR-ih-tn), combination of (1) a word meaning characteristic of the middle class of the period and its interests in "deals" and profits and (2) a word meaning characteristics of those strictly moral and   thrifty.

(1) *bourgeois* is French and related to the Late Latin *burgus* for castle; a bourgeois was a commoner living in a medieval town. From same base: bourg, bourgeoisie.
(2) *puritan* is derived from Late Latin *puritas*, purity. A Puritan belonged to the Protestant group which, in the 16th and 17th centuries, wanted to reform and purify the Church of England. From same base: puritanic, puritanically.

shrewd (shrood), sharp, wise, artful. From Middle High German *schrouwel*, devil. Original meaning modified over the years from evil to mischievous to sharp. (The word *shrewish* retains old meaning of evil-tempered.)

From same base: shrew, shrewdly, shrewdness.

Synonyms: knowing, cunning, clever, cautious, prudent, careful, watchful, mindful, wary, guarded, canny.

Antonyms: rash, unthinking, unreasoning, thoughtless, foolish, frivolous, ignorant, unintelligent, senseless.

Language Uses and Abuses

Four more Latin phrases

The only Latin phrases you'll find in this book are those in common use. Perhaps you've already seen, heard, or used these?

ad infinitum (odd in-fin-EE-tum *or* odd in-fin-EYE-tum), without end, to infinity. "The speaker was boring, mainly because he kept repeating the same things ad infinitum."

ad nauseam (odd NAH-zay-ahm), toward sickness, enough to make one sick. If an individual talks about a vacation to the point that it makes you nauseous, you could say, "He talked about his vacation ad nauseam." Caution: Saying or writing *ad nauseum* (last two letters *um*) is a common mistake, both in spelling and in pronunciation. Tacking an "m" on the end of the word *nausea* gets it right.

terra firma is pronounced as it looks and means firm ground. If flying or boating makes you feel a bit queasy, you could afterwards say, "I'm glad to be back on terra firma."

status quo (STAYT-us   kwoh), a state of affairs existing at a particular time. Speaker: "We should limit the terms of members of Congress." Opponent: "I prefer the status quo; let the people decide how long one should hold office."

Quick Checks on Comprehension

In each line below, highlight or check off the word or phrase that best matches the meaning of the word to the left.

extravagant	indirect, liberal, garrulous, positive
aristocrat	autocrat, bureaucrat, socialite, diplomat
dominated	directed, fanatical, wasteful, certain
indulge	coerce, mend, cherish, favor
shrewd	restive, unequal, cautious, nimble

In each line below, highlight or check off the two synonyms.

prudent, gaudy, guarded, aristocratic
mutual, shortsighted, gratify, sustain
opinionated, controlled, supervised, generated
noble, inspector, blue blood, director
extreme, exonerated, extricated, excessive

In each line below, highlight or check off the two antonyms.

stingy, prominent, lavish, harmless
showy, noisome, mastered, spirited
persuade, nurture, thwart, pursue
soulful, ignorant, trusting, cunning

If unsure about your comprehension choices, please see Appendix A.

The word payoff awaits—just don't procrastinate!

New Word-Choices
From Karen Armstrong, <u>A History of God</u>
(New York, NY: Alfred A. Knopf, 1994), p. xix f.

This book will not be a history of the <u>ineffable</u> reality of God itself, which is beyond time and change, but a history of the way men and women have <u>perceived</u> him from Abraham to the present time. Men and women started to worship gods as soon as they became recognizably human. This was not simply because they wanted to <u>propitiate</u> powerful forces; these early faiths expressed the wonder and mystery that seem always to have been an essential <u>component</u> of the human experience of this beautiful yet terrifying world. Like art, religion has been an attempt to find meaning and value in life, despite the suffering that flesh is heir to. Like any other human activity, religion can be abused, but it seems to have been something that we have always done. It was not tacked on to a <u>primordially</u> <u>secular</u> society by <u>manipulative</u> kings and priests but was natural to humanity. Indeed, our current <u>secularism</u> is an entirely new experiment, unprecedented in human history.

ineffable (in-EF-uh-bl), too overpowering or too sacred to be
  expressed in words, indescribable. From Latin *ineffabilis* (negative
  prefix *in*, not, + *effabilis*, utterable), not utterable.
<u>From same base</u>: ineffability, ineffableness, ineffably.
<u>Synonyms</u>: indescribable, inexpressible, unutterable,unspeakable.

perceive (pur-SEEV), to feel, become aware of, understand. From
  Latin *percipere* with the same meaning.
<u>From same base</u>: perceiving, perceived, perceivable, perceivably.

Synonyms: feel, note, observe, discern, distinguish, sense, grasp, understand, conceive, see, realize, apprehend, discover, behold.
Antonyms: mistake, misunderstand, misjudge, misconceive, overlook, confuse, ignore.

propitiate (pruh-PISH-ee-<u>ayt</u>), to cause to be favorably disposed. From Latin *propitiatus*, pp. of *propitiare*, to conciliate.
From same base: propitiating, propitiated, propitiable.
Synonyms: conciliate, placate, reconcile, appease, expiate.

component (kum-POH-nent), a basic part. From Latin *componens*, prp. of *componere*, to put together.
Synonyms: part, portion, fraction, division, segment, item, factor, detail, constituent, element.

primordially (prih-MOR-dee-uh-lee), first in time, original. Adverb from Late Latin *primordialis*, existing from the beginning.
From same base: primordially.
Synonyms: primevally, primally, primitively, primarily, venerably, prehistorically, traditionally.
Antonyms: recently, presently, lately, eventually.

secular (SEK-yoo-lur), concerned with life on earth, not with religion. From Late Latin *saecularis*, worldly, profane.
From same base: secularly, secularism, secularistic, secularistically.
Synonyms: mundane, temporal, worldly, earthly, lay, unholy, unconsecrated, unsanctified.
Antonyms: sacred, spiritual, hallowed, sanctified, holy, divine, religious, heavenly, celestial.

secularism (SEK-yuh-luh-riz-um), adherence to non-religious values. Also from Late Latin *saecularis* + noun-forming *ism*.

manipulative (muh-NIP-yuh-<u>lay</u>-tiv), controlling shrewdly and deviously for one's own purposes. From Latin *manipulus*, a handful, also a company (maniple) of foot soldiers.
From same base: manipulate, manipulating, manipulated, manipulatable.
Synonyms: controlling, working, wielding, handling, using, utilizing, domineering, dictatorial, dominating, regulating.

Language Uses and Abuses

Pesky pronouns and prepositions

Your interest in vocabulary is evidence that you know more about the use of personal pronouns than to be making errors like these:

> Member of a college basketball team in reference to a player on a rival team: "Him and me are good friends."
> Professional football analyst: "There's no love lost between he and his opponent."

Nevertheless, there is a first person "pronoun trap" into which it is easy for anyone to fall. Examples:

> He talked with Shirley and I about our insurance.
> She wrote a letter to my cousin and I.
> My father took my brother and I on a fishing trip.
> Between Ken and I, we could hardly lift the trunk.
> The instructor complimented Marian and I.

Unfortunately, the "I" may slip into that second position, even though we know that transitive verbs and prepositions are followed by *object* forms and that "me" is the *object* form of the personal pronoun "I."

In dealing with "preposition traps," *between* is used for relationships involving <u>two</u> persons or things, and *among* for relationships involving <u>three</u> or more persons or things:

> The five of us agreed among ourselves that the choice for the skiing trip was between Colorado and Idaho.

Quick Checks on Comprehension

In each line below, highlight or check off the word or phrase that best matches the meaning of the word to the left.

ineffable	insupportable, inexpressible, lackadaisical, radical
perceive	receive, sense, pretend, forbid
propitiate	placate, precipitate, negotiate, prorate
component	emolument, port, part, plane
primordially	erratically, primitively, proportionally, extraordinarily

| secular | popular, worldly, presumptive, niggardly |
| manipulative | pejorative, appealing, dominating, nominating |

In each line below, highlight or check off the two synonyms.

surveying, controlling, compromising, regulating
mundane, immune, earthly, surrealistic
pretentiously, primevally, prehistorically, incomprehensibly
increment, segment, sediment, element
conciliate, ameliorate, appease, surcease
preserve, terminate, observe, discern
unutterable, unspeakable, unbearable, unacceptable

In each line below, highlight or check off the two antonyms.

understand, refuse, misjudge, underscore
appropriately, traditionally, warily, recently
literal, unusual, temporal, spiritual

If unsure about your comprehension choices, please see Appendix A.

Use a new word today or you may have to pay!

DAY 10

New Word-Choices
Robert L. Carter, speech on
"The Criminal Justice System Is Infected with Racism,"
Vital Speeches of the Day, 62 (March 1, 1996) 10, p. 291.

I was fortunate to have become a civil rights litigator at a propitious period in the history of race relations. It was a time of change. The dichotomy between the country's egalitarian protestations and its mandated racial differentiations had begun to cause disquiet. The civil rights lawyers were succeeding in convincing the Supreme Court to infuse the 14th and 15th amendments with new life and meaning as guarantors of equal rights for blacks. Until that time, as you know, neither provision had been of much benefit to blacks.

litigator (LIT-ih-gayt-er), one who brings a dispute or claim before a court of law. From Latin *litigatus*, pp. of *litigare*, to dispute, bring suit, and, in turn from *lis* (genitive litis), dispute, + *agere*, to do, be party to.
From same base: litigate, litigating, litigated, litigation.

propitious (pruh-PISH-us), attended by favorable circumstances.
From Latin *propitius*, favorable.
From same base: propitiously, propitiousness.
Synonyms: auspicious, lucky, favorable, advantageous, promising, beneficial, encouraging, providential.
Antonyms: unfavorable, unlucky, inauspicious, disadvantageous, discouraging, unfortunate, disastrous, disconcerting, adverse.

dichotomy (dy-KOT-uh-mee), a division into two parts or classes. From Greek *dicha* (dicho), in two, and *tome*, a cutting. From same base: dichotomize, dichotomizing, dichotomized, dichotomous, dichotomously.

egalitarian (ih-<u>gal</u>-ih-TAIR-ee-un), relating to or believing in racial and social equality. From French *égalitaire* with same meaning, and, in turn, from *égalité*, equality.
<u>From same base</u>: egalitarianism.
<u>Synonyms</u>: friendly, democratic, human, thoughtful, considerate.

protestation (<u>praw</u>-teh-STAY-shun), the act of asserting positively, a strong declaration or affirmation; an objection of some kind. From Late Latin *protestatio* with same meaning.
Synonyms: objection, declaration, affirmation, allegation, complaint, claim, assertion.

mandated (MAN-dayt-ed), required, authorized, ordered. From Latin *mandatus*, pp. of *mandare*, to put into one's hand (*manus*), entrust.
<u>From same base</u>: mandate, mandating, mandatory, mandatorily.
<u>Synonyms</u>: commanded, ruled, directed, authorized, dictated, enjoined, demanded, instructed, decreed, prescribed, ordained, imposed.
<u>Antonyms</u>: petitioned, solicited, entreated, beseeched, implored, sought, appealed.

differentiation (<u>dif</u>-ur-EN-shee-<u>ay</u>-shun), a difference, unlikeness. From Middle Latin *differentiatus*, pp. of *differentiare*, to differ.
<u>From same base</u>: differentiate, differentiating, differentiated.
<u>Synonyms</u>: difference, unlikeness, disparity, divergence, dissimilarity, contrast, distinction, variation.
<u>Antonyms</u>: similarity, concurrence, accord, accordance, agreement, assent, harmony, concord, congruity.

infuse (in-FYOOZ), to instill, inspire, pour into. From Latin *infusus*, pp. of *infundere* (*in* + *fundere*, to pour), to pour in.
From same base: infusing, infused, infusion.
Synonyms: instill, inspire, pour into, imbue, indoctrinate, fill.

amendment (uh-MEND-ment), a revision or correction of a law, in
this instance, of the Constitution. From Old French *amendement*
with same meaning, and, in turn, from *amender*, to change..
From same base: amend, amending, amended, amendable,
amendatory.
Synonyms: alteration, correction, change, revision, improvement,
reformation

guarantor (GAIR-en-tur), one who gives a pledge of support or gives
assurance that some right will be protected or that something will be
done. From Old French *garantir*, to make a pledge or agreement..
From same base: guarantee, guaranteeing, guaranteed.
Synonyms: subsidizer, supporter, sustainer, patron, backer, sponsor.

provision (pruh-VIZH-un), a part of a total document or agreement;
the act of providing or the state of being provided. From Latin
provisio, a foreseeing, and, in turn, from *provisus*, pp. of *providere*,
to provide for, make preparation for.
From same base: provide, providing, provided, provisional,
provisionally.
Synonyms: proviso, condition, prerequisite, requirement, stipulation.

Language Uses and Abuses

Using action words

It pays to use action words (the "active voice" if you remember that
term from earlier school days). Your own experience tells you it is
more interesting to hear or read sentences like "The governor vetoed
the bill" or "We won the game" instead of their passive versions, "The
bill was vetoed by the governor" or "The game was won by us." The
first sentences leave no doubt about who did what to what; you see
living human beings in action. The second versions are indirect and
less appealing. So the rule-of-thumb is this: Try to give your readers
and listeners as much action as possible.

Quick Checks on Comprehension

In each line below, highlight or check off the word or phrase that best
matches the meaning of the word to the left.

litigator   legislator, innovator, claimant, applicant
propitious   enterprising, calling, renewing, promising
dichotomy   division, suspicion, inception, creation
egalitarian   autocratic, democratic, esoteric, plutocratic
protestation   affirmation, elation, probation, prevarication
mandated   subscribed, prescribed, inscribed, proscribed
differentiation   disparity, probity, asperity, alacrity
infuse   entail, profuse, refuse, instill
amendment   incision, apparition, alteration, punctuation
guarantor   collaborator, sponsor, elector, enumerator
provision   premonition, aspiration, stipulation, cession

In each line below, highlight or check off the synonyms.

supposition, condition, condiment, requirement
supporter, innovator, patron, matron
allocation, correction, elaboration, revision,
admire, inspire, subdue, imbue
politeness, impasse, unlikeness, contrast
enjoined, purloined, imposed, decreed
remark, margin, objection, complaint
friendly, considerate, energetic, suspicious
economical, beneficial, providential, informational

In each line below, highlight or check off the antonyms.

pernicious, auspicious, discouraging, foraging
commanded, elucidated, petitioned, absconded
improvisation, lucidity, variation, congruity

If unsure about your comprehension choices, please see Appendix A.

Swing and sway but don't put those words away!

DAY 11

New Word-Choices
From Victor J. Riley, Jr., speech on "Moving Beyond Rhetoric,"
Vital Speeches of the Day, 61 (March 1, 1995) 10, p. 313.

Your <u>commitment</u> [that of The Urban League] to jobs—through training, education, and placement—has been <u>commendably</u> steady. But, as successful as you are in training students, you need to be sure that good jobs are available on the other side of graduation day.

Yes, there's checkbook <u>philanthropy</u>. Yes, there are <u>mentor</u> programs. Yes, there are summer <u>internships</u> and <u>adapting</u> schools and set asides and paying for scholarships and <u>corporate</u> campaigns to help our schools, etc. All of these are <u>genuine</u> and important. And I am not <u>disparaging</u> or dismissing them. They are clearly part of the larger <u>formula</u> and will continue to be <u>indispensable</u>. But now can we not step up to the plate and do the right thing that is needed? And that is providing jobs.

commitment (kuh-MIT-ment), a promise or pledge to do something; the state of being committed. From Latin *committere*, to entrust, + *ment*, suffix indicating noun.
<u>From same base</u>: commit, committing, committed, committal, committee.
<u>Synonyms</u>: promise, consignment, engagement, pledge, assignment.

commendably (kuh-MEND-uh-blee), praiseworthily, laudably. Adverb from Latin *commendare*, to commend, render agreeable.
<u>From same base</u>: commendable.
<u>Synonyms</u>: praiseworthily, laudably, approvingly, creditably, admirably, splendidly, spectacularly, brilliantly.

Antonyms: censurably, culpably, blamefully, reprehensibly,
objectionably, reproachably, reprovably.

philanthropy (fih-LAN-thruh-pee), the act of making humanitarian
donations for the benefit of worthy groups, organizations, or
institutions. From Greek *philos* (phil), love, + *anthropos* (anthrop),
man or mankind, + *y*, suffix indicating noun.
From same base: philanthropic, philanthropical, philanthropically,
philanthropist.
Synonyms: kindness, benevolence, generosity, sympathy, compassion,
charity.
Antonyms: selfishness, niggardliness, pitilessness, cruelty,
oppressiveness, stinginess, covetousness, greediness.

mentor (MEN-tur), one who undertakes to advise, help, and befriend
a younger person. After the Greek mythological character, Mentor,
advisor to Odysseus in Homer's Odyssey.

internship (IN-turn-ship), a period of in-service training, medical or
otherwise. From Latin *internus*, inward, internal.
From same base: intern, internal.

adapting (uh-DAPT-ing), bringing into conformation with,
modifying to fit current or new conditions. From Latin *adaptare*, to
fit to.
From same base: adapt, adapted, adapter.
Synonyms: suiting, fitting, conforming, harmonizing, adjusting,
accommodating.
Antonyms: misfitting, misplacing, deranging, disjoining, dislocating.

genuine (JEN-yoo-in), being of the origin, descent, or character
claimed. From Latin *genuinus*, natural, real.
From same base: genuinely, genuineness.
Synonyms: real, tested, proven, true, natural, legitimate, authentic,
honest, sincere, actual, unquestioned.
Antonyms: false, deceitful, unreal, untrue, unnatural, deceptive,
questionable, clouded, fallacious, spurious.

corporate (KOR-pur-it), of or relating to a corporation. From Latin
corporatus, pp. of *corporare*, to make into a body (*corpus*).
From same base: corporately.

disparage (dis-SPARE-ij), to speak slightingly of, show disrespect for. From Old French *desparagier*, to lower from rank, to discredit.
From same base: disparaging, disparagingly, disparaged.
Synonyms: belittling, depreciating, deprecating, decrying, discrediting, dishonoring, undervaluing, underrating.
Antonyms: praising, eulogizing, acclaiming, approving, lauding, applauding, commending, complimenting, flattering, recommending.

formula (FOR-myoo-la), an exact or prescribed method for doing something, making something, or preparing something. From Latin *formula*, established form, rule, principle.
From same base: formulary.

indispensable (in-dih-SPEN-suh-bl), essential, absolutely necessary. From negative prefix *in*, not, + Middle Latin *dispensabilis*, not important, something that can be done without.
From same base: indispensably, indispensability.
Synonyms: essential, necessary, needed, fundamental, basic, required, prerequisite.
Antonyms: nonessential, unnecessary, needless, superfluous, useless, redundant, uncalled for, unwanted.

Language Uses and Abuses

Some combining forms in action

The "parts" of Latin verbs which often provide combining forms are the present infinitive and the past participle. For instance, the Latin present infinitive "to love" and the past participle, "loved," appear below with their combining forms in parentheses. English meanings of the combining forms come next on the same line. Each set of the six Latin verb forms below is followed by examples of English words derived from those forms.

amare (ami), to love; *amatus* (amat), loved.
  amiable (AY-mee-uh-bl), friendly, kindly.
  amateur (AM-uh-<u>chuur</u>), one who engages in a sport or other
    activity for the pleasure of it.

capere (cap), to take, hold; *captus* (capt), taken, held.
  capacious (kuh-PAY-shus), roomy; able to hold much.

captivate (KAP-tih-<u>vayt</u>), to charm, fascinate (i.e., take captive).

cedere (ced), to yield; *cessus* (cess), yielded.
  cede (seed), to give up, yield, transfer ownership.
  cession (SESH-un), the ceding of rights or territory to another.

dicere (dic), to speak, say; *dictus* (dict), spoken, said.
  diction (DIK-shun), a manner of speaking, choice of words.
  dictum (DIK-tum), a formal statement or pronouncement.

facere (fac), to make, do; *factus* (fact), made, done.
  facile (FAS-il), smooth, glib; easy to perform or do.
  faction (FAK-shun), a group of people operating within and often in opposition to a larger group.

mittere (mitt), to send; *missus* (miss), sent.
  mittimus (MIT-ih-mus), a warrant or writ for putting into prison a person convicted of a crime. Literally, the Latin word means "We send [the convicted person to prison]."
  missive (MIS-iv), a written letter or message [sent off to someone].

spectare (spec), to watch; *spectatus* (specta), looked at, watched.
  specter (SPEK-tur), a ghostly apparition.
  spectacle (SPEK-tuh-kul), a large public show, exhibition.

Quick Checks on Comprehension

In each line below, highlight or check off the word or phrase that best matches the meaning of the word to the left.

commitment   endorsement, procurement, pledge, amendment
commendably   understandably, laudably, surely, formally
philanthropy   compassion, progression, effrontery, respect
adapting   erasing, accepting, eradicating, conforming
genuine   marvelous, tested, new, ordinary
disparaging   dissenting, berating, belittling, besieging
indispensable   indirect, required, responsible, tutorial

In each line below, highlight, or check off the two synonyms.

irresistible, essential, basic, supportive

discrediting, supervising, abbreviating, underrating
cynical, authentic, persistent, actual
suggesting, authorizing, harmonizing, fitting
sympathy, charity, vision, indignation
handily, profoundly, approvingly, praiseworthily
success, promise, misfortune, assignment

In each line below, highlight or check off the two antonyms.

kindness, solitude, opposition, greed
moderating, dislocating, accommodating, elaborating
seasonable, prodigal, questionable, legitimate
commending, marking, generating, deprecating
dilated, essential, uncalled for, prohibited
sufficiently, culpably, quietly, admirably

If unsure about your comprehension choices, please see Appendix A.

On every day in every way, a new word is your best play.

New Word-Choices
From Robert P. Forrestal, speech on "Inflation,"
Vital Speeches of the Day, 61 (March 1, 1995) 10, p. 297.

Another way of looking at wage and price <u>behavior</u> suggests that the economy is less prone to <u>inflation</u> than it has been in the recent past, in part because the expectational setting has changed. Think about it this way: The Fed has been fighting inflation for more than 15 years—a time during which a <u>generation</u> of Americans came to expect recurring inflation at some point in a business <u>expansion</u>. But the Fed succeeded in bringing inflation down, even during the current expansion. It would therefore seem likely that this success would have <u>implications</u> beyond the mere fact that inflation is lower than ever. One implication might be that actions by the Fed have changed the <u>economic</u> <u>environment</u> by weakening the very forces that in the past may have led to <u>generalized</u> inflation.

behavior (bih-HAYV-yur), the way a person or thing acts or functions. From Old English prefix *be* as intensifier + Old French *aveir* (*avoir*), to have in hand, control, possess.
<u>From same base</u>: behavioral, behaviorally.
<u>Synonyms</u>: deportment, manners, bearing, conduct, policy, attitude.

inflation (in-FLAY-shun), growth, the state of being enlarged. From Latin *inflatio*, an enlarging by blowing into.
<u>From same base</u>: inflationary.
<u>Synonyms</u>: distention, expansion, swelling, exaggeration, dilation.
<u>Antonyms</u>: deflation, shrinking, condensation, compression.

generation (jen-uh-RAY-shun), the period of roughly thirty years between the birth of one human-being group and that of the next; the act or process of bringing into being. From Latin *generatus*, pp. of *generare*, to bring into being, produce.

From same base: generational, generative, generator.

Synonyms: formation, race, kind, production, reproduction, creation, caste, age, era, span, period.

Antonyms: destruction, extinction, demolition, abolition, extirpation, dissolution, obliteration, breakdown.

expansion (ik-SPAN-shun), a spreading or increasing in size, scope. From Late Latin *expansio* with same meaning.

From same base: expanse, expansionary.

Synonyms: amplification, extension, widening, magnification, augmentation, increase, dilation, enlargement, development.

Antonyms: decrease, reduction, decline, deflation, contraction, constriction, shrinkage.

implication (im-plih-KAY-shun), something hinted or suggested from which an inferences can be drawn; an act indicating involvement or showing connection with. From Latin *implicatio*, an entwining.

Synonyms: involvement, inference, connection, entanglement, compromise, denotation.

Antonyms: separation, disentanglement, disconnection, removal.

economic (ek-uh-NOM-ik), pertaining to the development or management of wealth. From Greek *oikonomikos*, having to do with management of a household (*oikos*) or estate.

From same base: economical, economically, economics.

environment (en-VYE-run-ment), the external circumstances or conditions that affect the existence or development of individuals or things. From Old French *environner*, to surround, encircle.

From same base: environmental, environmentally.

generalized (JEN-ur-ah-lyz-ed), broad, widespread in application. From Middle English *generalisen*, to make widespread.

From same base: generalize, generalizing.

Synonyms: broad, widespread, extensive, extended, stretched.

Language Uses and Abuses

Troublesome singulars and plurals

criterion (kry-TEER-ee-un), **criteria** (kry-TEER-ee-uh).
A Greek word meaning a standard or rule by which something can be judged. The plural, *criteria,* is too often misused as the singular form. For example, "In electing a judge, the primary criteria we should insist upon is integrity." It shouldbe "...the primary criterion we should insist upon is integrity."

phenomenon (feh-NOM-eh-non), **phenomena** (feh-NOM-eh-nah).
A Greek word meaning an extremely unusual thing or occurrence. Again, the plural is sometimes misused as the singular. For example, "A shooting star is a phenomena we seldom see." It should read "...is a phenomenon we seldom see."

prospectus (pruh-SPEK-tus), **prospectuses** (pruh-SPEK-tuh-sez).
A Latin word meaning a formal document containing details on a proposal for an undertaking of some kind; also a statement on features and attractions of an established institution, college, etc. The plural form is not, as many assume, *prospecti.* If you are speaking of a number of such documents or statements, the correct plural form is *prospectuses.*

alumnus (uh-LUM-nus), **alumni** (uh-LUM-nigh).
alumna (uh-LUM-nah), **alumnae** (uh-LUM-nigh).
When speaking of "alums," some care is in order. An alumnus is a male graduate; an alumna, a female graduate. Jane Doe is an alumna of the University of Virginia; Joe Doe is an alumnus. The women graduates of that institution are alumnae; the male graduates are alumni. When referring to both male and female graduates of an institution, however, alumni is used. (Plurals of both words are pronounced in exactly the same way.)

Quick Checks on Comprehension

In each line below, highlight or check off the word or phrase that best matches the meaning of the word to the left.

behavior   obligation, conduct, product, peril

inflation   infraction, participation, section, distention
generation   era, inspiration, proneness, expectancy
expansion   appeasement, increase, recurrence, impediment
implication   economy, environs, involvement, legend
generalized   expensive, broad, admirable, profitable

In each line below, highlight or check off the two synonyms.

extensive, meshed, contained, widespread
preference, inference, perfection, connection
dilation, development, environment, sentiment
creation, extirpation, reproduction, expectation
retribution, swelling, distention, solution
manners, containment, prudence, deportment

In each line below, highlight or check off the two antonyms.

shrinking, operation, dilation, sanction
satisfaction, production, deprivation, demolition
decrease, ordeal, sentiment, enlargement
prohibition, turbulence, entanglement, separation

If unsure about your comprehension choices, please see Appendix A.

To win more from life's tray, use a new word today!

DAY 13

New Word-Choices
From Susuma Yoshida, speech on
"New Challenges for Japanese Companies,"
Vital Speeches of the Day, 61 (March 1, 1995) 10, p. 304.

Few people in America fully realize how great the communication barrier is for Japanese. Here is an example which illustrates the current status of the so-called "perception gap" between the two nations. A few years ago, after a mission of U.S. Senators had met in Tokyo with high level officials of the Japanese government, one Senator spoke to a Japanese friend about his impression of the meeting:

> The Japanese dignitaries received us with utmost courtesy and seemed to listen carefully to our comments. After the meeting, members of our mission unanimously agreed none of us had clearly understood the points the Japanese probably wanted to make. We also shared the impression that a chilly atmosphere prevailed during the meeting. We were left with the feeling that the Japanese had become even more arrogant than before.

The next morning, a Tokyo newspaper reported on the same meeting, with a comment made by one of the high-ranking Japanese officials:

> We extended our utmost courtesy to the U.S. delegation. We tried to be good listeners instead of strongly pushing our own views, and we feel they appreciated that.

barrier (BARE-ih-ur), an obstacle or obstruction. From Old French *barrière*, a wall, stockade or anything "barring" passage.

Synonyms: bulwark, obstacle, obstruction, rampart, restriction, hindrance, prohibition, restraint, barricade.
Antonyms: admittance, opening, passage, entrance, road, way, transit.

status (STAY-tus), state, condition; relative position or rank. From Latin *status*, a standing or position.
Synonyms: condition, state, standing, position, situation, rank, station.

perception (pur-SEP-shun), the act of becoming aware of   something through the senses; of coming to understand. From Latin *perceptio*, a grasping through senses and mind.
From same base: perceptional.
Synonyms: sensory experience, sensitivity, sensitiveness, sensibility, understanding, comprehension, intuitiveness, discernment.

impression (im-PRESH-un), an effect produced by some source   or influence on the mind, senses, or feelings. From Latin *impressio*, a pressing into or upon.
From same base: impressional, impressionable, impressionability, impressionably, impressionistic, impressionistically, impressionism.
Synonyms: effect on the mind, sensation, feeling, notion, conception, view, inspiration, conception, thought, abstraction.
Antonyms: insensitivity, indifference, apathy, detachment, disinterest.

dignitary (DIG-nih-tare-ee), one holding a high, official   position. From Latin *dignitas*, worth, dignified position.
From same base: dignity.

mission (MISH-un), an individual or group sent forth with authority to perform a certain task or reach a certain objective. From Latin *missio*, a sending off, a sending away.
From same base: missionary, missioner.
Synonyms: commission, delegation, deputation, legation, agency.

unanimously (yoo-NAN-ih-mus-ly), without dissent; with the agreement of all involved.   Adverb from Latin *unus* (un), one, + *animus* (animus), mind, will, disposition + ending *ly*.
From same base: unanimous, unanimity.
Synonyms: harmoniously, conformably, consistently, congruently.

atmosphere (AT-mus-feer), any surrounding element or pervasive influence. From Greek *atmos* (atmos), vapor, + *sphaira* (sphere), sphere.
From same base: atmospheric, atmospherical, atmospherically.

arrogant (EHR-uh-gant), overbearing, haughty, full of self-importance. From Latin *arrogans*, prp. of *arrogare*, to be proud without justification.
From same base: arrogantly, arrogance.
Synonyms: haughty, overbearing, self-important, disdainful, supercilious, proud, imperious, pompous, affected.
Antonyms: lowly, humble, unassuming, bashful, backward, servile, submissive, timid, afraid, unobtrusive.

Language Uses and Abuses

Using precise words

On the general subject of being clear, we've already suggested that you use language that is direct, to the point, and active in "voice." Another way to be clear is to stay away from words that are not exact.

For example, words like *walk*, *house*, *street*, *dog*, *beautiful*, and *good* are a part of everyone's vocabulary. However, overused words like those are of little help in holding anyone's attention. The following are more descriptive ways to say *walk*: saunter, hurry, stride, march, amble, tramp, tread, stroll, strut, swagger, limp, hobble, parade, shuffle, etc. Some alternatives to the other routine words at the beginning of the paragraph above: mansion, shaded lane, terrier, striking, and excellent. In short, we listen more attentively to those who speak and write in accurate and descriptive terms.

Quick Checks on Comprehension

In each line below, highlight or check off the word or phrase that best matches the meaning of the word to the left.

barrier	proponent, union, restraint, material
status	apparatus, rank, exodus, habitation
perception	aggression, sensitivity, termination, retribution
impression	feeling, mood, reaction, imposition
dignitary	oracle, lackey, high official, lieutenant

utmost	brightest, quickest, tallest, greatest
mission	delegation, operation, incursion, generation
unanimously	susceptibly, silently, harmoniously, idly
arrogant	defeating, conscious, complacent, disdainful

In each line below, highlight or check off the two synonyms.

sardonic, haughty, wealthy, imperious
conformably, wrongly, consistently, indubitably
summation, interrogation, deputation, legation
conception, thought, reference, sufferance
suspension, comprehension, understanding, elevation
standing, lancing, soliciting, position
salvage, obstacle, rack, bulwark

In each line below, highlight or check off the two words antonyms.

location, obstruction, passage, lineage
sensation, renovation, pulsation, apathy
overbearing, reptilian, servile, civilian

If unsure about your comprehension choices, please see Appendix A.

On your very busy way, use a bright, new word today!

DAY 14

New Word-Choices
From Warren Christopher, speech on "American Foreign Policy,"
<u>Vital Speeches of the Day</u>, 61 (March 1, 1995) 10, p. 290 f.

We have contributed to historic progress in <u>resolving</u> conflict, backing democracy, and promoting development in countries around the world. But we must not rest on our <u>laurels</u>. <u>Aggression, tyranny,</u> and <u>intolerance</u> still <u>undermine</u> political <u>stability</u> and economic development in <u>vital</u> regions of the world. Americans face growing threats from the <u>proliferation</u> of weapons of mass destruction, <u>terrorism, and international crime.</u> And a number of problems that once seemed quite distant, like environmental <u>degradation,</u> <u>unsustainable</u> population growth, and massmovements of refugees now pose immediate threats to emerging democracies and to <u>global</u> prosperity.

resolving (rih-ZOLV-ing), solving or removing by explaining; finding a solution or answer to a problem; coming to a decision. From Latin *resolvere*, to unbind, untie, loosen, open.
<u>From same base</u>: resolve, resolved, resolvedly, resolvable, resolvability.
<u>Synonyms</u>: deciding, willing, persisting, determining, intending, planning, concluding, meaning.

laurels (LOR-ulz), honor or distinction gained by outstanding achievement. Seldom appears in singular. From Latin *laurus*, an evergreen from which, in ancient times, sprigs were woven into wreaths to crown the winners of contests.
<u>From same base</u>: laureled, laureate.

aggression (uh-GRESH-un), hostile behavior; unprovoked attack. From Latin *aggressio* with same meaning.
Synonyms: inroad, offense, encroachment, attack, invasion, warlikeness, belligerence, hostility.
Antonyms: submission, compliance, deference, obedience, subordination, submissiveness, docility, surrender, appeasement, defeatism, homage.

tyranny (TIR-uh-nee), absolute power unjustly exercised. From Greek *tyrannos*, absolute sovereign or ruler.
From same base: tyrant, tyrannical, tyrannically.
Synonyms: despotism, dictatorship, autocracy, absolutism, oppression.

intolerance (in-TOL-ur-ense), lack of respect for or direct opposition to the beliefs or opinions of others. From Latin *intolerantia*, insolence, unbearable conduct.
From same base: intolerant, intolerantly.
Synonyms: prohibition, inhibition, interdiction, hindrance, prevention, restriction, censure, restraint, opposition, obstruction, insolence.
Antonyms: permission, indulgence, concession, recognition, authorization, warrant, submission.

stability (stuh-BIL-ih-tee), the state or quality of being fixed, firm, steady. From Latin *stabilitas*, firmness, durability, steadfastness.
Synonyms: firmness, durability, steadfastness, constancy, immutability.
Antonyms: movability, unsteadiness, mobility, mutability, restlessness.

vital (VIGHT-ul), necessary or essential. From Latin *vitalis*, essential to life (*vita*).
From same base: vitally, vitality.
Synonyms: necessary, essential, indispensable, required, prerequisite, imperative, obligatory.
Antonyms: unnecessary, nonessential, dispensable, redundant, useless, extravagant, unsuitable, superfluous, needless, optional, worthless.

proliferation (pro-LIF-uh-ray-shun), rapid spreading, growth, production, or reproduction. From Latin *proles*, offspring, + *ferre*, to produce, + *tion*, suffix indicating noun.
From same base: proliferate, proliferating, proliferated, prolific, prolifically.

Synonyms: productivity, fertility, creativity, potency, virility, reproduction, procreation.
Antonyms: unproductiveness, unproductivity, infertility, sterility, barrenness, fruitlessness.

terrorism (TER-uh-<u>riz</u>-um), use of force or threats to demoralize or intimidate. From Latin *terrere*, to frighten.
From same base: terrorize, terrorizing, terrorized, terror, terrorist, terroristic, terrorization.
Synonyms: intimidation, demoralization, discouragement, anarchism, anarchy, coercion, violence, dissuasion.
Antonyms: encouragement, invigoration, animation, inspiration, exhilaration, stimulation, instigation.

degradation (<u>deg</u>-ruh-DAY-shun), a downgrading or bringing into contempt. From Late Latin *degradatio*, a bringing down (*de*) in rank or grade (Latin *gradus*).
Synonyms: baseness, meanness, dishonor, disgrace, debasement, degeneracy, dissipation, removal, dismissal.
Antonyms: honor, exaltation, elevation, admiration, praise, reward, merit, ascendancy, superiority.

unsustainable (<u>un</u>-suh-STAYN-uh-bl), not supportable. From Latin negative prefix *un*, not, + *sustinere*, to hold up, support.
From same base: sustain, sustaining, sustained, sustainable, sustainably, sustenance.
Synonyms: insupportable, unbearable, unrelievable, insufferable, unendurable, unfavorable.
Antonyms: maintainable, supportable, bearable, relievable, sufferable, endurable, favorable.

Language Uses and Abuses

More similar-sounding pairs + a triplet

affect is a verb meaning to have an influence on. "His disability did not affect his positive attitude toward life."
effect is both a verb and a noun. As a verb, effect means to bring about. "Her strong case effected a reversal in the members' views." As a noun, effect means a result. "His remarks had no effect me."

ingenious (in-JEEN-yus) means clever, inventive. "When it comes to making excuses, Jeff is really ingenious."

ingenuous (in-JEN-yoo-us) means innocent, simple, artless; candid, frank. "He is too ingenuous to be successful in that kind of business."

adverse (ad-VURS) means working against, unfavorable. "If there was anything she didn't like, it was adverse criticism." "The adverse effects of the San Francisco earthquake will be felt for a long time."

averse (uh-VURS) means unwilling, reluctant. "He was averse to committing himself to any one position."

assure is to promise with confidence. "He assured us that tickets would be available at a later date."

ensure is to make certain. "We mailed our reservations early to ensure that we'd get good seats."

insure is to protect in the legal or financial sense. "We insured our home against hurricane damage."

Quick Checks on Comprehension

In each line below, highlight or check off the word or phrase that best matches the meaning of the word to the left.

resolving   persisting, concluding, insisting, assuring
aggression   relocation, attack, repack, nullification
tyranny   socialism, aphorism, absenteeism, despotism
intolerance   restraint, nuisance, precedence, drudgery
stability   periphery, supremacy, constancy, ecstasy
vital   obligatory, exploratory, virile, perennial
proliferation   subversion, ratification, polity, productivity
terrorism   subversion, intimidation, direction, division
degradation   implantation, surrender, credence, dishonor
unsustainable   unendurable, unlearned, unprecedented, uncouth

In each line below, highlight or check off the two synonyms.

insupportable, unrelievable, unbelievable, inexcusable
duress, firmness, fecklessness, steadfastness
degeneracy, lassitude, disgrace, disaffection

demoralization, fraternization, discouragement, dismay
retired, required, expired, imperative
hindrance, revenge, instance, censure
statesmanship, relevancy, autocracy, dictatorship
debasing, descending, deciding, determining
fertility, unity, creativity, passivity
inability, offense, hostility, suspense

In each line below, highlight or check off the two antonyms.

supposition, invasion, promotion, submission
supposition, opposition, suspension, permission
heedlessness, unsteadiness, creativity, durability
needless, dignified, essential, equivocal
reenactment, element, procreation, barrenness
sentiment, dissuasion, encouragement, demoralization
dismissal, subservience, abolition, admiration
favorable, unsubstantiated, unbearable, feasible

If unsure about your comprehension choices, please see Appendix A.

A new word a day keeps the ennui away!

New Word-Choices
From Vicki Kemper, "A Citizen for All Seasons,"
Common Cause Magazine, 21 (Spring, 1995) 1, p. 12 f.

And at this time when millions of Americans have given up on government and public service and given in to cynicism and passivity, Esther Peterson at 88 is perhaps more remarkable than ever, a rare breed of patriot. While others mourn its passing, she remains unabashedly committed to both the wondrous idea and the ordinary labor of participatory democracy. In contrast to the prevailing voices that speak only of getting government off our backs and out of our lives, she continues to call for a government of, by and for people who care about more than their own narrow interests—even as she embodies the current buzzwords "volunteerism" and "individual responsibility." And though she worries that 1990s politics is too often reduced to soundbites, and frets that public participation often amounts to no more than negativism and name-calling on talk radio, she continues to believe that one person can make a difference and, even more important, that people working together can do anything.

cynicism (SIN-uh-siz-um), belief that everyone is motivated by selfishness and material interests. From Greek *kynikos*, dog-like, shifty.
From same base: cynic, cynical, cynically.
Synonyms: incredulity, skepticism, suspicion, unbelief, disbelief, distrust, doubt.
Antonyms: belief, trust, credence, confidence, reliance, acceptance, conviction.

passivity (pas-SIV-ih-tee), submission without opposition or resistance; state or quality of being inactive, submissive. From Late Latin *passivitas* with same meaning.
Synonyms: inactivity, acquiescence, submission, compliance, deference, obedience, subordination, submissiveness, resignation, humility, docility, surrender, indulgence.
Antonyms: defiance, opposition, disobedience, revolt, insubordination, confrontation, challenge.

unabashedly (un-ah-BASH-ud-lee), boldly; not ashamedly. Negative prefix *un*, not, + *abashedly*. From Old French *esbahir*, to make ashamed, ill at ease.
From same base: unabashed.
Synonyms: boldly, bravely, fearlessly, intrepidly, resolutely, courageously, audaciously, daringly.
Antonyms: timidly, fearfully, apprehensively, anxiously, solicitously, nervously, shyly.

committed (kuh-MIT-id), bound to, devoted to, pledged. From Latin *committere*, to entrust.
From same base: commit, committing, committal, committee.
Synonyms: trusted, entrusted, relegated, delegated, promised, assigned, consigned.
Antonyms: desisted, stopped, ceased, kept from, idled.

wondrous (WUN-drus), wonderful beyond measure. From Middle English *wundres*, out of the ordinary.
From same base: wonder, wonderful, wonderfully, wondering.
Synonyms: amazing, surprising, astonishing, stupefying.
Antonyms: routine, anticipated, expected, common, predicted.

participatory (par-TIS-ih-puh-TOR-ee), taking part in or sharing with others. From Latin *participatus*, pp. of *participare*, to share.
From same base: participate, participating, participated.
Synonyms: sharing, using, joining, cooperating, taking part in, partaking.

prevailing (pree-VAY-ling), currently strong, holding sway at the present time. From Latin *praevalere*, to be strong, hold sway.
From same base: prevail, prevailing, prevailed, prevalent, prevalence, prevalently.

Synonyms: predominant, general, universal, common, sweeping, all-embracing, comprehensive, widespread.
Antonyms: isolated, sporadic, exclusive, uncertain, partial, restricted.

embody (em-BOD-ee), to put into definite or visible form, make concrete. From prefix *em*, in, + Old English *bodig*, trunk, chest.
From same base: embody, embodying, embodied, embodiment.
Synonyms: incorporate, embrace, integrate, contain, include, comprise.

buzzword (BUZ-wurd), a word coined in recent years to cover current jargon in a particular field; in the context-paragraph above, the field is social and political action.

volunteerism (vol-un-TEER-ism), the practice of volunteering, in this instance, to be politically active and supportive of democratic action on all fronts. From Latin *voluntarius*, voluntary.
From same base: volunteer, volunteering, volunteered, voluntary.

soundbite (SOUND-bite), another current reference coined to cover the very short, bites-of-sound statements or advertisements common to radio and television.

fret (fret), to worry, be troubled. From Old English *fretan*, to devour, knaw away.
From same base: fretting, fretted, fretful, fretfully, fretfulness.
Synonyms: chafe, gall, corrode, disturb, agitate, anger, vex, annoy.
Antonyms: soothe, calm, comfort, soften, please, placate, smooth, heal.

negativism (NEG-uh-tih-viz-um), skepticism; an attitude characterized by doubting and questioning. From Latin *negativus*, opposite to something, in denial of it.
From same base: negative, negatively, negativeness, negativist.
Synonyms: abrogation, confutation, denial, cancellation, refutation, revocation, nullification, refusal, skepticism.

Language Uses and Abuses

Still more similar-sounding pairs

continual and **continually** apply to that which happens over and over again. "Wars in Europe seem to be continual." "Their business relationship is continually interrupted by arguments."

continuous and **continuously** apply to that which goes on without interruption. "Going to a movie has the advantage of its being continuous—no commercials." "We were continuously at odds throughout that discussion about what to do next."

credible, believable. "His story was credible; it had the ring of truth."

credulous, gullible, easily convinced. "No matter how outrageous the story she told him, he was credulous to the extreme."

incredible, unbelievable. "His survival in the face of hardship is incredible."

incredulous, unbelieving. "When the lawyer told us we had no arguable case, we were incredulous."

discreet, tactful, especially in dealing with others; careful about respecting confidences. "When confiding in her, you could depend on her being discreet."

discrete, not attached to others, made up of separate parts. "I was amazed by his command over hundreds of discrete items of information about European history."

principal is, first, a noun meaning either a chief person (e.g., a school principal, the principal in a play) or, secondly, financial capital. "Because of bad times, keeping his principal intact was difficult." The word is also an adjective meaning major or foremost: "Her principal goal was a degree in sociology."

principle is a noun only and means an important axiom, fundamental truth, law, doctrine, rule of conduct, motivating force. "High moral principles governed every aspect of Eleanor Roosevelt's life."

Quick Checks on Comprehension

In each line below, highlight or check off the word or phrase that best matches the meaning of the word to the left.

cynicism	praise, distrust, confidence, insolence
passivity	sublimation, propriety, docility, asperity
unabashedly	superbly, eloquently, succinctly, boldly

committed	enervated, delegated, extricated, sublimated
wondrous	worrisome, suspicious, mystifying, astonishing
participatory	liking, sharing, parting, adorning,
prevailing	general, separate, forlorn, colossal
fret	resolve, agitate, waste, protect
embody	change, succeed, contain, suborn
negativism	denial, referral, pretense, solecism

In each line below, highlight or check off the two synonyms.

revocation, convocation, evocation, confutation
anger, corrode, suppress, narrate
excuse, benefit, embrace, comprise
failing, sweeping, common, mastering
joining, rationing, petitioning, cooperating
helping, surprising, exhorting, amazing
promised, perplexed, effortless, entrusted
bravely, accordingly, daringly, sparingly
propinquity, humility, impression, submission
humanism, proficiency, skepticism, suspicion

In each line below, highlight or check off the two antonyms.

spout, doubt, credence, reference
compliance, cessation, defiance, gradation
carefully, woefully, fearlessly, timidly
persistent, desisted, assigned, persisted
astonishing, enabled, expected, insulted
ephemeral, sporadic, acrylic, general
volunteer, annoy, placate, enunciate

If unsure about your comprehension choices, please see Appendix A.

A new word a day and you'll be on your way!

New Word-Choices
From Vernon E. Jordan, Jr., speech on
"The Business Community and Government,"
Vital Speeches of the Day, 61 (March 15,1995) 11, p. 335 f.

Americans don't want big government, but they also don't want small government—government that abandons its responsibility to protect its weakest and most <u>vulnerable</u> citizens. Americans don't like taxes and deficits, but they also don't like being hustled into policies that throw a few dollars to the middle class, throw thousands to the wealthy, and throw the poor into the streets.

The clash of ideas in Washington today is a good thing. It is important to have your ideas challenged and to be forced to defend them. That is the <u>essence</u> of the democratic process. But there is more to the democratic process: the <u>inevitability</u> of <u>compromise</u> and the need to develop <u>bipartisan</u> <u>consensus</u> on <u>critical</u> national issues. Unfortunately, much of what comes out of Washington these days goes against the grain of the democratic process. We hear a take-no-prisoners <u>rhetoric</u> and <u>demonization</u> of liberal views that bring political <u>discourse</u> down to the level of radio talk-show extremism.

The journalist, H.L. Mencken, once wrote that he mistrusted most the man who "...always attacks his opponents, not only with all arms but with snorts and <u>objurgations</u>, who is always filled with moral <u>indignation</u>, and who is incapable of imagining honor in an <u>antagonist</u>, hence incapable of honor himself." That is an <u>eloquent</u> plea for civil political discourse.

vulnerable (VUL-ner-uh-bl), capable of being hurt or damaged.
  From Latin *vulnus*, wound.
<u>From same base</u>: vulnerably, vulnerability.

Synonyms: exposed, unprotected, accessible, unguarded, powerless, helpless, infirm, indefensible, assailable.

Antonyms: protective, conservative, defensive, secure, inviolable, invulnerable, unassailable.

essence (ES-ense), the fundamental or distinctive quality of something. From Latin *essentia*, something that is, exists.

inevitability (in-EV-ih-ta-bil-ih-tee), quality or state of being unavoidable or unpreventable. From Latin *inevitabilis*, that which cannot be avoided or prevented.

From same base: inevitable, inevitably.

Synonyms: certainty, sureness, definiteness, undeniability, inescapability, surety.

Antonyms: uncertainty, doubt, question, qualm, hesitation, insecurity, doubtfulness, vagueness, confusion.

compromise (KOM-pruh-mize), adjustment by means of concession; the result of such concession. From Latin *com*, together with others, + *promittere*, to promise, concede.

From same base: compromise, compromising, compromised.

Synonyms: adjustment, arrangement, settlement, conciliation, arbitration, agreement, concession, accommodation.

Antonyms: disagreement, altercation, strife, dispute, quarrel, dissension, wrangling, controversy, contention.

bipartisan (by-PAR-tih-zn), representing or supported by the members of two parties. From Latin *bi*, by two, into two, + *partire*, to divide.

From same base: bipartisanship, bipartite, bipartition.

consensus (kun-SEN-sus), general agreement, collective opinion. From Latin *consensus* (*con*, with others, + *sensus*, feeling, attitude).

Synonyms: compliance, acquiescense, confirmation, ratification, endorsement, affirmation, agreement.

Antonyms: dissension, refusal, noncompliance, protestation, contradiction, disagreement, discordance, denial, objection.

critical (KRIT-ih-kul), decisive, crucial; analytical. From Greek *kritikos*, critical, able to discern, express judgment.

From same base: critic, critically.

Synonyms: important, crucial, decisive, acute, grave, key, material, momentous, significant, substantial, serious, weighty.
Antonyms: unimportant, insignificant, immaterial, inconsequential, trivial, trifling, unessential, noncritical.

rhetoric (RET-ur-ik), insincere and artificial speaking or writing in contrast to the original Greek (*techne*) *rhetorike*, (the art of) speaking persuasively.
From same base: rhetorical, rhetorically, rhetorician.

demonization (DEE-mun-ih-zay-shun), a making into a demon; bringing under the influence of demons. From Greek *daimon*, evil-spirit, fate.
From same base: demonize, demonizing, demonized, demonic,demonically, demonism.

liberal (LIB-ur-ul), favoring progress or reform; also, as noun, one having progressive opinions or convictions. From Latin *liberalis*, relating to freedom.
From same base: liberally.

discourse (DIS-kors), formal or informal debating of issues or exchange of ideas. From Latin *discursus* with same meaning.
From same base: discourse (verb), discoursing.
Synonyms: argument, debate, lecture, conference, discussion.

objurgation (OB-jur-gay-shun), act of rebuking severely,   scolding. From Latin intensive prefix *ob* + *jurgatus*, pp. of *jurgare*, to rebuke, scold.
From same base: objurgate, objurgating, objurgated, objurgator.
Synonyms: rebuke, abuse, execration, condemnation, criticism, vituperation, reprobation.
Antonyms: praise, applause, commendation, approval.

indignation (in-dig-NAY-shun), the anger or scorn resulting from injustice, ingratitude, meanness. From Latin *indignatio* with same meaning.
Synonyms: anger, wrath, ire, resentment, scorn, displeasure,fury, rage, passion, animosity, exasperation, irascibility, acrimony, bitterness.

<u>Antonyms</u>: calmness, coolness, gentleness, modesty, humility,
patience, forbearance, toleration, tranquillity, restraint, equanimity,
self-control.

antagonist (an-TAG-un-ist), one who actively opposes,   resists, is
   hostile. From Greek preposition *ant*, against, + *agein*, to struggle, +
   ist, suffix indicating noun.
<u>From same base</u>: antagonize, antagonizing, antagonized, antagonistic,
antagonistically, antagonism.
<u>Synonyms</u>: foe, rival, adversary, opponent, detractor, competitor,
defamer, vilifier, defiler.
<u>Antonyms</u>: friend, benefactor, helper, assistant, supporter, associate,
companion, adherent, protector.

eloquent (EL-uh-kwent), fluent, forceful, persuasive. From Latin
   eloquens, prp. of *eloqui*, to speak out.
<u>From same base</u>: eloquently, eloquence.
<u>Synonyms</u>: moving, voluble, smooth, glib, prepared, convincing,
. persuasive, inciting, inducing, stimulating.
<u>Antonyms</u>: dissuasive, discouraging, restraining,disheartening,
deterring, repressing, hindering, suppressing,constraining, restricting.

Language Uses and Abuses

Introducing prefixes as guides to meaning

Knowing the meaning of the more common prefixes is helpful in
understanding and remembering words, especially when you already
have some idea of the sense of the words to which they are attached.
We begin with two words from this Day's context-paragraphs.

bipartisan. The *bi* is Latin with these meanings: two, having two, on
   both sides, in two ways, in two directions. Examples:

   bipartisan, representing or supported by two parties.
   biped, any two-footed animal.
   bilateral, two-sided, as in a two-country treaty.
   biplane, an aircraft having two wings.
   biweekly, occurring or coming out once every two weeks.
   bimonthly, occurring or coming out once every two months.

antithesis. The Greek *anti* means   against; it is here coupled with *thesis*, a position taken. The resulting noun means opposition to a position taken or the balancing of ideas, one against the other. Other examples of *anti* as a prefix:

antiaircraft, guns or missiles used for defense against enemy planes.
antibiotic, something operating against the growth of bacteria.
antidote, anything that counteracts poison or anything else. p
antifreeze, works against freezing in car radiators, etc.
antipathy, a strong feeling against something or somebody.
antisocial, against the basic principles of society.

Note: The Latin *ante*, sometimes confused with the Greek *anti*, means *before* in time or order. Examples:

antecedent, coming before in time or order.
anteroom, room before a larger, more important room.
antedate, to precede in time, to come before a later stated date.

Quick Checks on Comprehension

In each line below, highlight or check off the word or phrase that best matches the meaning of the wordto the left.

vulnerable   reckless, helpless, insufferable, marginal
inevitability   utility, passivity, certainty, liability
compromise   policy, settlement, arrangement, anticipation
consensus   indignity, perplexity, assurance, agreement
critical   normal, political, tenuous, crucial
discourse   destiny, inference, conference, assistance
objurgation   criticism, witticism, aneurism, sophism
indignation   frustration, suspicion, glorification,   acrimony
antagonist   purist, rival, thief, arsonist
eloquent   inducing, producing, subduing, liking

In each line below, highlight or check off the two synonyms.

voluble, inseparable, persuasive, obtuse
assistant, detractor, protector, adversary
scorn, nationality, monstrosity, animosity
expiration, restraint, rebuke, reprobation

reprehension, debate, discussion, rebate
grave, brave, serious, abstemious
feral, compliance, referral, acquiescence
concession, partition, accommodation, induction
tentativeness, contentiousness, sureness, definiteness

In each line below, highlight or check off the two antonyms.

unprotected, immune, secure, suspected
equity, surety, confusion, infusion
exercise, essence, strife, agreement
confirmation, policy, objection, rhetoric
erudition, commendation, condemnation, extirpation
erosion, passion, prestige, self-control
companion, competitor, hostage, prisoner
preferring, deterring, inciting, exciting
boorish, urbane, outlandish, sacrificial

If unsure about your comprehension choices, please see Appendix A.

Rome wasn't built in a day; keep the words coming your way!

New Word-Choices
From Rodger Schlickeisen, "Connecting with Wolves,"
<u>Defenders of Wildlife</u>, 70 (Winter, 1994/95) 1, p. 5.

Surely humans have an <u>innate</u> <u>psychological</u> need for the beauty and <u>inspiration</u> of unspoiled nature, although this need is becoming difficult to satisfy on our increasingly crowded planet. For all of its existence, after all, humanity has been an <u>integral</u> part of the natural world around us. And <u>evolutionary</u> <u>biologists</u> such as Harvard's Edward O. Wilson believe we retain a powerful <u>genetic</u> <u>affinity</u> for that natural world.

But rather than acting as partners in the natural <u>community</u> of life, humans have become primarily <u>exploiters</u> and conquerors of nature. Many view nature almost <u>exclusively</u> as an economic <u>resource</u>, or even as an <u>obstacle</u> to be overcome. But riches cannot cure the psychological <u>maladies</u> that seem increasingly part of modern <u>urbanized</u> existence.

Americans, despite our wealth as a nation, are <u>obsessed</u> with human problems and stressed by the <u>incessant</u> demands and communications overload that modern society imposes. Feelings of <u>alienation</u> are all too common.. Few of us have the time or means to escape more than occasionally to places where it is possible simply to enjoy the beauty of nature, to gain fresh <u>perspective</u>. Because the need to feel a part of nature is <u>inherent</u> in each of us, we <u>subconsciously</u> seek to restore our lost connection with nature. Perhaps more than anything else, the cause of wolf recovery provides that opportunity.

innate (ih-NAYT), inborn, not acquired. From Latin *innatus*, pp. of *innasci*, to be born, grow, arise in.
<u>From same base</u>: innately.

Synonyms: inborn, inbred, natural, native, ingrained, congenital, intrinsic, immanent, internal.

Antonyms: extrinsic, incidental, superimposed, superficial, transient, casual, external, accidental.

psychological (<u>sigh</u>-kuh-LOJ-ih-kul), having to do with the mind and with mental and emotional processes.   From Modern Latin *psychologia* based on Greek *psyche* (psycho) mind, + *logos* (log), study of, + *y*, suffix indicating noun.

From same base: psychologically, psychology, psychologist.

inspiration (<u>in</u>-spuh-RAY-shun), creative feeling or impulse. From Late Latin *inspiratio* with same meaning.

From same base: inspirational, inspirationally.

Synonyms: grasp, acumen, sagacity, understanding, impulse, comprehension, imagination, impression, sensation, feeling, emotion.

Antonyms: stupidity, idiocy, folly, futility, insensibility, apathy, unconcern, indifference.

integral (in-TEG-rul), essential, necessary for completeness.   From Latin *integer*, complete, whole.

From same base: integrally.

Synonyms: complete, total, essential, necessary, fundamental, elemental, vital.

Antonyms: secondary, accessory, auxiliary, subsidiary, incomplete, unnecessary, part, partial, deficient.

evolutionary (<u>ev</u>-uh-LOO-shun-ary), concerned with origin of life through descent from other forms.   From Latin *evolutio*, development, progressive change.

From same base: evolution, evolutionist.

biologist (by-OL-uh-jist). An expert on the science of life and living things.   From Greek *bios* (bio), life, and *logos* (log), the study or science of, + *ist*, suffix indicating noun.

From same base: biology, biological.

genetic (jen-ET-ic), of the origin of something, how it comes to be the way it is. From Greek *genesis*, origin, source.

From same base: genesis, genetics, geneticist.

affinity (uh-FIN-uh-tee), close relationship, union, natural attraction. From Latin *adfinitas*, relationship by marriage, union of any kind.
Synonyms: attachment, inclination, partiality, close relationship, resemblance, connection, affiliation, association, linkage.
Antonyms: disunion, separation, disengagement, disintegration, detachment, isolation.

exploiter (ek-SPLOYT-ur), one who takes advantage of others or of resources. From Latin *explicatus,* pp. of *explicare,* to use, (and later) to make unethical use of.
From same base: exploit, exploiting, exploited, exploitable.

exclusively (ek-SKLOO-siv-lee), entirely, to the elimination of all other considerations. From Middle Latin *exclusivus*, shut out.
From same base: exclusivity.
Synonyms: entirely, totally, wholly, completely, fully, solely.

resource (ree-ZORS), natural advantage or source. From Old French *resourdre*, to spring up again, rise up anew.
From same base: resourceful, resourcefully, resourcefulness.

obstacle (OB-stuh-kl), something standing in the way, hindrance, obstruction. From Latin *obstaculum* with same meaning.
Synonyms: obstruction, bar, barrier, hurdle, blockage, hindrance, interference, restriction, impediment, encumbrance.
Antonyms: aid, assistance, help, support, liberation, deliverance.

malady (MAL-uh-dee), disease, illness, sickness. From Old French *malade*, sick, infirm.

urbanized (UR-buh-nighzd), rendered city-like in character. From Latin *urbanus*, of a city (*urbs*).
From same base: urbanize, urbanizing, urbanized, urban, urbane, urbanely, urbanism, urbanist, urbanite, urbanity, urbanologist.

obsessed (ob-SES-ed), state of being preoccupied, troubled in mind. From Latin *obsessus*, pp. of *obsidere*, to beseige.
From same base: obsess, obsessing, obsessed.
Synonyms: preoccupied, engrossed, absorbed, musing, troubled, rapt, immersed, unobservant.

incessant (in-SES-nt), endless, continuing without   interruption.
   From Latin prefix *in*, not, + *cessans*, prp. of *cessare*, to cease.
From same base: incessantly.
Synonyms: endless, unending, ceaseless, eternal, perpetual,
interminable, continual, unremitting.
Antonyms: intermittent, periodic, recurrent, occasional.

alienation (ayl-yuh-NAY-shun), separation, an aversion of   feeling.
   From Latin *alienatio*, a separation between persons, a distancing.

perspective (pur-SPEK-tiv), point of view on the relative importance
   of things or circumstances. From Late Latin *perspectivus*, seen
   through, looked through.
From same base: perspectively.

inherent (in-HEER-ent), basic, inborn. From Latin *inhaerens*, prp. of
   inhaerere, to cling to, cleave to.
From same base: inherence.
Synonyms: inborn, innate, natural, inseparable, native, intrinsic,
ingrained, congenital, inbred, indispensable.
Antonyms: superfluous, superficial, extrinsic, incidental,
superimposed, supplemental, subsidiary, fortuitous, casual, external,
accidental.

subconsciously (sub-KON-shus-lee), not clearly or wholly conscious.
   Adverb from Latin prefix *sub*, below, + *conscius*, having feeling or
   knowledge.
From same base: subconscious, subconsciousness.

Language Uses and Abuses

Combining forms from the Greek

We are indebted to the ancient Greeks for close to 10% of the words in
our language, so knowing some of the more common Greek combining
forms can help us understand and remember the meanings of many
words. With pronunciations and combining forms within parentheses,
a few examples follow.

biology (by-OL-uh-jee), the study of the processes of life. From *bios*
   (bio), life, + *logos* (log), study of, + *y* as noun indicator.

geology (jee-OL-uh-jee), the study dealing with the physical nature, structure, and development of the earth's crust. From *gaia* (geo), earth, + *logos* and *y* as above.

graphology (gra-PHOL-uh-jee), the study of handwriting. From *graphe* (graph), writing, + *logos* and *y* as above.

pathology (puh-THOL-uh-jee), the study of the nature of disease. From *pathos* (path), disease, + *logos* and *y* as above.

biography (by-OG-ruh-fee), one's life story told by someone else. From *bios* as above + graphia (graph), writing, + *y* as noun indicator.

autobiography (aw-tuh-by-OG-ruh-fee), one's life story told by one's self. From *autos* (auto), self, + *bios* as above, + *graphia* and *y* as above.

photography (fuh-TOG-ruh-fee), the art or process of producing images through exposure to light. From *phos* (photo), light, + *graphia* and *y* as above.

geography (jee-OG-ruh-fee), the science describing the physical features of the surface of the earth. From *gaia* (geo), earth, + *graphia* and *y* as above.

Quick Checks on Comprehension

In each line below, highlight or check off the word or phrase that best matches the meaning of the word to the left.

innate	appropriate, irate, natural, special
inspiration	unction, sensation, aspersion, notion
integral	necessary, exemplary, wary, emotional
affinity	velocity, acuity, linkage, brokerage
exclusively	entirely, supposedly, reliably, carefully
obstacle	carrier, pinnacle, spectacle, barrier
obsessed	possessed, accessed, ordered, absorbed
incessant	subconscious, impressive, unending, unbending
inherent	native, alienated, invading, indebted

In each line below, highlight or check off the two synonyms.

ingrained, inured, inspired, inseparable
pointless, endless, unremitting, unspoken
transient, exposed, preoccupied, unobservant
hindrance, vacancy, impediment, supplement

inexplicably, wholly, completely, absurdly
exoneration, condiment, attachment, connection
total, ethereal, lateral, vital
repulse, impulse, emotion, suspension
congenital, quizzical, usual, inborn

In each line below, highlight or check off the two antonyms.

superficial, pathetic, political, intrinsic
imposing, enjoying, understanding, indifference
responsible, essential, deficient, terminal
isolation, delineation, persecution, affiliation
impertinence, obstruction, assistance, imposture
occasional, conscious, ceaseless, careless
stable, extrinsic, possible, inseparable

If unsure about your comprehension choices, please see Appendix A.

Keep the gremlins away—use a new word today!

DAY 18

New Word-Choices

From Tom Rogers, "Turkey: Where East Meets West and Old Meets New," <u>Michigan Alumnus</u>, 101 (March/April, 1995) 4, p.53.

The Ottoman Empire, which reached its peak under Suleyman the <u>Magnificent</u> (1520-66), once stretched across present-day Turkey to Vienna in today's Austria. But Suleyman's successors lacked his skill at pumping <u>vitality</u> into the far-flung empire. By the time that the Ottoman Empire came tottering into the twentieth century, it was known as "The Sick Old Man of Europe." Some holdings had <u>splintered</u> off into new countries like Greece. The rest had become <u>pawns</u> in the map making dictated by the great powers of Europe.

The Ottoman Empire's disastrous alliance with Germany during World War I set the stage for final <u>dismemberment</u>. Afterward, only the fierce <u>nationalism</u> of a soldier named Mustapha Kemal kept most of the remaining empire intact. Kemal <u>wrenched</u> his country into the twentieth century: he abolished the <u>sultanate</u> and formed a republic; he transformed the Muslim nation into a secular state; he <u>Romanized</u> the Turkish alphabet; he Europeanized and industrialized Turkey.

magnificent (mag-NIF-ih-sent), presenting an imposing appearance, splendid, superb. From Late Latin *magnificens* with same meaning and, in turn, from Latin *magnus* (magni),great, + *facere*, to make.
<u>From same base</u>: magnificence, magnificently.
<u>Synonyms</u>: grand, splendid, noble, superb, sublime, princely, royal, stately, brilliant, majestic, spectacular, imposing.
<u>Antonyms</u>: plain, common, ordinary, normal, informal, dull, unpretentious, commonplace, ungraceful, inartistic.

vitality (vy-TAL-ih-tee), mental or physical vigor, energy. From Latin *vitalitas* with same meaning.
Synonyms: vigor, energy, animation, liveliness, stamina, strength.
Antonyms: languor, lethargy, inertia, apathy, stupor, inactivity.

splinter (SPLIN-tuhr), to break into pieces, fragments. From Middle Dutch *splinte*, to break or split into pieces.
From same base: splintering, splintered, splintery.
Synonyms: break, shatter, smash, fracture, rupture, split, crush, crumble, fragment.
Antonyms: rebuild, restore, reinstate, reestablish, renew, reconstruct, reproduce, reorganize.

pawn (pawn), person or group used at another's will. From Middle English *poun*, a foot soldier.

dismemberment (dis-MEM-bur-ment), a forcible division into parts, pieces. From Old French *desmembrer*, to pull or cut to pieces.
From same base: dismember, dismembering, dismembered.
Synonyms: division, partition, segmentation, apportionment.

nationalism (NASH-uh-nl-iz-um), devotion to one's own country or to its independence. From Latin *natio*, tribe, race, people.
From same base: nationalistic, nationalistically, nationality, nationalist.

wrench (rench), to twist violently, move or force with great effort. From Middle English *wrenchen* with same meaning.
From same base: wrenching, wrenched.
Synonyms: compel, twist, dragoon, wrest, wring, squeeze.
Antonyms: unwind, straighten, untwist, untangle, unbend, uncoil.

sultanate (SUL-tn-ayt), government presided over by a sultan. From Arabic *sultan*, ruler.
From same base: sultan, sultana (wife of a sultan).

Romanized (row-man-IZD), changed to the Roman alphabet as opposed to the Turkic. From Latin *Romanus*, Roman.
From same base: Romanize, Romanizing, Romanized, Romanism, Romanist.

Language Uses and Abuses

What's in a name?

onyma (onym) is Greek for *name*. Thus, we have words like...

synonym (SIN-uh-nim), a word having the same or almost the same meaning as another word. From *syn*, with, + *onym*.

antonym (AN-tuh-nim), a word that has the opposite meaning or close to the opposite in meaning of another word. From *ant(i)*, against, + *onym*.

acronym (AK-ruh-nim), a word combining initial letters or letters and syllables of a series of words (e.g., SEATO, TLC). From *acr(o)*, at the tip of, + *onym*.

pseudonym (SOOD-uh-nim), a false, fictitious, or pen name. From *pseud(o)*, false, + *onym*.

nomen (nomen, nomin) is Latin for *name*...

nomenclature (NOH-men-klay-chur), the system of names used in a specific branch of learning. From *nomen + calator*, a caller or crier.

nominal (NOM-in-ul), in name only; very small compared to expectations. From *nomin* + adjectival ending.

nominate (NOM-ih-nayt), to propose someone as a candidate. From *nominatus*, pp. of *nominare*, to name and, in turn, from *nomin* + verbal ending.

So seeing *onyma* or *nomen* in a word is already to have a first clue to its meaning.

Quick Checks on Comprehension

In each line below, highlight or check off the word or phrase that best matches the meaning of the word to the left.

magnificent	vital, common, stately, perfect
vitality	animosity, vigor, credulity, inactivity
totter	resist, protect, alter, falter
splinter	break, rake, blister, filter
disastrous	harmful, wayward, hollow, spiteful
dismemberment	utilization, impairment, erudition, division

wrench   bench, proscribe, annul, twist

In each line below, highlight or check off the two synonyms.

compress, wrest, compel, dispel
partition, exception, apportionment, insolvency
carnivorous, courageous, calamitous, catastrophic
endure, resolve, shatter, smash
stagger, progress, waver, dwindle
shock, energy, dignity, stamina
brilliant, transformed, imposing, surprising

In each line below, highlight or check off the two antonyms.

plain, zealous, ambitious, majestic
foresight, strength, petition, lethargy
sketch, lurch, deter, stroll
crush, restore, mask, succeed
reticent, traditional, privileged, unfortunate
retract, wring, instigate, straighten

If unsure about your comprehension choices, please see Appendix A.

For an exciting foray, use a new word today!

New Word-Choices
From John F. Lewis, speech on
"The Choice and Voucher Debate: The Price of Democracy,"
<u>Vital Speeches of the Day</u>, 61 (March 15, 1995) 11, p. 328.

It <u>infuriates</u> the <u>advocates</u> of choice that public schools must deal with unions. An <u>independent</u> school principal simply reassigns a teacher to another class, or directs the teacher to coach soccer. The public school principal has to sit down and bargain, and nothing moves unless the union says, "O.K." Worse, to <u>terminate</u> an <u>incompetent</u> or <u>inefficient</u> public school teacher costs lots of money and countless <u>administrative</u> hours. And if you do the courageous thing and spend the money, the public climbs all over you for fiscal <u>irresponsibility</u>. So, no one terminates no one.

To me, it is no answer to our public school problems to setup a <u>dual</u> system and watch as one set of independent-school youngsters gets an education <u>unfettered</u> by what a democracy means, while others—typically <u>impoverished</u>—must go to schools where the rules of democracy are and must, by law, be applied. This is no choice as I understand choice. Good old <u>capitalistic</u> choice is <u>predicated</u> on an even playing field. But because of laws democracy has thrust upon them, public schools cannot change most of the very reasons that <u>underlie</u> decisions by choice advocates to find fault with them.

infuriate (in-FYUUR-ee-<u>ayt</u>), to enrage, make furious. From Middle
    Latin *infuriatus*, intensifier *in* + pp. of *furiare*, to enrage.
<u>From same base</u>: infuriate, infuriating, infuriated, infuriatingly.
<u>Synonyms</u>: anger, goad, madden, exasperate, incense, inflame, agitate, irritate, provoke, craze, nettle.

Antonyms: soften, mollify, soothe, calm, pacify, appease, conciliate, reconcile, moderate.

advocate (AD-vuh-<u>kayt</u>), to favor, defend, recommend. From Latin *advocatus*, pp. of *advocare*, to call, summon.
From same base: advocate, advocating, advocated, advocator.
Synonyms: support, favor, defend, recommend, champion, maintain, promote, advance, forward, justify.
Antonyms: attack, oppose, assail, resist, obstruct, restrain, deny, thwart, confront, contradict, retaliate, protest.

independent (<u>in</u>-dee-PEN-dnt), self-reliant, not depending on others or upon a system. From Latin negative prefix *in*, not, + *dependens*, prp. of *dependere*, to rely on.
From same base: independently, independence, independency.
Synonyms: free, separate, unrestricted, unconfined, alone, sovereign, autonomous, self-reliant, self-sufficient.
Antonyms: dependent, subordinate, subservient, reliant, subject.

terminate (TUR-muh-<u>nayt</u>), to bring to an end. From Latin *terminatus*, pp. of *terminare*, to end, limit.
From same base: terminate, terminating, terminated, terminator.
Synonyms: stop, finish, close, break off, cease, desist, conclude, settle.
Antonyms: begin, start, commence, originate, institute, inaugurate, enter upon, initiate, introduce, set up.

incompetent (in-KOM-pih-tent), denoting lack of ability or skill. From Latin negative prefix *in*, not, + *competens*, prp. of *competere*, to be capable.
From same base: incompetently, incompetence.
Synonyms: unskillful, inexpert, bungling, unable, incapable, inadequate, unfit, inefficient, ineffectual, unhandy, unqualified, disqualified, unskilled, inept, unsuitable.
Antonyms: skillful, dexterous, expert, proficient, competent, deft, clever, talented, capable, knowing, masterly, able, skilled, informed, experienced, practical, efficient, trained, qualified, handy, adept.

administrative (ad-<u>min</u>-ih-STRAYT-iv), connected with management. From Latin *administratus*, pp. of *administrare*, to manage or direct, give out or dispense.

From same base: administer, administering, administered, administratively, administrable, administrator.

irresponsibility ir-ih-spon-sih-BIL-ih-tee), unreliability, shiftlessness. From Latin negative prefix *ir*, not, + *responsus*, pp. of *respondere*, to answer through official opinion.
From same base: irresponsible, irresponsibly.
Synonyms: uncertainty, indecision, unreliability, shiftlessness, hesitation, insecurity, confusion.
Antonyms: responsibility, accountability, encumbrance, burden, liability.

unfettered (un-FET-urd), unchecked as to freedom of movement or expression. From negative prefix *un*, not, + Old English *feter*, a shackle or chain for the feet.
Synonyms: unchecked, unbound, unchained, unleashed, unrestrained, unrestricted, unlimited, uncurbed.
Antonyms: checked, bound, chained, leashed, restrained, restricted, limited, curbed, blocked.

impoverished (im-POV-ur-ished), reduced to poverty. From Middle English *empoverishen*, to make poor, deprive of strength or resources.
From same base: impoverish, impoverishing, impoverishment.
Synonyms: poor, indigent, destitute, beggared, needy, penniless.
Antonyms: wealthy, affluent, independent, prosperous, moneyed, rich.

capitalistic (cap-ih-tul-IS-tik), characteristic of an economic system in which most of the means of production are privately owned. From Latin *capitalis*, of the head (*caput*).
From same base: capitalize, capitalizing, capitalized, capital, capitalism, capitalist, capitalistically.

predicate (PRED-ih-kayt), to assume or affirm as a necessary base. From Latin *praedicatus*, pp. of *praedicare*, to proclaim, declare.
From same base: predicating, predicated.

underlie (un-der-LYE), to lie under or beneath; be the basis for. From Middle English *underlien*, to lie under.
From same base: underlay (past tense), underlain (past participle).

Language Uses and Abuses

Greek numbers as prefixes

Among the words analyzed for Day 16 was bipartisan, the *bi* for "two" and partisan for "parties."   Many other Latin and Greek number-associated prefixes offer similar keys to understanding words. Today, we note a few Greek examples:

monos, one, single, only
monotheism (MON-uh-thee-iz-um), belief in one god; from *mono* + *theos*, god.
monopoly (muh-NOP-uh-lee), exclusive right to sell; from *mono* + *polein*, to sell.

dis, di (before consonants), twice, two, twofold
dilemma (dih-LEM-uh), difficult choice between two unpleasant alternatives; from   *di* + *lemma*, proposition.
diphasic (dy-PHAYZ-ik), having two phases; from   *di* + *phasis*, stage in a cycle.

tria, tri, three
triarchy (TRY-ar-kee), government by three rulers; from *tri* + *archos*, leader.
trilogy (TRIL-uh-jee), a unified series of three plays, novels, or other works; from   *tri* + *logos*, written work (with *logos* as "word" or "work" instead of "study of."

tetra, four
tetragram (TET-ruh-gram), any word of four letters; from *tetra* + *gramma*, something written.
tetragon (TET-ruh-gon), a quadrangle; from *tetra* + *gonon*, angle.

pente, five
pentagon (PEN-tuh-gon), a plane figure with five angles and five sides, as in Pentagon, the five sided building housing the U.S. military establishment; from *pente* + *gonon*, angle.
pentathlon (pen-TATH-lun), an athletic contest in which each contestant takes part in five events; from *pente* + *athlon*, contest.

hex, six

hexameter (hek-SAM-ih-tur), a line of verse containing six metrical feet; from *hex* + *metron*, measure.

hexapod (HEK-sa-pod), any insect with six legs; from *hex* + *podos*, foot.

deka, ten

Decameron (deh-KAM-ur-un), tales told over a period of ten days by Boccaccio in order to while away the time during a medieval plague; from *deca* + *hemera*, day.

decade (DEK-ayd), a period of ten years; from *deca* + *ade* (standard ending).

kilo, a thousand

kilogram (KIL-uh-gram), 1000 grams; from *kilo* + *gramma*, gram in weight.

kilometer (ki-LOM-ih-tur), 1000 meters; from *kilo* + *metron*, meter.

Quick Checks on Comprehension

In each line below, highlight or check off the word or phrase that best matches the meaning of the word to the left.

infuriate	subdue, pursue, provoke, invoke
advocate	champion, narrate, pinion, placate
independent	notorious, intrigued, infamous, separate
terminate	expose, close, oppose, offend
incompetent	able, inane, inconvenient, incapable
irresponsibility	sobriety, inequity, parity, unreliability
unfettered	unchecked, unreasoned, unable, unique
impoverished	supportive, needy, unctuous, established

In each line below, highlight or check off the two synonyms.

lavish, poor, superannuated, indigent
unbound, unimpressed, unleashed, unequal
determination, uncertainty, hesitation, unanimity
bungling, dull, inept, insipid
cease, pole, desist, peel
subjugated, free, expurgated, sovereign
unbend, defend, recommend, suspend

anger, tease, calculate, inflame

In each line below, highlight or check off the two antonyms.

soothe, endorse, predict, agitate
hearten, watch, thwart, favor
prone, alone, expedient, dependent
conclude, initiate, correlate, exude
courted, informed, settled, inexpert
reunion, indecision, responsibility, mobility
unchained, unprepared, indicted, restricted
subverted, beggared, affluent, pompous

If unsure about your comprehension choices, please see Appendix A.

The game is to play! Use a new word today.

DAY 20

New Word-Choices
From Richard W. Riley, speech on "Turning the Corner:
From a Nation at Risk to a Nation with a Future,"
<u>Vital Speeches of the Day</u>, 61 (March 15, 1995) 11, pp. 345, 347.

I [as Secretary of Education] do not <u>sanction</u> <u>federal</u> <u>intrusion</u> into state and local decision making. I did not come to Washington to save the job of a <u>bureaucrat</u> or to defend old ways of doing business. I am a strong supporter of applying ample doses of American <u>ingenuity</u> and <u>creativity</u> in our educational system. We need to encourage ideas such as <u>charter</u> schools and public school choice; be <u>flexible</u> and recognize that students learn in many different ways.

I am an advocate of <u>accountability</u> in public education. That is one important reason why I do not support using public tax dollars for private school <u>vouchers</u>. Above all, we need to avoid the trap that has so often befallen American education: the <u>inability</u> to maintain a sustained drive for excellence. Too often we get distracted by the fad of the moment. What we need now, more than ever, is some old-fashioned American <u>tenacity</u> to stay on course.

So what does this mean to those of us who are a part of the public <u>dialogue</u> about the future of American education? We need to listen to one another. There is a difference between <u>constructive</u> criticism and the <u>articulation</u> of deeply held <u>convictions</u> on one hand and the tendency by some, on the other hand, to define just about everything in public education as useless and, at the extreme, even corrupt.

sanction (SANGK-shun), to approve, confirm, allow. From Latin *sanctus*, pp. of *sancire*, to confirm.
<u>From same base</u>: sanctionable.

Synonyms: confirm, approve, allow, commend, ratify, authorize,
permit, warrant, indulge, advocate, encourage.
Antonyms: disapprove, disparage, denounce, object, blame, censure,
prohibit, inhibit, restrain, hinder, exclude.

federal (FED-ur-ul), of, by, or having to do with the   central
government. From Latin *foedus* (feder), a league, compact, or treaty.
From same base: federally, federalism, federalist.

intrusion (in-TROO-zhun), the act or condition of   encroaching or
forcing upon. From Middle Latin *intrusio* with same meaning.
From same base: intrusive, intrusively, intrusiveness.
Synonyms: trespassing, infringement, invasion, inquisitiveness.
Antonyms: diffidence, shyness, wariness, caution, timidity.

bureaucrat (BYOOR-uh-krat), an official who adheres rigidly to a set
routine.   From French *bureau* (bureau), writing   table or desk, +
Greek *kratos* (crat), rule, power.
From same base: bureaucracy, bureaucratic, bureaucratically.

ingenuity (in-jeh-NOO-ih-tee), the quality of being   inventive, clever.
From Latin *ingenuitas*, frankness, cleverness, inventiveness.
Synonyms: cleverness, inventiveness, shrewdness, cunning, wisdom.
Antonyms: stupidity, unintelligence, incapacity, simplicity, inanity.

creativity (kree-ay-TIV-ih-tee), the power or skill to bring   into
existence. From Middle Latin *creativus*, brought into being through
skill, imagination, art.
From same base: creative, creatively, creativeness.
Synonyms: imagination, enterprise, fancifulness, verve, inspiration,
originality, invention, imagery.
Antonyms: imitation, emulation, simulation, plagiarism, actuality,
realness, objectivity.

charter (CHAHR-tur), authorized to specialize in a certain area or
areas. From Latin *charta*, a formal document, letter, or poem. (The
Magna Charta or Magna Carta, great charter, was a bill of rights
forced on King John of England in 1215 A.D.)
From same base: chartered, charterer.

flexible (FLEK-sih-bl), easily persuaded, willing to change, open to compromise. From Latin *flexibilis*, that which can be bent; adapted, changed.
From same base: flexibly, flexibility.
Synonyms: pliant, supple, adaptable, changeable, pliable, yielding, limber, lithe, bending, docile, tractable.
Antonyms: stiff, unbending, stubborn, unyielding, inflexible, rigid, resistant, obstinate, constrained.

accountability (uh-kownt-uh-BIL-ih-tee), obligation of an individual, group, or organization to be responsible for and justify certain acts or action. From Old French *aconter*, to tell, report, + Latin *habilitas*, aptitude, suitability.
From same base: accountable, accountably, accountableness.
Synonyms: answerability, responsibility, amenability, liability, punishability, blameworthiness, censurability.
Antonyms: irresponsibility, unreliability, untrustworthiness, blamelessness, guiltlessness.

voucher (VOW-chur), a paper stating holder may authorize the use of a specified sum for the education of a child or teenager in a private school. From Old French *vocher*, to attest, affirm.
From same base: vouch, vouching, vouched.

inability (in-uh-BIL-ih-tee), the state of being unable; lacking in power. From Latin negative prefix *in* + *habilitas*, aptitude, suitability.
Synonyms: powerlessness, impotence, incapability, disablement, disability, incapacity, impairment, futility.
Antonyms: ability, aptitude, knack, flair, talent, competence, efficiency, proficiency, adequacy, capability, capacity, initiative, genius, prowess, cleverness.

tenacity (teh-NAS-ih-tee), the quality of holding on, holding strongly (opinions, etc.), holding firmly. From Latin *tenacitas*, a holding firm.
From same base: tenacious, tenaciously.
Synonyms: toughness, perversity, stubbornness, obstinacy, persistence, retentiveness, cohesiveness, resistance.
Antonyms: looseness, laxity, fragility, frailty, timidity, instability, infirmity of purpose.

dialogue (dy-uh-LAWG), a talking together, conversation, discussion. From Greek *dialogos*, a conversation.

constructive (kun-STRUK-tiv), tending to build, improve, advance. From Middle Latin *constructivus*, helping to build.
From same base: constructively, constructiveness.
Synonyms: creative, productive, fertile, original, inventive, ingenious, clever, prolific.
Antonyms: destructive, unproductive, infertile, unoriginal, ruinous, corrosive, abrasive, impotent, unfruitful.

articulation (ahr-tik-yuh-LAY-shun), a statement or utterance; the way in which parts are joined together--as in the sounds of speech. From Latin *articulatio* with same meaning.

conviction (kun-VIK-shun), the state of being certain; a strong belief. From Late Latin *convictio* with same meaning.
Synonyms: creed, persuasion, supposition, notion, impression, opinion, view, conclusion, judgment, theory, assumption.
Antonyms: delusion, illusion, misconception, superstition. uncertainty,

Language Uses and Abuses

The Latin *magnus* as a combining form

Discussion of the word charter (above) led to mention of the Magna Charta. We also have the word *magnus* in Albertus Magnus (Albert the Great), a German philosopher of the same period and, from the earlier 7th Century, Charlemagne (Charles the Great), Emperor of the Western Roman Empire.

Typical examples of *magnus* (magn, magni) in our language:

magnanimous (mag-NAN-ih-mus), great-minded, generous. From Latin *magnus* + *animus*, mind.
magnate (MAG-nayt), an important or influential person in any field. From Late Latin *magnas* (plural *magnates*), great man.
magnificence (mag-NIF-ih-sense), stately or imposing beauty; richness of furnishings, color, dress. From *magnus* + *facere*, to make, do.

magnificent (mag-NIF-ih-sent), presenting an imposing appearance. Same derivation as for word above. (For use in context, see Day 18.)

magnify (MAG-nih-<u>fy</u>), to make larger, increase the size of. Same derivation as for the two words above.

magniloquent (mag-NIL-uh-kwent), speaking or spoken in a great or grandiose style. From *magnus + loquens*, prp. of *loqui*, to speak.

magnitude (MAG-nih-<u>tood</u>), greatness or importance. From *magnus* + a suffix standard for many Latin nouns and for English nouns derived from them.

Quick Checks on Comprehension

In each line below, highlight or check off the word or phrase that best matches the meaning of the word to the left.

sanction	invent, approve, submit, examine
intrusion	infringement, supplement, temperament, increment
ingenuity	energy, propriety, inventiveness, largess
creativity	avidity, originality, aridity, supremacy
flexible	acceptable, probable, capable, adaptable
accountability	timidity, placidity, liability, inability
inability	impotence, arrogance, license, innocence
tenacity	insistence, innocence, forbearance, persistence
constructive	eruptive, deceptive, abrasive, productive
conviction	unction, admonition, assumption, inception

In each line below, highlight or check off the two synonyms.

overview, creed, inception, persuasion
impressive, creative, inventive, perspective
toxicity, laxity, instability, affability
disability, utility, veracity, incapacity
liability, virility, responsibility, culpability
jubilant, pliant, puerile, docile
expression, imagination, euphemism, enterprise
fiction, cleverness, wisdom, carelessness
shyness, verbosity, creativity, caution
show, allow, recognize, authorize

In each line below, highlight or check off the two antonyms.

denounce, pronounce, pretend, commend
perseverance, wariness, endurance, inquisitiveness
liquidity, shrewdness, stupidity, tepidity
invention, prevention, lucubration, imitation
tractable, unyielding, unappealing, stable
punishability, practicality, blamelessness, liability
tenacity, futility, efficiency, temerity
fragility, kindness, acrimony, toughness
lugubrious, ingenious, perspicacious, unoriginal
opinion, union, doubt, opposition

If unsure about your comprehension choices, please see Appendix A.

Put more twist on the play—use a new word today!

New Word-Choices
Samuel Hazo, speech on "Fear of Feelings: Change the Rhythm
and the Walls of the City Will Shake,"
Vital Speeches of the Day, 62 (March 15, 1996) 11, p. 338.

The <u>ultimate</u> <u>casualty</u> at a time of a <u>degeneration</u> of language—in which the expression of both <u>precise</u> thought and precise feeling is not even regarded as a <u>desideratum</u>—is public <u>discourse</u> itself. <u>Diogenes</u> would say that the <u>currency</u> of social life at such a time has been <u>debased</u>. Take much of what passes for political debate, for example, Of course, we all know that genuine political <u>oratory</u>, like <u>acoustical</u> music, has been <u>adulterated</u> by electronic <u>enhancement</u>. Thus, speech-making is no longer an art but a <u>technique</u> in which public men and women are often little more that mouths for speech writers. In short, they "mouth" instead of speak. They do not feel the words at all. Often in <u>compensation</u> some mouthers think that making a point forcefully requires them to raise their voices, as if mere volume <u>signifies</u> emphasis and conviction.

The general fault with the public <u>utterances</u> of many political leaders is that they seem to be somehow detached from what they are saying. This makes them seem <u>vacuous</u> even when they are discussing serious subjects. They begin to sound like men and women who have never in their lives faced the possibility of sudden <u>extinction</u> or injury, never been brushed by tragedy's wing.

ultimate (UL-tih-mit), fundamental, final, last of a series. From Latin
 ultimus, last, highest, greatest.
<u>From same base</u>: ultimately, ultimatum.
<u>Synonyms</u>: fundamental, final, last, highest, greatest, extreme,
maximum, remotest, terminal, eventual, absolute.

casualty (KAZ-yoo-ul-tee), one who or one which is destroyed. From
Middle Latin *casualitas*, an unfortunate happening.
Synonyms: sufferer, victim, pawn.

degeneration (dee-JEN-uh-ray-shun), the condition of being
degraded, debased. From Late Latin *degeneratio* with same
meaning, and, in turn, from Latin *de*, from, + *genus*, kind, race,
species.
From same base: degenerate, degeneracy, degenerative,
degeneratively.
Synonyms: deterioration, decay, corruption, decline, degradation,
decadence, baseness, disgrace, dishonor, abasement, debasement. .
Antonyms: honor, elevation, exaltation, admiration, praise, reward,
merit, reward, ascendancy, superiority.

precise (prih-SEIS), sharply and clearly defined. From Latin
praecisus, pp. of *praecidere*, to cut off, be brief.
From same base: precisely, precision, preciseness.
Synonyms: accurate, definite, exact, authentic, strict, genuine,
rigorous, particular, exacting, inflexible, austere.
Antonyms: inexact, careless, negligent, faulty, erroneous, misleading,
deceiving, lax, false, ambiguous, uncertain.

desideratum (deh-sid-er-RAW-tum), something needed and wanted.
From neuter form of *desideratus*, pp. of Latin *desiderare*, to
desire, want.

Diogenes (dye-AW-jen-eez), a Greek philosopher noted for his austere
life style and for his cynical attitude toward the rest of society and its
material interests.

currency (KUR-en-see), general use, acceptance; money, medium of
exchange. From Latin *currens*, prp. of *currere*, to run, be going on.
From same base: current, currently.

debase (dee-BAYCE), to degrade, lower in worth. From Latin *de*,
down from, + *basis*, base, anything from which a start is made.
From same base: debasing, debased, debasement.
Synonyms: degrade, impair, humble, corrupt, dishonor, taint, shame,
adulterate, abase, contaminate, disgrace, vitiate.
Antonyms: elevate, enhance, lift, improve, help, raise.

oratory (OR-uh-tor-ee), public speaking. From Latin *oratorius*, of a speaker, and, in turn, from *orator*, a speaker.
From same base: orator, oratorical, oration.
Synonyms: rhetoric, discourse, speech, eloquence.

acoustical (uh-KOOS-tih-kul), artificially constructed and transmitted to the ear; having to do with the control of sound. From Greek *akoustikos*, of or for hearing, and, in turn, from *akouein*, to hear.
From same base: acoustic, acoustics, acoustically, acoustician.

adulterate (uh-DUL-tuh-rayt), to make impure by mixing in other ingredients. From Latin *adulteratus*, pp. of *adulterare*, to falsify.
From same base: adulterating, adulterated, adulterant, adulteration, adulterator, adulterer, adulterous, adultery.
Synonyms: debase, mix, defile, corrupt, contaminate, muddle, confuse.
Antonyms: purify, clarify, clear, refine, improve, free, cleanse, filter.

enhancement (en-HANSE-ment), an increasing in volume or augmentation of sound, in this instance through electronic means. From Vulgar Latin intensive *in* + *altiare*, to raise; the latter is, in turn, from Latin *altus*, high.
From same base: enhance, enhancing, enhanced, enhancer.
Synonyms: improvement, intensification, augmentation, enlargement, increase, embellishment.

technique (tek-NEEK), manner of performance. From Greek *teknikos*, in a workmanlike manner, and, in turn from *tekne*, the manner whereby a thing is gained.
From same base: technic, technical, technically, technichality, technician.
Synonyms: method, methodology, way, fashion, procedure, means, system, approach, style.

compensation (kom-pen-SAY-shun), a making amends for a shortfall or lack of a thing or quality. From Latin *compensatio* with same meaning.
From same base: compensate, compensating, compensated, compensationally, compensator, compensatory,
Synonyms: payment, remuneration, wage, salary, allowance, stipend, recompense, reward, indemnity, amends, return, emolument, profit, benefit, gain.

Antonyms: penalty, fine, loss, forfeiture, deprivation, confiscation, damage, sequestration.

signify (SIG-nih-fy), to mean, amount to. From Latin *significare*, to
   be a sign or indication of, and, in turn, from *signum* , sign, + *facere*,
   to make.
From same base: signifying, signified, signifiable, significance,
significant, significantly, signification.
Synonyms: mean, amount to, indicate, disclose, signal, communicate,
evince, express, tell, inform.
Antonyms: nullify, neutralize, preclude, refute.

utterance (UT-ur-ense), that which is spoken or written. From
   Middle English *uttren*, to put forth, speak, or express audibly.
From same base: utter, utterable, utterer.
Synonyms: expression, assertion, declaration, proclamation,
pronouncement.

vacuous (VAC-yoo-us), empty of substance, inane. From Latin
   vacuus, void, worthless.
From same base: vacuously, vacuousness.
Synonyms: vacant, void, empty-headed, blank, dumb, inane.

extinction (ek-STINGK-shun), annihilation, abolition, destruction.
   From Latin *exstinctus*, pp. of *exstinguere*, to put out, quench.
From same base: extinguish, extinguishing, extinguished, extinct.,
extinguishable.
Synonyms: annihilation, abolition, destruction, a putting out.

Language Uses and Abuses

Reviewing a few a's and b's

all ready means "entirely prepared."
already means "before now" or "by now."
   "They were all ready to catch the bus, but it had already gone by."

all right—always two words, never *alright.*

all together means "acting in concert" or "gathered in one place."

altogether means "completely." "The rumor that the club members never meet all together is altogether false."

being as, **being that** are poor substitutes for "because" and should be avoided. "Being as I haven't had time to get ready, I don't expect to do well in the contest" should begin with "Because I haven't had time...."

besides is an adverb meaning "furthermore" or "in addition." It is also a preposition meaning "in addition to."
beside is a preposition meaning "next to." All three uses in one: "Besides, several others besides you wanted to sit beside her."

but, hardly. Using *not* with these words, already negative in themselves, creates a double-negative. "You haven't got but a few minutes to do that job" should be "You have but a few minutes...." "I couldn't hardly hear her" should be "I could hardly hear her."

Quick Checks on Comprehension

In each line below, highlight or check off the word or phrase that best matches the meaning of the word to the left.

ultimate	estimate, eventual, proximate, lamentable
casualty	royalty, ally, victim, pilgrim
degeneration	fiction, frustration, degradation, animation
precise	nice, ordinary, luminous, definite
debase	erase, abase, suppose, oppose
oratory	discourse, resource, laboratory, lavatory
adulterate	eliminate, expectorate, contaminate, prate
enhancement	projection, pronouncement, increase, impound
technique	system, rhythm, critique, pique
compensation	entry, gain, pain, periphery
signify	purify, exemplify, disclose, amplify
utterance	impedance, sufferance, assertion, assumption
vacuous	intelligent, energetic, apprehensive, inane
extinction...	indoctrination, summation, destruction, innovation

In each line below, highlight or check off the two synonyms.

inception, prohibition, abolition, annihilation

vain, void, vital, vacant
expression, function, dilation, declaration
irritate, indicate, salivate, mean
intent, payment, raiment, stipend
way, pay, poach, approach
improvement, emolument, element, embellishment
profess, impress, confuse, corrupt
speech, teaching, eloquence, sequence
shame, repair, impair, proclaim
revere, rigorous, austere, prosperous
rally, disgrace, dismay, decay
sufferer, fawn, pawn, explorer

In each line below, highlight or check off the two antonyms.

incline, decline, efficiency, ascendancy
exact, superfluous, obvious, ambiguous
humble, enhance, stumble, advise
recount, apprehend, defile, cleanse
allowance, annoyance, emolument, predicament
provide, signal, nullify, purify

If unsure about your comprehension choices, please see Appendix A.

Make it easier to convey—use a new word every day!

New Word-Choices
From Madeleine K. Albright, speech on
"The United States and the United Nations,"
Vital Speeches of the Day, 61 (April 1, 1995) 12, p. 354 f.

The power of the United Nations Charter can be found not only in its eloquence, but in its origins. The authors of those <u>lofty</u> <u>ideals</u> understood well the <u>lethal</u> nature of <u>isolationism</u>'s <u>siren</u> call. The battle-hardened generation of Roosevelt, Churchill, and DeGaulle viewed the U.N. as a practical response to an inherently <u>contentious</u> world; a necessity not because relations among states could ever be brought into perfect <u>harmony</u>, but because they cannot. However, just as military power is advanced by the integration of sea power with air and <u>amphibious</u> <u>capabilities</u>, so our diplomacy is advanced by the integration of <u>unilateral</u> with <u>coalition</u> and more broadly <u>multilateral</u> approaches. Multilateral steps complement bilateral and unilateral efforts; they do not substitute for them.

The Administration has continued <u>strategies</u> to improve and reform U.N. peacekeeping so that it better serves our interests. Peacekeeping has the <u>capacity</u>, under the right circumstances, to separate <u>adversaries</u>, maintain ceasefires, <u>facilitate</u> the delivery of <u>humanitarian</u> relief, enable refugees and displaced persons to return home, <u>demobilize</u> <u>combatants</u> and create conditions under which political reconciliation may occur and free elections may be held. In so doing, it can help to <u>nurture</u> new democracies, lower the global tide of refugees, reduce the likelihood ot unwelcome <u>interventions</u>, and prevent small wars from growing into larger conflicts.

lofty (LAWF-tee), noble, sublime; very high (e.g., a lofty peak). From Old English *lyft*, air, sky.

From same base: loftier, loftiest, loftily, loftiness.
Synonyms: high, elevated, exalted, stately, dignified, tall, towering, eminent, soaring, arrogant, haughty, conceited.
Antonyms: low, depressed, modest, diffident, retiring, timid, bashful, timorous, unobtrusive, unpretentious, shy, demure, reserved, unassuming.

ideal (eye-DEE-ul), a worthy model or goal; something in its most perfect form. From Greek *idea*, the look of a thing; an opinion or belief. (Not to be confused with the adjective, **ideal**, perfect, excellent.)
From same base: idealize, idealizing, idealized, ideally, idealization, idealism, idealistic, idealistically, idealist, ideality.
Synonyms: model, goal, pattern, prototype, standard, target, aim, mission, objective.

lethal (LEE-thul), deadly, fatal, causing death. From Latin *letalis*, deadly, mortal, and, in turn, from *letum*, death.
From same base: lethally.
Synonyms: deadly, fatal, mortal, destructive, deathly.
Antonyms: life-giving, refreshing, invigorating, reviving, freshening, strengthening, curative, healthful.

isolationism (eye-suh-LAY-shuh-niz-um), the belief that one's country should not be involved in international alliances, treaties, etc. From Italian *isolato*, set apart, placed alone, and, in turn, from Latin *insula*, island.
From same base: isolation.
Synonyms: separation, segregation, disconnection, dissociation, quarantine, seclusion, insulation.

siren (SIGH-run), enticing, irresistible, dangerously attractive. From Greek *Seirenes*, the mythical Sirens on the south coast of Italy whose songs were thought to entice sailors to their deaths.

contentious (kun-TEN-shus), ever ready to argue, quarrel, fight. From Latin *contentio*, struggle, strife.
From same base: contention, contentiously, contentiousness.
Synonyms: fractious, unruly, pugnacious, irritable, hot-tempered, fiery, excitable, irascible, disputatious, passionate, impetuous.

Antonyms: peaceful, quiet, inoffensive, modest, retiring, agreeable, good-natured, friendly, kind, sympathetic, tolerant, calm, composed, forgiving.

harmony (HAR-muh-nee), a state of order or agreement; pleasing sounds. From Greek *harmonia*, an orderly combination of parts or sounds.
From same base: harmonize, harmonizing, harmonized, harmonization.
Synonyms: concord, agreement, unison, accord, unanimity, unity, uniformity, consistency, conformity.
Antonyms: discord, disagreement, discordance, opposition, strife, disunion, antagonism, conflict, contention.

amphibious (am-FIB-ee-us), that can operate on both land and water. From Greek *amphibios* (*amphi*, two, + *bios*, life), living a double life.
From same base: amphibiously, amphibian, amphibiotic.

capability (kay-puh-BIL-ee-tee), the quality of having the capacity or ability to do something. From Late Latin *capabilis*, being able to do things well.
From same base: capable, capably, capableness.
Synonyms: ability, competency, qualification, suitability, adequacy, efficiency, skill.
Antonyms: inability, incompetency, unsuitability, inadequacy, inefficiency, unsuitability, incapability.

unilateral (yoo-nih-LAT-ur-ul), pertaining to, existing on, or involving one side or nation. From Latin *unus* (uni), one, + *latus* (later), side, + adjective ending *al*.
From same base: unilaterally, unilateralism.

coalition (koh-ah-LISH-un), a temporary alliance of factions or nations for some specific purpose. From Middle Latin *coalitio* with same meaning.
From same base: coalitionist.
Synonyms: combination, alliance, confederation, league, union, treaty, compact.
Antonyms: separation, disagreement, difference, divergence, contention, dispute.

multilateral (<u>mul</u>-tih-LAT-ur-ul), pertaining to, existing   on, or involving more than two sides or nations.   From   Latin *multus* (multi), many, + *latus* (later), sided + adjective ending *al*.
From same base: multilaterally.

strategy (STRAT-ih-jee), a plan or action for securing some   end. From Greek *strategein*, to plan, take charge, lead.
From same base: strategic, strategically, strategist.

capacity (kuh-PAS-ih-tee), the ability or qualification for, or to do, something.   From Latin *capacitas* with same meaning.
Synonyms: capability, competence, aptitude, talent, faculty, aptness, genius, ability, gift, skill.
Antonyms: incompetence, inability, awkwardness, inefficiency, unskillfulness, ineptness, inadequacy.

adversary (AD-vur-<u>sehr</u>-ee), one who actively opposes or fights another or others.   From Latin *adversarius*, antagonist, opponent.
Synonyms: foe, enemy, opponent, antagonist, competitor, rival.
Antonyms: friend, comrade, companion, acquaintance, associate, colleague.

facilitate (fah-SIL-ih-<u>tayt</u>), to make easy or easier.   From   Latin *facilis*, easy, + suffix *ate*, to be or become.
From same base: facilitating, facilitated.
Synonyms: expedite, simplify, smooth, ease.
Antonyms: complicate, trouble, inconvenience, hamper,encumber, impede, entangle.

humanitarian (hyoo-<u>man</u>-ih-TAIR-ee-un), promoting the welfare of humanity.   From Latin *humanitas*, humanity.
From same base: humanity, humanitarianism.
Synonyms: kind, benevolent, sympathetic, compassionate, gentle, kind-hearted, charitable.
Antonyms: barbarous, pitiless, cruel, merciless, rude, fierce, savage, brutal.

demobilize (dee-MOH-beh-<u>lize</u>), to disband troops.   From Latin prefix *de*, away from, off, + *mobilis*, movable, active.
From same base: demobilizing, demobilized.

combatant (kom-BAT-nt), individual, group, or nation engaged in fighting. From Latin prefix *com*, with, + *battuere*, to beat or knock.
From same base: combat, combating, combated,
combative,combatively, combativeness.
Synonyms: fighter, contender, contestant, battler, warrior,belligerent, soldier.

nurture (NUR-chur), sustain, educate. From Latin *nutrire*, to nourish.
From same base: nurturing, nutured, nurturance, norturer.
Synonyms: nourish, nurse, train, sustain, foster, support, cherish.

intervention (in-tur-VEN-shun), any interference in the   affairs of others, especially of other nations.   From Late   Latin *interventus* (Latin *inter*, between, + *ventus*, pp. of *venire*, to come) , a coming between, intervention, interference.
From same base: interventionist, interventionism.
Synonyms: interference, intrusion, opposition, obtrusion,
meddlesomeness, interposition, interjection, officiousness.

Language Uses and Abuses

Latin numbers as prefixes

On Day 19, we noted words with Greek number-prefixes. In today's context-paragraphs, we've seen the Latin-based *unilateral* in use. Now we follow with *unus* again and with other common Latin number-prefixes with one typical English example for each.

unus, one
uniform (YOO-nih-form), always one and the same, never changing in form or   manner; from *unus* + *forma*, form, figure, shape.
primus, first
primer (PRIM-ur), a simple book for teaching children to read, a beginning book on almost any subject; from *primus* (prim) + noun ending

duo, two
duality (doo-AL-ih-tee), of two, composed of two parts or kinds, as in "duality of purpose;" from *duo* (dual) + noun-ending.

secundus, second

secondary (SEK-un-dare-ee), coming after the first, as in secondary school; from secundus (second) + adjective ending.

tres, three

triennial (try-EN-ee-ul), happening every three years or lasting for three years; from *tres* + *annus*, year.

tertius, third

tertiary (TUR-shee-<u>air</u>-ee), third in order of time, degree; from *tertius* + adjective ending,

quattuor, four

quatrain (KWA-trayn), a stanza or poem of four lines, usually rhyming; from *quattuor* + noun ending.

quartus, fourth

quartet (kwor-TET), any group of four things persons, performers, voices,   instruments; from *quartus* + noun ending..

quinque, five

quinquefoliolate, (<u>kwin</u>-kweh-FOH-lee-uh-lit), a plant with five leaflets per leaf; from *quinque* + *foliatus*, leafy.

quintus, fifth

quintuplet (kwin-TUP-lit), any of five offspring born at a single birth; from *quintus* + *plexus*, folded, intertwined.

sex, six

sextet (seks-TET), any collection of six things or persons, performers, singers, musicians; from *sex* + noun ending.

sextus, sixth

sextant (SEK-stant), sixth part of a circle; an instrument used by navigators to determine position; from *sextus* + noun eding.

centum, hundred

century (SEN-chuh-ree), any period of one hundred years; from *centum* + noun ending.

mille, thousand

millennium (mih-LEN-ee-um), any period of a thousand years; from *mille* + *annus*, year, + noun ending.

Quick Checks on Comprehension

In each line below, highlight or check off the word or phrase that best matches the meaning of the word to the left.

lofty   turbulent, eminent, present, omniscient
ideal   pedestal, model, mold, focus
lethal   special, peripheral, local, mortal
isolationism   fusion, radical, seclusion, intrusion
contentious   specious, respectful, irritable, jealous
harmony   degree, subsidy, accord, fortune
capability   atrocity, humility, ensemble, skill
coalition   compact, impact, extract, morale
capacity   sentimentality, asperity, ability, zealotry
adversary   luminary, penalty, client, foe
facilitate   ease, remonstrate, crease, elevate
humanitarian   culpable, capable, conventional, charitable
combatant   fugitive, lodger, fighter, logger
nurture   suture, future, foster, ouster
intervention   infusion, intrusion, integration, elation

In each line below, highlight or check off the two synonyms.

recognition, opposition, interpolation, interference
sprain, sustain, train, entrain
battler, sustainer, contender, retainer
rude, morose, frail, brutal
simplify, electrify, expedite, explore
antiquarian, antagonist, extremist, rival
politeness, aptness, genius, detachment
league, nepotism, union, arrangement
ingenuity, inability, inadequacy, instability
concord, discord, unanimity, charity
fiery, inscrutable, lackadaisical, impetuous
insulation, speculation, inspiration, segregation
productive, deadly, niggardly, destructive
facet, epilogue, objective, goal
erratic, reserved, preserved, timid

In each line below, highlight or check off the two antonyms.

arrogant, expectant, unassuming, presuming

deathly, willful, breathless, healthful
laconic, youthful, unruly, tolerant
uniformity, deformity, enormity, conflict
complexity, efficiency, perversity, inadequacy
dispute, request, motivation, alliance
talent, instinct, generosity, ineptness
relative, enemy, predecessor, friend
smooth, encourage, impede, mutiny
elegant, cruel, simple, gentle

If unsure about your comprehension choices, please see Appendix A.

Ahoy there and belay! Use a new word today!

New Word-Choices
From Andrew R. Cecil, speech on
"Moral Values of Liberalism and Conservatism,"
Vital Speeches of the Day, 61 (April 1, 1995) 12, p. 371.

The conflict between modern liberals and conservatives arises when attempts are made to transform the limited powers of government into a paternalistic state, or when the state fails to alleviate disharmonies arising in society. In the United States, liberalism and conservatism have never served as party creeds. We have liberal and conservative Democrats as well as liberal, moderate, and conservative Republicans. Neither of the major political parties has a doctrinaire set of principles that stand in fierce opposition to those of the other. The lines of distinction between the platforms of the two parties are not clearly drawn. There are no meaningful differences between the ultimate goals sought by the two parties. The Democrats have a tendency to use the government to furnish social services on a wider scale than the Republicans, who place greater faith in private initiative and in the individual's ability to shape his or her destiny.

One of the principal qualities of our party system has been an atmosphere of mutual tolerance, resulting in the tradition of responsible opposition engaged in legitimate activity and adherence to the rules of constitutional procedure and fairness. The spirit of political tolerance is sustained even in election years, when the political chips are piled high and campaigns tend to inflame the participants. No punitive action is taken by the winners against those who opposed them. Any attempt to transcend the bounds of what is legal, moral, and civil will turn the momentum in favor of the opposition.

paternalistic (puh-TER-nul-<u>is</u>-tik), care or control in the manner of a father looking after his children. From Latin *paternus*, of a father, and, in turn, from *pater*, father.
<u>From same base</u>: paternal, paternally, paternalism, paternalistically, paternity.

alleviate (uh-LEE-vee-<u>ayt</u>), to reduce, decrease, make easier to bear. From Late Latin *alleviatus*, pp. of *alleviare*, to make light.
<u>From same base</u>: alleviating, alleviated, alleviation.
<u>Synonyms</u>: mitigate, lessen, soften, lighten, reduce, decrease, moderate, abate, relieve, remove, lessen.
<u>Antonyms</u>: increase, intensify, heighten, magnify, augment, aggravate.

disharmony (dis-HAHR-muh-nee), a state of discord, disorder, or disagreement. From Greek negative prefix *dis* + *harmonia*, a state of accord; a pleasing concord of sounds.
<u>From same base</u>: disharmonious.
<u>Synonyms</u>: discordance, disorder, disagreement, dissonance, discordance, opposition, strife, disunion, deviation, antagonism, conflict, dissension, contention.
<u>Antonyms</u>: concord, agreement, unison, accord, concordance, concurrence, union, unanimity, unity, uniformity, conformity, amity, agreeableness.

creed (kreed), a statement of beliefs, principles, doctrines. From Latin *credere*, to believe.
<u>Synonyms</u>: faith, belief, conviction, credence, ideology, trust, acceptance, conclusion, doctrine.
<u>Antonyms</u>: skepticism, unbelief, incredulity, suspicion, cynicism, distrust, disbelief, doubt.

moderate (MOD-uhr-it), holding ideas or views that are "in the middle," not given to extremes. From Latin *moderatus*, pp. of *moderare*, to keep within reasonable bounds.
<u>From same base</u>: moderate, moderating, moderated, moderately, moderateness.
<u>Synonyms</u>: limited, sparing, reasonable, fair, temperate, modest, ordinary, steady, regulated, lenient, tolerant.
<u>Antonyms</u>: large, considerable, extensive, excessive, extravagant, liberal, unlimited, intemperate, indulgent.

doctrinaire (DOK-trih-NAIR), impractically rigid, unbending. From Latin *doctrina*, that which is imparted by teaching.
From same base: doctrine, doctrinal, doctrinally.
Synonyms: positive, immovable, unchangeable, unbending, rigid, opinionated, dictatorial, imperious, arrogant, domineering.
Antonyms: uncertain, wavering, doubtful, hesitating, skeptical, dubious, unsettled, hesitant, indecisive.

opposition (aw-puh-ZISH-un), the act of confronting or serving as a check on an individual or group. From Latin *oppositio*, an opposing.
From same base: oppositional.
Synonyms: resistance, obstruction, confrontation, checking, withstanding, restraint, thwarting, counteraction,retaliation, contradiction.
Antonyms: cooperation, fraternization, concurrence, confirmation, endorsement, sanction, commendation, support,acclaim.

distinction (dih-STINGK-shun), the act of separating or marking off by differences. From Latin *distinctio*, the finding of a difference.
From same base: distinct, distinctly, distinctness, distinctive, distinctively, distinctiveness.
Synonyms: differential, feature, marking, peculiarity, difference, variance, dissimilarity, distinctness.
Antonyms: similarity, resemblance, likeness, affinity, conformity.

initiative (ih-NISH-uh-tiv), the act of taking the first step or making the first move. From Middle Latin *initiativus* with same meaning.
Synonyms: beginning, introduction, commencement, start, opening, inauguration, opening.

destiny (DES-tuh-nee), what will happen to a person or thing in the future. From Old French *destiner*, to fasten down, make secure.
From same base: destine, destining, destined.
Synonyms: fate, decree, end, lot, fortune, judgment, predetermination, chance, finality, conclusion.

mutual (MYOO-choo-ul), felt, shared, or possessed in common. From Latin *mutuus*, on both sides, fastened to each other.
From same base: mutually, mutuality.

Synonyms: reciprocal, interchangeable, joint, identical, common, equivalent, similar, like.
Antonyms: separate, disconnected, disunited, distinct, detached, unshared, severed, dissimilar, unlike, unequal, different, divergent.

tolerance (TOL-ur-ense), recognition and respect for the beliefs and practices of others without sharing them. From Latin *tolerantia*, a bearing, enduring.
From same base: tolerant, tolerantly.
Synonyms: permission, allowance, endurance, indulgence, recognition, authorization, sanction, submission, respect.
Antonyms: prohibition, inhibition, interdiction, hindrance, disallowance, prevention, restriction, disapproval, censure, protest, restraint, opposition.

tradition (truh-DISH-un), a custom so long continued that it has almost the force of law. From Latin *traditio*, a handed-down instruction or guidance.
From same base: traditional, traditionally, traditionalism, traditionalist.
Synonyms: custom, habit, usage, convention, practice, routine, vogue.

legitimate (lih-JIT-ih-mit), lawful, legal, valid. From Latin *legitimus* with same meaning, and, in turn, from *lex*, law.
From same base: legitimately, legitimacy.
Synonyms: lawful, legal, valid, permissible, allowable, sanctioned, authorized, warranted, admitted, prescribed, equitable, fair, right, just.
Antonyms: unfair, unjust, unlawful, unsanctioned, illegal, illicit, disallowed, wrong, unconstitutional, prohibited, restricted, interdicted.

adherence (add-HEER-ens), state of sticking closely to the rules. From Latin *adhaerens*, prp. of *adhaerere*, to stick to.
From same base: adherent.
Synonyms: attachment, connection, concurrence, assent, union, cohesion, stickiness.
Antonyms: separation, division, disunion, looseness, disruption, disconnection, sunderance.

constitutional (kon-stih-TOO-shuh-nl), consistent with or following the laws and principles of the Constitution. From Latin *constitutio*, a regulation, order, ordinance.

From same base: constitution, constitutionally, constitutionality.

participant (pahr-TIS-ih-punt), one sharing or taking part in some activity. From *participans*, prp. of *participare*, to share with.

punitive (PYOO-nih-tiv), pertaining to punishing or bringing about punishment. From *punitivus*, a Middle Latin adjective with same meaning, and, in turn, from Latin *punire*, to punish.
From same base: punitively, punitiveness.
Synonyms: penal, corrective, disciplinary, grueling, avenging, retributive, revengeful, vindictive.
Antonyms: clearing, exonerating, discharging, forgiving, reprieving.

transcend (tran-SEND), to exceed, overstep, go beyond the limits of. From Latin *transcendens*, prp. of *transcendere*, to climb over.
From same base: transcending, transcended, transcendent, transcendently, transcendentally, transcendence.
Synonyms: go beyond, exceed, surpass, overtop, excel, outweigh, outrival, predominate, prevail, overreach.

momentum (moh-MEN-tum), strength or force moving in a particular direction. From Latin *momentum*, movement, impulse.
Synonyms: impetus, force, push, energy, vigor, strength, might, power, compulsion, pressure, dynamics.
Antonyms: inaction, weakness, abeyance, standstill, languor, hesitation, impotence, enervation, failing.

Language Uses and Abuses

Expressing ideas vividly

In talking or corresponding with individuals or groups, you already know how important it is to express your ideas clearly and appropriately. Whenever possible, you will also want to take the lively or vivid-scene approach, that is, to make use of realistic "scenes" or descriptions which can be readily visualized by the listener. Here's one "scene" from a talk by Edward L. Flom, an officer of Florida Steel:

One of the hardest tasks of leadership is understanding that you are not what you are, but what you're perceived to be by others. A perfect example of this is what happened in New York City when I was about ten or eleven.   Preferring not to be delayed, my father made a U-turn in the middle of 5th Avenue and was promptly stopped by one of New York's finest. For those of you who knew my father, he was very intelligent, very articulate, very calm, and also was a transplanted Yankee. When the policeman asked if he had any idea of what he had done, my father said, in a slow Southern drawl, "Man, back home we always whip around to go the other direction." Then the officer shook his head and said, "Just please proceed on home."

"Short stories" from your own experience or from that of others are an easy way to enliven your speaking or writing.   Stories or no stories,.when you do take care in choosing the vivid-language approach, you'll find it that much easier to keep listeners or readers absorbed in your message.

Quick Checks on Comprehension

In each line below, highlight or check the word or phrase that best matches the meaning of the word to the left.

alleviate	substantiate, demonstrate, lessen, overturn
disharmony	hegemony, conflict, credence, infinity
creed	sorrow, belief, attitude, intention
moderate	temperate, acrimonious, eminent, arduous
doctrinaire	unending, undone, unequal, unbending
opposition	sanction, confrontation, ostentation, union
distinction	difference, inference, preference, sufferance
initiative	increment, inducement, incitement, commencement
destiny	posterity, finality, opportunity, equity
mutual	common, simple, purposeful, intentional
tolerance	eminence, indulgence, importance, imagery
tradition	impression, levitation, custom, purview
legitimate	retained, hallowed, valid, emphatic
adherence	attachment, impairment, emolument, extension
punitive	demonstrative, stalwart, complete, corrective
transcend	exceed, proceed, impede, accede
momentum	course, force, gauntlet, tedium

In each line below, highlight or check off the two synonyms.

power, tandem, impetus, project
recede, surpass, continue, prevail

revolutionary, disciplinary, avenging, impinging
anticipation, connection, usurpation, link
illegal, ratified, prohibited, magnified
habit, profit, convention, declension
stolidity, hindrance, censure, pressure
severed, divergent, dejected, harmless
denial, respite, fate, chance
inauguration, elucidation, intersection, beginning
rapture, feature, marking, parking
reporting, checking, thwarting, supporting
opinionated, incompetent, frightened, domineering
lenient, personable, reasonable, exceptional
credence, reference, thrust, trust
pleasure, fatigue, disorder, strife
abate, create, reduce, induce

In each line below, highlight or check off the two antonyms.

mitigate, initiate, transcend, aggravate
order, accord, contention, impression
faith, doubt, wraith, range
steady, intemperate, ready, irrelevant
subordinate, impressive, positive, indecisive
gratification, support, compassion, counteraction
enormity, insouciance, variance, conformity
identical, perennial, distinct, succinct
resemblance, respect, restraint, respite
unlawful, traditional, exceptional, authorized
supposition, justification, separation, cohesion
revengeful, wonderful, challenge, pardon
suspense, vigor, weakness, happiness

If unsure about your comprehension choices, please see Appendix A.

Brighten your listeners' day with a sparkling new word we pray!

New Word-Choices
From Raymond W. Smith, speech on
"Advertising and the Interactive Age,"
<u>Vital Speeches of the Day</u>, 61 (April 1, 1995) 12, p. 360.

<u>Interactive</u> advertising represents a powerful new tool for reaching consumers—bringing the store to the buyer, rather than the other way around.   It combines the <u>immediacy</u> of full-motion video, the <u>targetability</u> of direct mail, and the two-way dialogue of catalogue sales.   It allows you to target a persuasive message at a <u>receptive</u> consumer who can tailor the information and act on it instantaneously. And at its heart is a powerful data base that will give you an immediate, precise measurement of buying behavior—which will let you see the link between the message and the action: the ultimate measure of advertising effectiveness

There will always be a role, of course, for the mass medium of television to create the shared experiences and symbols that <u>constitute</u> our common <u>identity</u>. As such, you will need to continue to do what you have done <u>peerlessly</u> over the years: create an emotional <u>identification</u> with a product through awareness ads and branding strategies. But you will also need to master the very different strengths of the new interactive medium. Not everyone will be able to make this difficult and delicate <u>transition</u>.   But those who do will find themselves at the forefront of a <u>dynamic</u> and growing new service industry.   Your value will come from offering a whole range of integrated services and from your ability to manage the <u>diverse</u> activities that will soon be compressed into a single <u>transaction</u>.

interactive (<u>in</u>-tur-AK-tiv), acting upon each other; here, action
   taking place between consumer and advertiser instead of the

consumer's playing a passive role as in the past. From Latin prefix *inter*, between or among, + *actus*, pp. of *agere*, to act.
<u>From same base</u>: interact, interacting, interacted, interactively.

immediacy (ih-MEE-dee-uh-see), occurring as one watches or absorbs through one or more of the senses. From Late Latin *immediatus*, having nothing coming between.
<u>From same base</u>: immediate, immediately.

targetability (TAHR-git-uh-BIL-uh-tee), ability to be sharply aimed or focused. Coined by speaker through joining *target* and *ability*. From Middle French *targette*, a small, round shield, + Latin *habilitas*, aptitude, suitability.

receptive (rih-SEP-tiv), inclined to respond favorably. From Middle Latin *receptivus* with same meaning.
<u>From same base</u>: receptively, receptivity, receptiveness.
<u>Synonyms</u>: recipient, open-minded, interested, receivable, favorable, acceptable, welcome.

constitute (KON-stih-<u>toot</u>), to make up, compose, be the elements of. From Latin *constitutus*, pp. of *constituere*, to set up, establish.
<u>From same base</u>: constituting, constituted.
<u>Synonyms</u>: form, make, compose, fashion, formulate, arrange, construct, draw up.
<u>Antonyms</u>: break, unmake, destroy, annul, ruin, disarrange, disperse.

identity (eye-DEN-tih-tee), distinctive character or characteristics shared by an individual or group. From Late Latin *identitas*, combining *idem*, same, and *essentitas*, essence.
<u>From same base</u>: identical, identically.
<u>Synonyms</u>: congruity, oneness, singleness, similarity, likeness, resemblance, affinity, conformity, kinship, unity.
<u>Antonyms</u>: unlikeness, dissimilarity, unrelatedness, difference, variation, disparity.

peerlessly (PEER-lis-lee), perfectly, supremely. Adverb from Latin *par*, equal, + Middle English suffix *les*, without, + adverb-forming *ly*.
<u>From same base</u>: peerless, peerlessness.

Synonyms: supremely, perfectly, gloriously, uniquely, inimitably, preeminently, matchlessly, superlatively, surpassingly, exquisitely, faultlessly, incomparably.

Antonyms: subordinately, imperfectly, secondarily, unimportantly, poorly, trivially, commonly, ordinarily, worthlessly, deficiently, defectively, inadequately.

identification (eye-den-tih-fih-KAY-shun), close association, connection or involvement with. From Late Latin *identificare*, combining *idem*, same, and *facere*, to make.

From same base: identify, identifying, identified, identifiable, identifiably.

transition (tran-ZISH-un), change from one situation or condition to another. From Latin *transitio*, a going across, a passing over.

From same base: transitional, transitionally.

Synonyms: change, shift, turn, break, conversion, deviation.

Antonyms: continuation, continuity, stability, permanence.

dynamic (dy-NAM-ik), energetic, forceful. From Greek *dynamikos* with same meaning, and, in turn, from *dynamis*, power, strength.

From same base: dynamical, dynamically, dynamics.

Synonyms: energetic, forceful, powerful, strong, vigorous, mighty.

Antonyms: weak, powerless, feeble, frail, impotent, unable, incapable, helpless, incompetent.

diverse (dih-VERS), different, varied. From Latin *diversus*, pp. of *divertere*, to turn aside.

From same base: diversely, diversiveness.

Synonyms: various, varying, varied, manifold, dissimilar, unlike, separate, distinct, discordant.

Antonyms: similar, like, alike, correspondent, resembling, harmonious, common, same.

transaction (tran-ZAK-shun), something carried on, performed, accomplished. From Latin *transactio* with same meaning.

From same base: transactional.

Synonyms: dealing, proceeding, business, act, affair, matter, deed, action, event, happening, activity, performance, undertaking, negotiation.

Language Uses and Abuses

Other Greek prefixes as guides to meaning

On Day 19, we listed Greek numbers serving as prefixes. Today, again with the goal of finding ways to determine and remember word meanings, we list other common Greek prefixes, each with one example.

ana, out of, up: **anachronism** (uh-NAK-ruh-niz-um), something out of its proper time (e.g., an old-time Victrola, a belief in witches); from *ana + chronos*, time.

apo, away: **apostasy** (uh-POS-tuh-see), desertion of one's faith, party, or principles; from *apo . + stasis*, standing, position.

epi, on, upon: **epigram** (EP-ih-gram), a short, witty verse or saying; from *epigramma* (*epi*, [something] on + *gramma*, that which is written) with same meaning.

eu, well: **eulogy** (YOO-luh-jee), a spoken or written piece of high praise ;from *eu + logos*, speech. (The *logos* in biology means study of; in eulogy, the *logos* is the same word with an alternate meaning.)

hemi, half; **hemisphere** (HEM-ihs-feer), half of a globe, half of the earth; from hemi + sphaira, sphere.

hetero, other: **heterosexual** (het-ur-uh-SEK-shoo-ul), pertaining to the other sex or to sexual desire for one of the opposite sex; from *hetero + sexualis*, involving sex.

kata (cata), down: **catastrophe** (kuh-TAS-truh-fee), a great and sudden disaster; from *kata + strophe*, an overturning, overthrowing.

pan, all: **pandemonium**, (pan-duh-MOH-nee-um), a riotous uproar; from *pan + daimon*, demon.

para, beside, alongside of: **paradox** (PEHR-uh-doks), a false, absurd, or contradictory statement; from *para + doxa*, an opinion, statement.

peri, around: **periscope** (PEHR-uh-skope), a viewing device, usually in a submarine, capable of being turned around for viewing in all directions; from *peri* + *skopos*, watcher.

proto, first: **prototype** (PROH-tuh-type), a first model on which other models or products are based; from *proto* + *typos*, model.

sym (before consonants), *syn*, with: **sympathy** (SIM-puh-thee), pity felt for another's suffering; from *sym* + *pathos*, feeling.

Quick Checks on Comprehension

In each line below, highlight or check off the word or phrase that best matches the meaning of the word to the left.

receptive	festive, interested, invested, corruptive
constitute	simplify, predict, form, expose
identity	lonesomeness, creativity, oneness, liability
peerlessly	supposedly, uniquely, hazily, uniformly
transition	change, audition, arrangement, location
dynamic	forceful, useful, spiteful, dutiful
diverse	dreaded, obliged, explicit, varied
transaction	proceeding, portent, maze, hazard

In each line below, highlight or check off the two synonyms.

action, compassion, reason, undertaking
competent, like, resembling, dissembling
allergic, energetic, flighty, mighty
corral, shift, turn, spurn
unjustly, perfectly, incomparably, superficially
ambiguity, unity, annuity, affinity
perceive, induce, formulate, draw up
reprehensible, acceptable, practical, welcome

In each line below, highlight or check off the two antonyms.

destroy, compose, oppose, imply
similarity, regularity, unlikeness, politeness
superbly, defectively, surpassingly, fitfully
inversion, conversion, stability, suitability

revengeful, impotent, vigorous, pretentious
harmonious, hilarious, resolute, discordant

If unsure about your comprehension choices, please see Appendix A.

Let no one say nay—use a new word today!

New Word-Choices

From James Q. Wilson, speech on "What to do About Crime,"
<u>Vital Speeches of the Day</u>, 61 (April 1, 1995) 12, p. 375 f.

There are now data that show any fair-minded observer rather <u>conclusively</u> that after <u>controlling</u> for income and for every racial or <u>ethnic</u> group, those children raised in single-parent families headed by never-married young women are <u>materially</u> worse off in terms of school <u>achievements</u>, <u>delinquency</u>, and emotional problems. These risks are greater for boys than for girls.

What can we do to supply an <u>adequate</u> environment for these children? Our goal should be to <u>alter</u> expectations, so that boys will not grow up believing that sexual exploitation and the reputation thereby acquired is their main <u>objective</u>, and girls will not think that sexual <u>experimentation</u> leading to the <u>formation</u> of independent households is their goal. Boys and girls will grow up thinking that romance, commitment, and marriage are the goals they ought to seek.

I believe that welfare reform ought to be linked to crime control; the two are part of an <u>indissoluble</u> whole. I believe that this might help solve the <u>acute</u> American problem of juvenile violence. I am not convinced that it would help the worldwide problem of property crime. In other countries we have many different kinds of welfare systems, yet they, too, have rapidly <u>escalating</u> rates of property crime and drug abuse.

data (DAY-tuh), facts or figures from which conclusions may be
  drawn, information. From *datus*, pp. of *dare*, to give, hand over.
<u>From same base</u>: datum (singular form of plural above).

conclusively (kun-KLOO-siv-lee), decisively, undoubtedly. Adverb from *conclusivus*, pp. of *concludere*, to conclude, bring to an end.
From same base: conclusive, conclusiveness.
Synonyms: decisively, undoubtedly, reasonably, analytically, doubtlessly, unquestionably, rationally, inductively.

controlling (kun-TROLL-ing), allowing for, paying due heed to factors of, restraining the free roll of. From Latin prefix *contra*, against, + *rotula*, a small wheel.
From same base: control, controlled, controllable, controllability, controller.
Synonyms: checking, restraining, allowing for, influencing, regulating, holding, ruling, governing, directing, guiding, repressing, hindering, preventing, coercing.
Antonyms: letting go, abandoning, giving up, relinquishing, renouncing, leaving, quitting, forsaking.

ethnic (ETH-nik), descriptive of a people of the same origin as distinguished by customs, characteristics, language, common history, etc. From Greek *ethnikos*, foreign.
From same base: ethnical, ethnically, ethnicity.

materially (muh-TEER-ee-uh-lee), to a considerable degree or in an important way. Adverb from Middle Latin adjective, *materialis*, of substance, of matter.
From same base: material, materialism, materialistic, materialistically.
Synonyms: solidly, sensibly, tangibly, substantially, corporally, bodily, physically.
Antonyms: immaterially, insensibly, spiritually, airily, mistily, bodilessly.

achievement (uh-CHEEV-mnt), an accomplishment, a goal attained. From Old French *achever*, to finish, + suffix *ment*, condition of.
From same base: achieve, achieving, achieved, achievable.
Synonyms: accomplishment, exploit, deed, feat, attainment, performance, act, action, completion, fulfilment.
Antonyms: failure, cessation, neglect, negligence, carelessness, loss, deprivation, defeat, misfortune, waste, forfeiture.

delinquency (dih-LING-kwen-see), a fault, offense, failure to meet obligations (such as regular school attendance). From Latin *delinquens*, prp. of *delinquere*, to commit a fault, leave undone.
From same base: delinquent, delinquently.
Synonyms: neglect, fault, omission, offense, oversight, omission, default, negligence, laxness.
Antonyms: care, solicitude, responsibility, concern, interest, regard, vigilance, caution, consideration.

adequate (AD-ih-kwit), equal to what is required. From Latin *adaequatus*, pp. of *adaequare*, to make equal.
From same base: adequately, adequacy, adequateness.
Synonyms: adapted, suited, suitable, sufficient, enough, equal, fit, fitting, fitted, competent, capable, qualified, satisfactory.
Antonyms: inadequate, unsuited, unsuitable, insufficient, disqualified, unqualified, unfit, incompetent, inferior, unequal, unsatisfactory.

alter (AWL-tur), to change, make different. From Middle Latin *alterare*, to modify, and, in turn, from Latin *alter*, other.
From same base: alterable, alteration.
Synonyms: change, transform, make different, modify, reduce, regulate, diversify, shift, veer, turn, twist, reconstruct.
Antonyms: keep, retain, let stand, preserve, maintain, hold, persist, stay, sustain, continue.

objective (ub-JEK-tiv), a goal or end. From Middle Latin *objectivus*, thrown or put before.
From same base: objectively, objectiveness.
Synonyms: object, goal, end, aim, aspiration, purpose, design, intention, scheme, outlook.
Antonyms: beginning, introduction, premise, cause, origin, inception, initiation, initiative.

experimentation (ik-sper-ih-men-TAY-shun), discovering or testing through trial and error. From Middle Latin *experimentatio*, testing, proving.
Synonyms: testing, proving, verifying, trying, attempting, examining, practicing, exercising, endeavoring, undertaking.

formation (for-MAY-shun), a forming or being formed. From Latin *formatio* with same meaning.

Synonyms: fabrication, organization, composition, fashioning, forging, contriving, devising, molding, shaping, production, creation, origination, invention.

indissoluble (in-dih-SOL-yuh-bl), incapable of being separated, broken, destroyed. From Latin prefix *in*, not, + *dissolubilis*, that can be broken or destroyed.
From same base: indissolubly, indissolubility.

acute (uh-KYOOT), sharply severe, serious, critical. From Latin *acutus*, pp. of *acuere*, to sharpen.
From same base: acutely, acuteness.
Synonyms: sharp, keen, intense, severe, serious, critical, penetrating, pointed.
Antonyms: dull, stupid, chronic, obtuse, uncritical.

escalating (ES-kuh-layt-ing), gradually increasing. From Latin prefix e, out of, upward, + scalae, a flight of stairs, a scaling ladder.
From same base: escalate, escalated, escalation, escalator.
Synonyms: increasing, growing, intensifying, multiplying, redoubling, surging, rising, expanding, extending, amplifying.
Antonyms: decreasing, diminishing, reducing, lessening, curtailing, minimizing, reducing, contracting, shrinking.

Language Uses and Abuses

More combining forms from Greek and Latin

You've noticed that many of our words are made up from Greek and Latin combining forms. You've seen, for example, that the Greek *phil* (love) + *anthrop* (man) = philanthropy, a regard for humanity marked by charity of various kinds. You've seen also that *auto* (self) + *bio* (life) + *graph* (writing) = autobiography, the story of one's life written by one's self. And for a Latin example, *multi* (many) + *part* (part) + suffix *ite* = multipartite, having many parts. In addition to defining a word, a good dictionary provides its makeup and makes it almost impossible to forget its meaning. First, some Greek-based examples:

hippopotamus; from *hippos* (hippo), horse, + *potamos* (potomos), river.
dinosaur; from *deinos* (dino), terrifying, + *sauros* (saur), lizard.

oligarchy, rule by a few; from *oligos* (olig), few, + *archia* (archy), ruling.

Philadelphia, city of brotherly love; from *philos* (phil), love, +*adelphos* (adelphia), brother.

telescope, an instrument for viewing from a distance; *telos* (tele), end, + *scopos* (scope), viewer.

And from the Latin:

agriculture; from *ager* (agri), field, + *cultura* (cultura), cultivation of.

altocumulus, a relatively high formation of clouds; from *altus* (alto), high, + *cumulus* (cumulus), heap.

manuscript, a document written, typed, or word-processed by hand; from *manus* (manu), hand, + *scriptus* (script), written.

pedicure, care of the feet; from *pes* (pedi), foot, + *cura* (cure), care of.

Quick Checks on Comprehension

In each line below, highlight or check off the word or phrase that best mtches the meaning of the word to the left.

conclusively	attentively, decisively, sorely, lightly
controlling	understanding, guiding, harboring, sighting
materially	solidly, finally, superficially, strongly
achievement	feature, intent, creed, deed
delinquency	efficiency, vengeance, laxness, rancor
adequate	insolent, fanciful, satisfactory, morose
alter	imperil, transform, inform, perform
objective	origin, frenzy, dexterity, goal
experimentation	resting, testing, correcting, posting
formation	advising, devising, lauding, inviting
acute	acrid, pallid, critical, empirical
escalating	growing, flowing, mowing, promoting

In each line below, highlight or check off the two synonyms.

advocating, increasing, subordinating, expanding
penetrating, infiltrating, gaudy, sharp
molding, laying, shaping, breaking
lamenting, electrifying, proving, verifying
perception, beginning, enduring, inception

modify, produce, fructify, reduce
culpable, capable, qualified, specified
omission, provision, regret, neglect
exploit, act, subtraction, zeal
neglectfully, substantially, materially, indisputably
abandoning, importuning, forsaking, usurping
retroactively, undoubtedly, unquestionably, numbly

In each line below, highlight or check off the two antonyms.

giving up, supervising, making up, directing
imperceptibly, tangibly, spiritually, constantly
transaction, cessation, inspection, completion
matchless, laxness, fare, care
suited, treated, unqualified, dissatisfied
change, prepare, preserve, exchange
periodic, salutary, severe, uncritical
surging, purging, finishing, diminishing

If unsure about your comprehension choices, please see Appendix A.

From the righteous path don't stray—use a new word today!

New Word-Choices
From Peter Brimelow, <u>Alien Nation</u>
(New York, NY: Random House, 1995), pp. xv, xix.

There is a sense in which current <u>immigration</u> policy is Adolf Hitler's <u>posthumous</u> revenge on America. The U.S political elite <u>emerged</u> from the war <u>passionately</u> concerned to cleanse itself from all <u>taints</u> of racism or <u>xenophobia</u>. Eventually, it enacted the <u>epochal</u> Immigration Act of 1965. And this, quite accidentally, triggered a renewed mass immigration, so huge and so <u>systematically</u> different from anything that had gone before as to transform—and ultimately, perhaps, even to destroy—the one unquestioned victor of World War II: the American nation, as it had evolved by the middle of the twentieth century.

There is a <u>fundamental</u> distinction to be made between immigration in principle and immigration in practice. <u>Obeisance</u> to the former is preventing <u>observation</u> of the latter. The mass immigration so thoughtlessly triggered in 1965 risks making America an <u>alien</u> nation—not merely in the sense that the numbers of aliens are rising to levels last seen in the nineteenth century; not merely in the sense that America will become a freak among the world's nations because of the unprecedented <u>demographic</u> <u>mutation</u> it is inflicting on itself; and not merely in the sense that Americans themselves will become alien to each other, requiring an increasingly strained government to <u>arbitrate</u> between them.

immigration (<u>im</u>-ih-GRAY-shun), the act of coming into a new
    country to settle there. From Latin *immigratus*, pp. of *immigrare*, to
    move into.
<u>From same base</u>: immigrate, immigrating, immigrated.

Synonyms: ingress, ingression, introgression, entrance, entry, incoming, inflow.
Antonyms: egress, emergence, exit, emigration, exodus, migration, evacuation, withdrawal.

posthumous (POS-chew-mus), arising or continuing after one's death. From Late Latin *posthumus*, after death, and, in turn, from Latin *post*, after, + *humus*, ground (burial).
From same base: posthumously.

emerge (ih-MURJ), to rise out of. From Latin *emergere* with same meaning.
From same base: emerge, emerging.
Synonyms: come out, egress, exit, depart, go away, leave, withdraw, set out, migrate, emigrate, evacuate.
Antonyms: remain, stay, abide, linger, stand, carry on, sustain, maintain.

passionately (PASH-uh-nit-lee), ardently, fervently. Adverb from Middle Latin *passionatus*, ardent, fervent.
From same base: passionate.
Synonyms: ardently, fervently, vehemently, intensely, excitedly, precipitately, violently, intemperately.
Antonyms: stolidly, impassively, phlegmatically, apathetically.

taint (taynt), stain, blemish, trace of corruption, evil. From Old French *teindre*, to color, and, in turn, from Latin *tingere*, to tinge or color.
From same base: taint (verb), tainting, tainted, taintless.
Synonyms: tinge, color, tint, stain, dye.

xenophobia (zen-uh-FOH-bee-uh), a hatred or distrust of foreigners or strangers. From Greek *xenos* (xeno), stranger or foreigner, + *phobos* (phobia), fear.
From same base: xenophobe, xenophobic.

epochal (EP-uh-kl), denoting the beginning of a new and important period in history, or denoting a period in time noteworthy for any reason. From Greek *epechein*, to stop, pause, or extend over time.
From same base: epoch, epochally.

systematically (<u>sis</u>-tuh-MAT-ih-kuh-lee), methodically, regularly;
according to an orderly method or plan. From Greek adjective
systematikos and, in turn, from *systema*, a whole made up of parts.
<u>From same base</u>: systematic, systematical.
<u>Synonyms</u>: methodically, regularly, precisely, punctually, formally,
uniformly, steadily, constantly, habitually, customarily,
conventionally, periodically, recurrently, normally, ordinarily.
<u>Antonyms</u>: irregularly, imprecisely, informally, rarely,
unconventionally, uncertainly, casually, randomly, vaguely, unreliably,
aimlessly, indefinitely.

evolve (ih-VOLV), to develop, grow out of. From Latin prefix *e*, out
of, + *volvere*, to roll.
<u>From same base</u>: evolve, evolving.
<u>Synonyms</u>: uncover, unfold, disclose, enlarg, exhibit, extend.
<u>Antonyms</u>: curtail, shorten, abbreviate, narrow, lessen, confine.

fundamental (<u>fun</u>-duh-MEN-tl), basic, essential. From Latin
fundamentum, foundation.
<u>From same base</u>: fundamentally, fundamentalism, fundamentalist.
<u>Synonyms</u>: basic, essential, principal, primary, intrinsic, chief.
<u>Antonyms</u>: superficial, nonessential, subordinate, secondary, auxiliary.

obeisance (oh-BAY-sense), reverence for, attitude of respect for,
homage or courtesy to. From Old French *obeissant*, present
participle of *obeir*, to obey.
<u>Synonyms</u>: homage, reverence, courtesy, respect, deference,
allegiance.
<u>Antonyms</u>: disrespect, discourtesy, irreverence, disregard, disesteem,
defiance.

observation (<u>ob</u>-zur-VAY-shun), compliance with the law and
customs; a looking at. From Latin *observatio*, a watching.
<u>From same base</u>: observational.
<u>Synonyms</u>: observance, keeping, acknowledgment, adherence,
compliance, obedience, fulfillment.
<u>Antonyms</u>: nonobservance, nonobservation, nonperformance,
noncompliance, evasion, omission, neglect.

alien (AYL-yen), not one's own, strange. From Latin *alienus*,
  strange, foreign, and, in turn, from *alius*, another, someone of a
  different nature.
From same base: alienist, alienism.
Synonyms: strange, foreign, opposed, distant, remote, hostile,
contradictory, inappropriate, unlike, conflicting, contrary, estranged.
Antonyms: akin, alike, corresponding, appropriate, pertinent, relevant,
proper, congenial, native, friendly.

demographic (<u>dem</u>-uh-GRAF-ik), pertaining to the statistical science
  dealing with distribution, density, and other data on populations.
  From Greek *demos* (demo), people, + *graphein* (graphic), to write.
From same base: demography, demographically, demographer.

mutation (myoo-TAY-shun), change, alteration, a variation in basic
  characteristics. From Latin *mutatio* with same meaning.
From same base: mutational, mutationally.
Synonyms: change, alteration, permutation, variation, modification,
deviation, conversion.
Antonyms: continuation, permanence, stability, continuity, firmness.

arbitrate (AHR-bih-<u>trayt</u>), to settle disputes by acting as umpire
  between or among disputing individuals or parties. From Latin
  arbitratus, pp. of *arbitrari*, to judge, decide.
From same base: arbitrating, arbitrated.
Synonyms: decide, settle, judge, determine, conclude, rule, adjudicate.
Antonyms: waver, vacillate, doubt, hesitate, falter.

Language Uses and Abuses

Do you know anyone with a phobia or a mania?

Among the words analyzed for this Day is *zenophobia*. In the
examples below, we see again the value of becoming familiar with
combining forms as keys to meaning.

Among words ending with the Greek *phobia*, fear:

acrophobia (<u>ak</u>-ruh-FO-bee-uh), an abnormal fear of being in high
  places; Greek *akros* (acro), high + *phobia*.

agoraphobia (ag-uhr-ah-FO-bee-uh), an abnormal fear of being in public places; Greek *agora* (agora), market place + *phobia*.

hydrophobia (hy-druh-FO-bee-uh), an abnormal fear of water ; Greek *hydor* (hydro), water + *phobia*.

Among words ending with the Greek *mania,* madness:

bibliomania (bib-lee-uh-MAY-nee-uh), a compulsion to collect books; Greek *biblion* (biblio), book + *mania*.

kleptomania (klep-tuh-MAY-nee-uh), a compulsion to steal; Greek *kleptes* (klepto), thief + *mania*.

pyromania (pye-ruh-MAY-nee-uh), a compulsion to set fires; Greek *pyr* (pyro), fire + *mania*.

Quick Checks on Comprehension

In each line below, highlight or check off the word or phrase that best matches the meaning of the word to the left.

immigration   expiration, inflow, notation, replace
emerge leave,   preserve, moderate, surge
passionately   belatedly, suspiciously, intensely, calmly
taint   line, stain, spray, peril
systematically   peerlessly, ruinously, hardly, uniformly
evolve   remand, suspend, extend, intend
fundamental   unequal, imperial, equilateral, principal
obeisance   respect, caution, admiration, kindness
observation   reliance, position, compliance, ration
alien   notorious, strange, impressive, emotional
mutation   preservation, potion, change, creation
arbitrate   meditate, probate, decide, deride

In each line below, highlight or check off the two synonyms.

rattle, settle, conclude, preclude
variation, sophistication, protestation, deviation
congenial, loquacious, friendly, uninhibited
orchestration, observance, preference, adherence
umbrage, homage, preference, deference
essential, intrinsic, cathartic, perennial
disclose, impose, uncover, propose

normally, materially, ordinarily, inevitably
tint, swatch, cycle, color
credibly, fervently, fancifully, ardently
locate, depart, invite, withdraw
remonstrance, entrance, counseling, incoming

In each line below, highlight or check off the two antonyms.

ingress, progress, exit, permit
elevate, migrate, remain, sustain
stolidly, unavoidably, inherently, vehemently
supportively, colloquially, habitually, casually
pretend, extend, curtail, derail
palpable, nonessential, intimate, basic
reverence, romance, project, disrespect
acknowledgment, amendment, production, evasion
hostile, puerile, akin, joyful
conversion, probability, stability, installment
undermine, determine, waver, prefer

If unsure about your comprehension choices, please see Appendix A.

Don't be whimsical, don't be fey—just use a new word today!

New Word-Choices
From Benjamin Schwarz,
"The Diversity Myth: America's Leading Export,"
The Atlantic Monthly, 275 (May, 1995) 5, p. 57 f.

<u>Solipsism</u> is a <u>perennial</u> American temptation. In a <u>grotesquely</u> comic muddle of causes and <u>cultures</u>, Lyndon Johnson once sought to buy off the North Vietnamese with promises of a Great Society-style project along the Mekong. <u>Variants</u> of the cry "Why can't they be more like us?" have long served as a <u>staple</u> of American tourists and foreign-policy <u>mandarins</u> alike. We have made ourselves at home in the world, characteristically, by regarding it as America in the making.

Thus <u>imbued</u> with ourselves, we often get the world wrong. Mussolini was not an <u>impetuous</u> New Dealer, nor Ho Chi Minh a Democratic politician. The West Bank is not the American South, nor is the cause of the Palestinian homeland an <u>exotic</u> version of the black struggle for civil rights. Similarly, the ethnic <u>tumult</u> loosed by the end of the Cold War is not to be <u>assessed</u> by pious <u>invocations</u> of our multi-ethnic, multi-racial <u>heritage</u> of tolerance and civic <u>comity</u>. The blood-lettings in Bosnia, Rwanda, Chechnya, and Haiti have no <u>parallels</u> in the distorted idea of our past which we <u>trumpet</u> abroad. Not that they are <u>incommensurably</u> worse that anything in the American experience. Rather, the history we hold up as a light to nations is a <u>sanctimonious</u> <u>tissue</u> of myth and <u>self-infatuation</u>. We get the world wrong because we get ourselves wrong. Taken without <u>illusion</u>, our history gives us no right to preach—but it should prepare us to understand the brutal realities of nation-building at home and abroad.

solipsism (SOL-ip-<u>siz</u>-um), the idea that the self is the only thing that matters; egotistical self-concern. From Latin *solus*, alone, + *ipse*, self, + suffix *ism*.

perennial (puh-REN-ee-ul), unceasing, continuing through many years. From Latin *per*, through, + *annus*, year.
<u>From same base</u>: perennially.
<u>Synonyms</u>: unceasing, continual, constant, perpetual, lasting, unfailing, endless, persistent, permanent, ceaseless, everlasting.
<u>Antonyms</u>: fleeting, transient, evanescent, brief, transitory, passing, ephemeral, impermanent, vanishing, short-lived.

grotesquely (groh-TESK-lee), outlandishly, incongruously. From Italian *grottesca*, distorted (in reference to the distorted drawings often found in an early *grotta*, cave).
<u>From same base</u>: grotesque, grotesqueness.
<u>Synonyms</u>: fantastically, outlandishly, incongruously, oddly, absurdly, unnaturally, strangely.
<u>Antonyms</u>: normally, usually, customarily, ordinarily, conventionally, typically.

culture (KUL-chur), the ideas, customs, skills, arts, etc., of a given people at a given time. From Latin *cultura*, cultivation of the mind; cultivation of the soil.
<u>From same base</u>: culturing, cultured, cultural.
<u>Synonyms</u>: education, learning, scholarship, manners, refinement, knowledge, breeding, experience.
<u>Antonyms</u>: ignorance, boorishness, stupidity, stolidity, vulgarity, pretension, illiteracy.

variant (VEHR-ee-unt), a different or varying version. From Latin *varians*, prp. of *variare*, to vary.
<u>From same base</u>: variance.
<u>Synonyms</u>: variation, change, deviation, modification, mutation, fluctuation.
<u>Antonyms</u>: sameness, identicalness, conformity, congruity, uniformity.

staple (STAY-pul), a standard approach; a chief item or element in anything. From Middle Dutch *stapel*, a mart stocking foodstuffs and other items of trade.

mandarin (MAN-duh-rin), a pompous official holding high office in foreign policy or in some related field; a leading intellectual or political figure; a high official of China under the Empire. From Sanscrit *mantrin*, a counselor.

imbued (im-BYOOD), impressed (by ourselves, in this instance). From Latin *imbuere*, to saturate.
From same base: imbue, imbuing, imbued.
Synonyms: saturated, pervaded, colored, suffused, animated, inspired, impressed.
Antonyms: unsaturated, unimpressed, deficient, inadequate, lacking, uninspired, wanting.

impetuous (im-PECH-oo-us), rash, impulsive. From Late Latin *impetuosus*, rushing; acting with little thought.
From same base: impetuously, impetuousness, impetuosity.
Synonyms: rash, impulsive, furious, vehement, violent, hasty, headlong, headstrong, impulsive, fiery, passionate, fierce, heady, ardent.
Antonyms: calm, steady, slow, thoughtful, careful, considerate, meek, mild, patient, doubtful, peaceful, placid, quiet, controlled.

exotic (ig-ZOT-ik), fascinating, striking, enticing, strangely different. From Greek *exotikos*, foreign, outlandish.
From same base: exotically.
Synonyms: appealing, striking, enticing, strange, beguiling, bewitching, enthralling, engrossing, entrancing.

tumult (TOO-mult), agitation, commotion, disturbance. From Latin *tumultus*, a swelling, surging up.
From same base: tumultuous, tumultuously.
Synonyms: agitation, commotion, uproar, disturbance, violence, turbulence, disorder, vehemence, passion.
Antonyms: peace, quiet, restraint, calm, tranquillity, gentleness, moderation, patience.

assess (uh-SES), to measure, evaluate, estimate. From Latin *assessus*, pp. of *assidere*, to sit beside, assist, give advice.
From same base: assessment, assessor.
Synonyms: measure, evaluate, estimate, assist, advise, appraise, assay, appreciate, rate.

invocation (<u>in</u>-voh-KAY-shun), a calling upon, a reference to. From
Latin *invocatio* with same meaning.
<u>From same base</u>: invocational.

heritage (HEHR-ih-tij), something handed down from one's ancestors
(e.g., culture, tradition). From Latin *hereditas* with same meaning.
<u>Synonyms</u>: inheritance, legacy, patrimony, birthright.

comity (KOM-ih-tee), courtesy, civility, friendliness. From Latin
comitas with same meaning.

parallel (PEHR-uh-lel), similarity, connection, likeness, comparison.
From Greek *parallelos* (prefix *para*, side by side, + *allelos*, one
another), with same meaning.
<u>From same base</u>: parallelism.
<u>Synonyms</u>: similarity, connection, likeness, comparison, resemblance,
affinity, conformity, community, kinship, counterpart, duplicate.
<u>Antonyms</u>: difference, variance, divergence, variation, diversity,
dissimilarity, unlikeness, disparity.

trumpet (TRUM-pit), proclaim with fanfare, boast about. From
Middle English *trompette*, a brass-wind instrument with a blaring
tone.
<u>From same base</u>: trumpeting, trumpeted.
<u>Synonyms</u>: brag, boast, exult, vaunt, bluster, crow.

incommensurably (<u>in</u>-kuh-MEN-shur-uh-blee), immeasurably,
substantially, markedly. Adverb from Late Latin adjective
incommensurabilis (Latin prefix *in*, not, + *com*, together, +
mensurare, to measure), not measured by the same standard.
<u>From same base</u>: incommensurable, incommensurability.
<u>Synonyms</u>: immeasurably, substantially, markedly.

sanctimonious (<u>sangk</u>-tih-MOH-nee-us), making a display of
devotion, pretending righteousness. From Latin *sanctimonia*,
virtue, sacredness, and, in turn, from *sanctus*, holy.
<u>From same base</u>: sanctimoniously, sanctimoniousness.
<u>Synonyms</u>: preachy, self-righteous, pious, religionistic, hypocritical,
canting, feigning.

tissue (TISH-oo), a piece of soft, thin, perishable paper. From Middle English *tissu*, a thin, interwoven cloth.

self-infatuation (self-in-fach-oo-AY-shun), state of being carried away by a foolish and unreasonable love of self. From Old English reflexive pronoun *self* + *infatuation* from Late Latin *infatuatio*, foolish love or affection.

illusion (ih-LOO-zhun), false or misleading belief or opinion not in accord with the facts. From Latin *illusio*, a mocking, deceit.
From same base: illusional, illusionary.
Synonyms: fantasy, imagination, dream, vision, fancy, apparition, image.
Antonyms: reality, fact, actuality, happening, certainty, circumstance, episode, event.

Language Uses and Abuses

Other Latin prefixes as guides to meaning

In this section on Day 16, you encountered the Latin preposition *ante*, before (in time or order), as a prefix and partial clue to the meaning of words like *antecedent* and *antedate*. Then, on Day 22, we listed Latin numbers commonly serving as prefixes.

The context-paragraphs today included the words *interactive* and *transition*, both of which begin with Latin prepositions as prefixes and keys to meaning. Since Latin prepositions play a significant role as prefixes in our language, some of the more common of them appear below with English examples.

circum, around
circumvent (SUR-kum-vent), to get the better of or escape by going around; from *circum* + *ventus*, pp. of *venire*, to come, to arrive.
circumlocution (sur-kum-loh-KYOO-shun), a verbose style of speaking or writing, talking around a subject rather than about it.

contra, against
contradiction (kon-truh-DIK-shun), the act of speaking against what someone has said; from *contra* + *dictus*, pp. of *dicere*, to speak.
contraband (KON-truh-band), goods which it is against the law or treaty to import or export.

inter, between

interrupt (in-tur-RUPT), to come between or break into a discussion or action; from *inter* + *ruptus*, pp. of *rumpere*, to break.

intercellular (<u>in</u>-tur-SEL-yoo-lurt), situated between or among cells.

intra, within

intramural (in-truh-MYOOR-ul), taking place within the walls (e.g., within the walls of a school as in, for example, intramural sports; from *intra* + *murus*, wall.

intravenous (<u>in</u>-truh-VEEN-us), situated within or affecting the inside of a vein.

sub, under

subservient (sub-SUR-vee-ent), serving under in an inferior position; from *sub* + *serviens*, prp. of *servire*, to serve.

subordinate (suh-BOR-din-it), someone whose rank is under or below that of another; a clause that is less important than another.

super, above

superimpose (<u>soo</u>-pur-im-POHZ), to put, lay, or stack over something else; from *super* + *imponere*, to place upon.

supercilious (<u>soo</u>-pur-SIL-ee-us), exhibiting arrogance and personal superiority over others.

Quick Checks on Comprehension

In each line below, highlight or check off the word or phrase that best matches the meaning of the word to the left.

perennial	informal, internal, lasting, preening
grotesquely	strangely, expertly, soundly, sensibly
culture	premonition, education, impression, allusion
variant	elevation, position, duration, mutation
imbued	inured, inspired, tired, required
impetuous	headstrong, lucky, energetic, reticent
exotic	periodic, ascetic, enhancing, entrancing
tumult	insult, uproar, downpour, cult
assess	insist, evaluate, rectify, elevate
heritage	patronage, dotage, elegy, legacy
parallel	polarity, singularity, similarity, comity
trumpet	bluster, fester, pester, pander

incommensurably   nervously, immeasurably, cruelly, precisely
sanctimonious   storing, poring, feigning, appraising
illusion   fusion, apparition, infatuation, invocation

In each line below, highlight or check off the two synonyms.

reality, fealty, fact, probity
ludicrous, pious, self-effacing, self-righteous
substantially, inexorably, markedly, deplorably
produce, conduct, boast, exult
oneness, likeness, duplicate, extricate
patrimony, matrimony, birthright, insight
pressure, estimate, lapse, measure
innocence, indulgence, restraint, patience
striking, inciting, enthralling, pervading
calm, placid, altruistic, flagrant
opinionated, saturated, suffused, enervated
conformity, sameness, tameness, verbosity
importuning, learning, privilege, knowledge
oddly, importantly, morosely, absurdly
unveiling, spineless, unfailing, endless

In each line below, highlight or check off the two antonyms.

ephemeral, special, ceaseless, reeling
superbly, unnaturally, normally, probably
refinement, supplement, emptiness, boorishness
profundity, abrasion, deviation, uniformity
inspired, reconciled, unimpressed, recorded
indolent, violent, flaccid, placid
commotion, promotion, multiplicity, tranquillity
conformity, alacrity, verbosity, diversity
dream, bream, intent, event,

If unsure about your comprehension choices, please see Appendix A.

With joyous roundelay, try using a new word today!

DAY 28

New Word-Choices
From Dr. Benjamin M. Spock, <u>A Better World for Our Children</u>
(Bethesda, MD: National Press Books, 1994), p. 73 f.

Our nation is the most violent in the world, and it has been getting <u>progressively</u> worse in the twentieth century. The pioneers who settled this country in waves had to be aggressive to pull up roots and to survive in this harsh new land. They not only betrayed, <u>dispossessed</u> and <u>eradicated</u> the Native Americans, but each group of immigrants found ways to insult and abuse the next. The waves of largely European immigrants and generations of their American-born children eventually <u>fashioned</u> a new society. The very <u>multiplicity</u> of the groups now making up our population has contributed to the lack of a common <u>philosophy</u> and to the often <u>hostile</u> <u>rivalry</u> between groups.

African-Americans, starting as slaves, have had to contend with being unable to <u>disguise</u> their race as they've painfully tried to climb the ladder to <u>equality</u>. While many people of color have successful and <u>productive</u> lives, the problem of racial injustice is still with us. Too many young, urban <u>minority</u> males especially feel <u>disenfranchised</u> and cheated by society as a whole. Many minority males have been raised by single mothers who are themselves victims of poverty and other social injustices.

progressively (pruh-GRES-iv-lee), continuously moving forward.
Adverb from Middle Latin adjective *progressivus*, and, in turn, from
Latin *progressus*, pp. of *progredi*, to advance.
<u>From same base</u>: progressive, progressiveness.
<u>Synonyms</u>: enterprisingly, increasingly, forward, onward, ahead,
under way, in progress.

dispossess (<u>dis</u>-puh-ZES), to deprive of the possession of something like land, a home, etc. From Latin negative prefix *dis* + *possessus*, pp. of *possidere*, to hold, possess.
<u>From same base</u>: dispossessing, dispossessed.
<u>Synonyms</u>: expel, oust, evict, deprive, depose, drive out, banish, deport, exile, dislodge, seize, capture, appropriate, usurp, confiscate, expropriate, extort, eject, despoil.
<u>Antonyms</u>: restore, replace, reinstate, reestablish, reinstall, reinsert, return, rehabilitate, renew, renovate.

eradicate (ih-RAD-ih-<u>kayt</u>), to destroy, do away with. From Latin *eradicatus*, pp. of *eradicare*, to root out, get rid of.
<u>From same base</u>: eradicating, eradicated, eradication.
<u>Synonyms</u>: destroy, do away with, get rid of, exterminate, root out, annihilate, uproot, abolish, disperse, extinguish, devastate, kill, remove.
<u>Antonyms</u>: plant, implant, embed, settle, fix, establish, stabilize, institute, strengthen, fortify, secure, confirm.

fashion (FASH-un), to make, shape, mold. From Old French *faceon* with same meaning.
<u>From same base</u>: fashioning, fashioned, fashionable, fashionably, fashionableness.
<u>Synonyms</u>: shape, mold, design, create, plan, form, fabricate, manufacture.

multiplicity (<u>mul</u>-tuh-PLIS-ih-tee), the condition or quality of being varied, having many kinds. From Late Latin *multiplicitas* (*multus*, many, + *plicare*, to fold together), multiple.

philosophy (fih-LOS-uh-fee), a common approach to life, morals, character, and behavior; love of wisdom and the search for it. From *philos* (philo), love, + *sophia* (soph), wisdom.
<u>From same base</u>: philosopher, philosophic, philosophical, philosophically.

hostile (HOS-tl), unfriendly, antagonistic, having or expressing enmity. From Latin *hostilis* with same meaning.
<u>From same base</u>: hostilely, hostility.

Synonyms: unfriendly, antagonistic, contrary, adverse, inimical, belligerent.
Antonyms: friendly, devoted, amicable, loyal, conciliatory, well-disposed, kindly, agreeable.

rivalry (RYE-vul-ree), a striving to equal or excel. From Latin *rivalis*, one leaving near or using the same stream (*rivus*, river) as another.
From same base: rival, rivaling, rivaled.
Synonyms: opposition, competition, emulation, resistance, confrontation, contention, struggle, combat.
Antonyms: aid, assistance, help, support, cooperation, participation, unity, encouragement.

disguise (dis-GUYZ), to alter the appearance of. From prefix *dis*, opposite of, + Old French *guise*, manner, appearance.
From same base: disguising, disguised.
Synonyms: change, mask, conceal, camouflage, feign, hide, pretend, screen, cloak, cover, veil.
Antonyms: strip, bare, open, uncover, unmask, unveil, peel off, tear away.

equality (ih-KWOL-ih-tee), a state of being equal to others. From Latin *aequalitas* with same meaning.
Synonyms: parity, equivalence, parallelism, comparability, evenness.
Antonyms: inequality, disparity, inadequacy, deficiency, disparateness, unevenness.

productive (pruh-DUK-tiv), marked by effective results, by higher economic or professional attainments. From Middle Latin *productivus* with similar meaning.
From same base: productively, productivity, productiveness.
Synonyms: creative, inventive, prolific, ingenious, fertile, original, clever.
Antonyms: unproductive, unyielding, infertile, impotent, unfruitful, useless, unprofitable, ineffectual.

minority (my-NOR-ih-tee), a racial or other group smaller than and different from the larger group. From Latin *minor*, the smaller number or lesser part, + noun-ending *ity*.

disenfranchised (<u>dis</u>-en-FRAN-chizd), deprived of rights common to all citizens. From negative prefix *dis*, not, + Old French *franc*, free. <u>From same base</u>: disenfranchisement.

Language Uses and Abuses

More Latin prefixes as guides to meaning

To those Latin prefixes listed on Days 22 and 27, we now add a few more, again most of them serving originally as prepositions.

ab, away: **ablution** (ab-LOO-shun), a washing away as, for example, in a religious ceremony; from *ab* + *luere*, to wash.

ad, to: **adjutant** (AJ-uh-tent), an officer who helps a commanding officer with administrative duties; from *ad* + *iuvare*, to help.

ambi, both: **ambidextrous** (am-bih-DEK-strus), able to use both hands with equal ease; from *ambi* + *dextra*, the right hand (having, in other words, two right hands).

con, with: **convention** (kun-VEN-shun), a coming with or together; from *con* + *venire*, to come.

de, from: **demolish** (deh-MOL-ish), to pull down, tear down, smash; from *de* + *moliri*, to build, construct.

e or *ex* (before vowels), out of: **evoke** (ih-VOHK), to call forth, summon; from *e* + *vocare*, to call.

extra, outside of: **extralegal** (eks-truh-LEE-gul), outside of legal control; from *extra* + *legalis*, legal.

per, through: **perjury** (PUR-juh-ree), a breaking through the law, the breaking of an oath or any formal promise; from *per* + *ius* (later spelled *jus*), law.

post, after: **postnatal** (pohst-NAY-tl), occurring after birth; from *post* + *natalis*, having to do with birth.

pre, before: **preordain** (pree-or-DAYN), to decree, order, or arrange beforehand; from *pre* + *ordinare*, to ordain, order; authorize to perform the functions of a cleric.

semi, half: **semitropical** (sem-ee-TROP-ih-kul), having only some of the characteristics of the tropics; from *semi* + Greek *tropikos*, belonging to a turn of the sun.

ultra, beyond: **ultraconservative** (ul-truh-kun-SERV-uh-tiv), one who is conservative to an extreme degree; from *ultra* + *conservativus*, tending to follow traditions and resist change.

Quick Checks on Comprehension

In each line below, highlight or check off the word or phrase that best matches the meaning of the word to the left.

progressively	fortuitously, surprisingly, exceedingly, enterprisingly
dispossess	display, derogate, dissent, deprive
eradicate	interrogate, substantiate, devastate, initiate
fashion	fabricate, prevaricate, ingratiate, regulate
hostile	penitent, belligerent, petulant, somnolent
rivalry	subversion, intention, rejection, opposition
disguise	conceal, repeal, appeal, anneal
equality	rarity, asperity, regularity, parity
productive	covert, inventive, preventive, inductive

In each line below, highlight or check off the two synonyms.

prohibitive, creative, ingenious, specious
equivalence, restlessness, imperialism, parallelism
preen, lampoon, conceal, screen
simulation, cooperation, support, report
unfriendly, inimical, despicable, sociable
gorge, perform, form, mold
implant, uphold, uproot, remove
depict, evict, dislodge, disregard
forward, onward, wayward, inward

In each line below, highlight or check off the two antonyms.

seize, replace, raze, pace
perish, abolish, impoverish, establish
adverse, inverse, agreeable, reprehensible
persistence, insistence, resistance, assistance
revere, repeal, uncover, conceal
roughness, evenness, clarity, disparity
fertile, ruthless, unfruitful, unfaithful

If unsure about your comprehension choices, please see Appendix A.

With a new word as prey, use it the livelong day!

DAY 29

New Word-Choices
From Benjamin H. Alexander, speech on
"The Importance of Education in Today's America,"
Vital Speeches of the Day, 61 (April 15, 1995) 13, p. 403 f.

Excellence in education is possible today if we teach our students to master standard English, appreciate hard work, have self-respect and respect for others, seek values, and shun crass materialism. It should be an indictable crime to graduate students from high school who cannot read, write, and compute.

A teacher once told me that discipline is essential in our schools in order to teach reading—and all of you know she is correct. We must have special schools for pupils who will not obey. They must be removed from the classroom for the good of the majority, or those few students will always disrupt learning and cause chaos, so that too many pupils will move at a snail's pace, and into adulthood in ignorance.

We have failed in education because of public policies that have aided and abetted weak curricular content for students, soft classroom discipline, and lax graduation requirements. The notion has been advanced every so subtly that inner city children by and large are unable to achieve academically; that they have some sort of built-in deficiency that is exacerbated by the circumstances of their birth and the so-called "underprivileged" environment in which they are raised. This notion of a mental built-in deficiency caused by where you were born and raised is, of course, patently false.

excellence (EK-suh-lents), superiority, surpassing merit. From Latin
  excellentia with same meaning, and, in turn, from *excellens*, prp. of
  excellere, to excel.
From same base: excellent, excellently, excellency.
Synonyms: merit, quality, superiority, goodness, value, worth, lead,
eminence, power, influence, prestige.
Antonyms: inferiority, mediocrity, inadequacy, regression.

crass (kras), vulgar, coarse. From Latin *crassus*, thick, dense.
From same base: crassly, crassness.
Synonyms: vulgar, coarse, rough, gross, indelicate, crude, unrefined,
unpolished, inelegant, harsh.
Antonyms: refined, polished, delicate, elegant, fine.

materialism (muh-TEER-ee-uh-liz-um), an attitude that the only
  worthwhile goals in life are comfort, pleasure, and the gaining of
  "materials" like wealth and other possessions. From French
  materialisme with same meaning.

indictable (in-DYT-uh-bul), worthy of being charged in a court of
  law. From Middle English *enditable*, that should be indicted.
From same base: indict, indicting, indicted.
Synonyms: blameworthy, censurable, culpable, reprehensible,
reproachable, responsible, blameful, inexcusable, unpardonable,
unjustifiable.
Antonyms: forgivable, defensible, excusable, justifiable, pardonable,
remissable, absolvable.

compute (kum-PYOOT), to be capable of reaching a number by
  reckoning with other numbers. From Latin *computare*, to reckon.
From same base: computing, computed.
Synonyms: calculate, figure, reckon, tally, estimate, add.

majority (muh-JOR-ih-tee), the greater part or larger number within a
  group. From Middle Latin *maioritas* with same meaning, and, in
  turn, from Latin *maior*, greater.

disrupt (dis-RUPT), throw into disorder, block the orderly course of.
  From Latin *disruptus*, pp. of *disrumpere*, to break apart.
From same base: disrupting, disrupted, disruptive, disruptively.

<u>Synonyms</u>: disarrange, disorder, derange, disarray, disorganize, confuse, bewilder, perplex, confound, disorient.

chaos (KAY-aws), extreme confusion or disorder. From Greek *chaos*, infinite space, infinite darkness.
<u>From same base</u>: chaotic, chaotically.
<u>Synonyms</u>: confusion, disorder, snarl, shambles, disorganization.
<u>Antonyms</u>: harmony, order, system, method.

pace (payse), a step in walking, rate of movement. From Latin *passus*, a step.
<u>From same base</u>: pacing, paced.
<u>Synonyms</u>: speed, gait, rate, velocity, stride, step.

abet (uh-BET), to encourage. In "aided and abetted," abetted means encouraged. From Old French *abeter*, to incite.
<u>From same base</u>: abetting, abetted.
<u>Synonyms</u>: aid, assist, help, encourage, incite, stimulate, instigate, promote, uphold, embolden, support.
<u>Antonyms</u>: discourage, impede, obstruct, frustrate, hinder, baffle, counteract, dissuade, resist, confound, deter.

curricular (kuh-RIK-yuh-lur), pertaining to a set series of studies through which students "run." From Latin *currere*, to run.
<u>From same base</u>: curriculum.

lax (laks), lacking discipline or firmness. From Latin *laxus*, loose, slack.
From same base: laxly, laxness.
<u>Synonyms</u>: loose, slack, remiss, soft, flabby, careless, dishonorable, depraved, weak, immoral.
<u>Antonyms</u>: tight, firm, hard, muscular, moral, upright, conscientious, reliable, determined, observant, faithful, true, righteous, honorable, dutiful, honest.

subtly (SUT-lee), skillfully, cleverly, with discrimination. Adverb from Latin adjective *subtilis*, fine, precise.
<u>From same base</u>: subtle, subtleness, subtlety.
<u>Synonyms</u>: skillfully, cleverly, ingeniously, nicely, finely, perceptively.
<u>Antonyms</u>: dully, stupidly, slowly, perversely, idiotically, clumsily, awkwardly, senselessly, witlessly, foolishly.

academically (<u>ak</u>-uh-DEM-ih-kuh-lee), in the schools, in the educational process. Adverb from Latin adjective *academicus*, having to do with education.
<u>From same base</u>: academic, academical, academy.

deficiency (dih-FISH-un-see), incompleteness, the absence of something essential. From Latin *deficiens*, prp. of *deficere*, to lack.
<u>From same base</u>: deficient, deficiently.
<u>Synonyms</u>: inadequacy, insufficiency, scarcity, scantiness, incompleteness, deficit, shortcoming, shortage.
<u>Antonyms</u>: completeness, adequacy, sufficiency, suitability.

exacerbate (ig-ZAS-ur-<u>bayt</u>), to aggravate, make more severe. From Latin *exacerbatus*, pp. of *exacerbare*, to make angry.
<u>From same base</u>: exacerbating, exacerbated.
<u>Synonyms</u>: exasperate, irritate, make serious, intensify, exaggerate, make worse, make severe, annoy, provoke.

underpriviledged (<u>un</u>-dur-PRIV-lijd), deprived of certain material and social rights through poverty, discrimination, etc. From German *unter*, under, + Latin *privilegium*, a basic right guaranteed by government.

patently (PAT-nt-lee), clearly, obviously. From Latin *patens*, prp. of *patere*, to lie open.
<u>From same base</u>: patent (i.e., open to all).
<u>Synonyms</u>: apparently, plainly, clearly, obviously, unmistakably, manifestly, evidently, distinctly.
<u>Antonyms</u>: ambiguously, dimly, vaguely, indistinctly.

Language Uses and Abuses

"They're all alike."

In discussing choices of language in general, we earlier offered suggestions on how to express ideas clearly and vividly. To those positive approaches, we add the caution against stereotyping, the too-common assumption that all individuals in a particular group fall into a "standard mold" (Greek *stereos* + *typos*). If someone says, "People in the inner-city don't want to work," she or he is guilty of stereotyping.   And those who say politicians are skilled only in winning elections are similarly at fault.

Stereotypes are convenient classification baskets—all native Americans are the same, so they go in this basket; all Californians are the same, so they go in that one—and so on for instructors, activists, construction workers, stock brokers, Republicans, Orientals, the clergy, agnostics, Democrats, fundamentalists, farmers, Southerners, cab drivers, et al.   So, as we speak or listen, one fact should be kept in mind; what many regard as true of a group may not be true of individuals in it...and may not even be true of the group.

Quick Checks on Comprehension

In each line below, highlight or check off the word or phrase that best matches the meaning of the word to the left.

excellence	severity, reality, goodness, relaxation
crass	coarse, hoarse, bereft, indebted
indictable	reputable, generous, lax, blameworthy
compute	loan, reckon, perpetrate, initiate
disrupt	derange, display, denounce, disassociate
chaos	confusion, profusion, infusion, delusion
pace	pate, gate, strait, gait
abet	gamble, uphold, debate, surge
lax	pack, rack, crack, slack
subtly	finely, mutually, supremely, glumly
deficiency	ability, scarcity, plurality, elasticity
patently	manifestly, lightly, freely, combatively

In each line below, highlight or check off the two synonyms.

supportively, evidently, uncomplainingly, apparently
deficit, composite, shortage, portage
impressively, joyfully, clumsily, awkwardly
depraved, entranced, immoral, imperial
recede, obstruct, construct, impede
imbibe, stride, step, pride
snarl, snaffle, quarrel, shambles
refuse, confuse, bewilder, dazzle
calculate, regulate, figure, feature
culpable, reasonable, soulful, blameful
insignificant, elegant, refined, inclined

impropriety, superiority, gratitude, merit

In each line below, highlight or check off the two antonyms.

reciprocity, quality, monstrosity, mediocrity
astonished, viewed, polished, crude
censurable, reliable, excusable, susceptible
lunacy, harmony, confusion, profusion
promote, predict, subscribe, obstruct
noisy, content, firm, weak
cleverly, foolishly, improperly, movingly
shortcoming, incursion, flippancy, adequacy
superbly, solely, ambiguously, distinctly

If unsure about your comprehension choices, please see Appendix A.

If your language is gray, color it anew today!

New Word-Choices
From Richard L. Weaver II, speech on "Leadership for the Future:
Walking, Talking, and Working Together,"
<u>Vital Speeches of the Day</u>, 61 (May 1, 1995) 14, p.439.

The idea that women should <u>translate</u> their experiences into the male <u>code</u> in order to express themselves effectively, or in order to be accepted in a male-dominated workplace is an <u>outmoded, inconsistent,</u> subservient notion that should no longer be given credibility in modern society. The idea that women are the ones who need to change should be banished from our attitudes, banished from our thinking, and banished from our actions forever. As greater numbers of women and men work together, the <u>professional</u> <u>climate</u> has to change. To lead, we will need to talk with each other. To lead, we will need to work with each other, or, clearly, we will face the <u>consequences</u> of our unwillingness to change.

What we must adopt is a balanced perspective that <u>capitalizes</u> on the important <u>traits</u> of human beings—not men or women. If you think about it, effective leadership requires both <u>instrumental</u> and <u>expressive</u> responsibilities, both <u>task-oriented</u> and <u>socio-emotional</u> responsibilities. Good leaders need to be intelligent, assertive, and independent just as much as they need to be nurturing, <u>sensitive</u> and emotional. These are human qualities. The <u>concept</u> of an <u>androgynous</u> model of leadership—that is, a blending of masculine and feminine behavior—must be the accepted <u>norm</u>. This is what I mean by walking, talking, and working together.

translate (trans-LAYT), change into another way of speaking, into another mode of expression. From Latin *translatus*, pp. of *transferre*, to carry across.

From same base: translating, translated, translatable.

Synonyms: construe, render, reword, change, convert, transform.

Antonyms: misinterpret, misread, misconstrue, misconceive, misrender.

code (kohd), a set of signals or symbols used in communication and, in "male code," a way of communicating characteristic of males. From Latin *codex*, a wooden tablet for writing.

outmoded (owt-MOH-did), out of fashion, obsolete. From Old English *ut*, out, + Latin *modus*, mode, manner.

Synonyms: obsolete, outdated, unfashionable, olden, ancient, antiquated, archaic, antique, dated, timeworn, obsolescent.

Antonyms: new, modern, up-to-date, modernistic, ultramodern, streamlined.

inconsistent (in-kun-SIS-tunt), contradictory, lacking backing, not uniform. From Latin negative prefix *in*, not, + *consistens*, prp. of *consistere*, to stand together.

From same base: inconsistently, inconsistency.

Synonyms: unsteady, inconstant, contrary, unsuitable, varying, incompatible, contradictory.

Antonyms: steady, constant, suitable, compatible, stable, firm, uniform, steadfast.

professional (pruh-FESH-uh-nul), appropriate to or conforming to the set standards or principles of a certain activity. From Latin *professio*, an occupation, art, profession.

From same base: profession, professionally.

Synonyms: businesslike, practical, orderly, systematic, methodical, efficient, industrious, sedulous.

climate (KLY-mit), any prevailing conditions affecting life, activity, etc. From Greek *klima*, region, zone, and the weather associated with it.

From same base: climatic, climatically.

consequence (KON-sih-kwents), that which naturally follows as the result of a preceding action or condition. From Latin *consequens*, prp. of *consequi*, to follow after.
From same base: consequent, consequential, consequentially.
Synonyms: effect, result, outgrowth, end, issue, upshot,outcome.
Antonyms: cause, origin, beginning, preparation, source,commencement, rise, inception, start.

capitalize (KAP-ih-tl-eyz) on, to take advantage of, avail oneself of, exploit. From Latin *capitalis*, of the head (*caput*), capable of being put to beneficial use.
From same base: capitalizing, capitalized, capitalization, capitalist.
Synonyms: take advantage of, exploit, use, adopt, utilize, profit by, operate.

instrumental (in-struh-MEN-tl), pertaining to useful mechanical or technical abilities. From Middle Latin *instrumentalis*, serving as a means.
From same base: instrumentally, instrumentation.
Synonyms: contributory, conducive, promoting, helping, serving, accessory, useful.

expressive (ik-SPRES-iv), serving to indicate meaning or feeling or both. From Middle Latin *expressivus* with same meaning.
From same base: expressively, expressiveness.
Synonyms: eloquent, soulful, sentimental, poetic, oratorical, notional.

task-oriented (task-OR-ee-en-td), aimed at or concentrating on work (task). From Middle Latin *tasca*, a piece of work, and from Latin *oriens*, prp. of *oriri*, to adjust to a situation.

socio-emotional (SOH-see-oh-ih-MOH-shu-nl), having to do with personal relationships between and among fellow-workers as well as with the feelings and bonding associated with them. From Latin *socius*, ally, and from *emotus*, pp. of *emovere*, to stir up.

sensitive (SEN-sih-tiv), having appreciation or understanding; being emotionally or intellectually aware. From Middle Latin *sensitivus*, of the senses or sensation.
From same base: sensitively, sensitivity, sensitiveness.

Synonyms: predisposed, perceptive, susceptible, subject, prone, impressionable, liable, tender.

concept (KON-sept), generalized idea, view, thought. From *conceptus*, pp. of *concipere*, to imagine.
From same base: conceptual.
Synonyms: idea, view, thought, conception, theory, supposition, consideration, notion, opinion.

androgynous (an-DROJ-uh-nus), having the characteristics of both male and female. From Greek *andros* (andro), genitive form of *aner*, man, + *gyne* (gyno), woman.
From same base: androgyny.

norm (norm), a standard of conduct, an accepted way of behaving. From Latin *norma*, carpenter's square; a standard model or pattern, and, in turn, from Greek *gnomon* with same meaning.
Synonyms: standard, touchstone, yardstick, barometer, gauge.

Language Uses and Abuses

How word sources jog the memory

When you look up a word, a quick look at its source or sources helps you remember the word, its meaning, and its spelling.. The few examples below—three Latin, two Greek—point up the value of checking those sources.

aqua, water
aqueduct (AK-weh-dukt), a pipe or channel made for carrying water from a distant source; from *aqua* (aque) + *ductus* (duct), pp. of *ducere*, to lead, guide.
aquifer (AK-wih-fur), an underground layer of rock, sand, etc. containing or carrying water; from *aqua* (aqui) + *ferre* (fer), to carry.

caput, head
capital (KAP-ih-tl), a word of many meanings, one of which is the top part of a column or pillar; from *caput* (capit).
capitalism (KAP-ih-tl-iz-um), the economic system in which most of the means of production are privately owned; from *caput* (capit) with noun-forming ending.

gamos, a Greek word for wedding, marriage

monogamy (muh-NOG-uh-mee), the practice of having one spouse at
a time; from *monos* (mono), one, only, + *gamos* (gamy).

polygamy (puh-LIG-uh-mee), the practice of having more than one
spouse at a time; from *polys* (poly), many, + *gamos* (gamy).

genos, Greek for race, stock, family

genocide (JEN-uh-syd), the systematic extermination of an entire
people or national group; from *genos* (geno) + French suffix *cide*
from the Latin *caedere*, to kill.

generic (juh-NEHR-ik), referring to an entire kind, class, or group;
often used in reference to prescribed drugs; from *genos* (gener) +
adjective-forming ending.

lex, law

legal (LEE-gul), of or pertaining to the law; in conformity with the
law; adjectival form from *lex* (leg).

legislation (lej-is-LAY-shun), the act or procedure of enacting laws;
an officially enacted law or laws; from *lex* (legis) + *latio*, a bringing
forth, a proposing.

Quick Checks on Comprehension

In each line below, highlight or check off the word or phrase that best
matches the meaning of the word to the left.

translate	promote, reword, inundate, fascinate
outmoded	timeworn, remodelled, relegated, timely
inconsistent	unbroken, inaccurate, insensate, unsteady
professional	normal, efficient, coherent, unconcerned
consequence	disruption, outcome, inference, outlay
capitalize	rectify, allocate, adopt, preempt
instrumental	subordinate, expressive, conducive, persuasive
expressive	superlative, incremental, eloquent, sequential
sensitive	prohibitive, prone, obscure, flagrant
concept	riddle, idea, percept, precept
norm	pendulum, closure, stack, yardstick

In each line below, highlight or check off the two synonyms.

standard, proposition, page, gauge
potion, notion, opinion, bunion
partial, soulful, sentimental, elemental
reckless, hollow, liable, susceptible
fashioning, helping, ordering, serving
exploit, postpone, utilize, polarize
inspection, origin, source, resolution
social, practical, numerical, methodical
trustworthy, exceptional, varying, inconstant
separated, replete, outdated, obsolete
produce, change, fasten, convert

In each line below, highlight, or check off the two antonyms.

render, surrender, misread, repeat
parochial, unfashionable, insuperable, modern
conceptual, contrary, congenial, constant
upshot, report, roster, origin

If unsure about your comprehension choices, please see Appendix A.

Don't be in disarray—use a new word today!

New Word-Choices
From Edward O. Wilson, The Diversity of Life
(Cambridge, MA: Harvard University Press, 1992), p. 259.

The cutting of <u>primeval</u> forest and other disasters, fueled by the demands of growing human populations, are the overriding threat to biological <u>diversity</u> everywhere. But even the data that led to this conclusion, coming as they do mainly from <u>vertebrates</u> and plants, understate the case. The large, <u>conspicuous</u> <u>organisms</u> are the ones most <u>susceptible</u> to rifle shots, to overkill and the introduction of competing organisms. They are of the greatest immediate importance to man and receive the greater part of his <u>malign</u> attention.

Not many <u>habitats</u> in the world covering a kilometer contain fewer than a thousand species of plants and animals. Patches of rain forest and coral reef harbor tens of thousands of <u>species,</u> even after they have declined to a <u>remnant</u> of the original wilderness. But when the entire habitat is destroyed, almost all of the species are destroyed. Conservationists now generally recognize the difference between rifle shots and <u>holocausts</u>. They place <u>emphasis</u> on the <u>preservation</u> of entire habitats and not only on the <u>charismatic</u> species within them. They are uncomfortably aware that the last surviving herd of Javan rhinoceros cannot be saved if the remnant woodland in which they live is cleared, that harpy eagles require every scrap of rain forest around them that can be spared from the chainsaw. The <u>relationship</u> is <u>reciprocal</u>: when star species like rhinoceros and eagle are protected, they serve as umbrellas for all the life around them.

primeval (pry-MEE-vul), primitive, belonging to the first ages. From Latin *primus*, first, + *aevum*, age.

<u>Synonyms</u>: primitive, ancient, primal, primary, old, olden, immemorial, native, original, antique, venerable, traditional, prehistoric, distant, early.
<u>Antonyms</u>: modern, recent, late, present, future, eventual, approaching, impending, new, novel, up-to-date, coming, upstart, young.

diversity (dih-VUR-sih-tee), variety, difference. From Middle Latin *diversificare*, to make different.
<u>From same base</u>: diversification.
<u>Synonyms</u>: variety, difference, diversification, variance, distinctness, distinction, variation, dissimilarity, unlikeness, disparity.
<u>Antonyms</u>: similarity, resemblance, likeness, affinity, conformity, semblance, community, conformance.

vertebrate (VUR-tuh-brit), any animal having a backbone or spinal column. From Latin *vertebra*, a joint of the back, and, in turn, from *vertere*, to turn.
<u>From same base</u>: vertebra, vertebral.

conspicuous (kun-SPIK-yoo-us), clearly visible, striking. From Latin *conspicuus*, open to view, and, in turn, from intensifying prefix *com* + *specere*, to look at.
<u>From same base</u>: conspicuously, conspicuousness.
Synonyms: visible, striking, outstanding, eminent, noted, celebrated, prominent, commanding, well-known.
<u>Antonyms</u>: hidden, concealed, unseen, secret, mysterious, covered, obscure, unknown.

organism (OR-guh-niz-um), a live plant or animal. From Middle Latin *organizare*, to provide with an organized structure.
<u>From same base</u>: organismically.

susceptible (suh-SEP-tuh-bl), yielding readily to, open to. From Middle Latin *susceptibilis*, easily affected.
<u>From same base</u>: susceptibly, susceptibility, susceptibleness.
<u>Synonyms</u>: open, sensitive, impressionable, liable, subject, exposed, predisposed, prone.
<u>Antonyms</u>: insensible, insensitive, impassive, apathetic, dull, indifferent, unresponsive, unaffected, unimpressed, unmoved, unemotional.

malign (muh-LINE), to slander, defame. From Late Latin *malignare*,
   to speak evil of.
Synonyms: slander, defame, traduce, blacken, vilify, besmirch,
depreciate, revile, libel.
Antonyms: defend, vindicate, justify, praise.

habitat (HAB-ih-tat), the region or environment where a plant or
   animal is normally found. From Latin *habitare*, to have possession
   of, dwell in.
From same base: habitable, habitability.

species (SPEE-sheez), a group of organisms having a high degree of
   similarity, including a number of traits in common. From Latin
   species, outward appearance, kind.

remnant (REM-nent), a small part of, that which remains or is left
   over. From Old French *remenant*, prp. of *remaindre*, to remain
   behind.
Synonyms: remainder, residue, rest, balance, piece, fragment, relic,
surplus, refuse.
Antonyms: whole, entire, total, all, completeness, entirety, bulk, mass,
addition, increment, complement, supplement.

holocaust (HOL-uh-kawst), a wholesale destruction and loss of life.
   From Greek *holokauston*, burnt whole (*holos*, whole, + *kaustos*,
   burnt).

emphasis (EM-fah-sis), the special attention or importance given to
   something to make it stand out. From Greek *emphasis*, standing
   out.
From same base: emphatic, emphatically.
Synonyms: importance, consequence, significance, concern, stress,
prominence.

preservation (prez-ur-VAY-shun), a maintaining intact and
   undamaged. From Middle Latin *praeservatio* with same meaning.
Synonyms: protection, conservation, defense, safekeeping,
guardianship.

charismatic (kare-iz-MAT-ik), of or pertaining to extraordinary
   personal magnetism. From Greek *charisma*, grace, favor, talent.

From same base: charisma.
Synonyms: entrancing, captivating, fascinating, enchanting, delightful, winning, irresistible, attractive, magnetic.
Antonyms: disgusting, repugnant, revolting, horrible, forbidding, abominable, offensive, unpleasant, disagreeable.

relationship (rih-LAY-shun-ship), the quality or state of being connected. From Latin *relatio*, a bringing back.
From same base: relation, relational.
Synonyms: relation, connection, affiliation, association, interrelation, interdependence, dependence, reference, linkage, contact, integration.

reciprocal (rih-SIP-ruh-kul), mutual, corresponding, matching. From Latin *reciprocus*, returning, going backwards and forwards.
From same base: reciprocally.
Synonyms: mutual, corresponding, matching, correlative, interchangeable, changeable, dependent, interdependent.

Language Uses and Abuses

A word to the wise

The word *wise* is often unwisely and unnecessarily tacked on as a suffix to make adverbs out of nouns or adjectives. Examples:

"Moneywise, this is a good time to invest in bonds."
"She was not a very careful buyer, foodwise."

A sensible rule-of-thumb: When you use -*wise* as a suffix, use it only if it appears in a recent or current dictionary with that ending. Examples of correct usage:

"We always go clockwise when we run around this track."
"He wants his money back; otherwise, he's going to sue."

In the two sentences immediately below, the suffix -*ize* is similarly misused, this time to make verbs out of nouns or adjectives:

"Always sensitized to the latest polls, the candidate was careful to take positions in accord with them."
"The two companies were unable to finalize an agreement."

But some verbs do already and correctly have the *-ize* ending:

"The doctor was immunizing a number of children."
"Surgical techniques have been revolutionized in recent years."

Quick Checks on Comprehension

In each line below, highlight or check off the word or phrase that best matches the meaning of the word to the left.

primeval	eccentric, coequal, prehistoric, unique
diversity	subtlety, variety, specialty, notoriety
conspicuous	prominent, rigorous, contiguous, conducive
susceptible	predisposed, presumed, prejudiced, culpable
malign	consign, impale, encroach, revile
remnant	spate, residue, retinue, grate
emphasis	impatience, nonsense, reticence, importance
preservation	innovation, unction, protection, compunction
charismatic	magnetic, caustic, graphic, metallic
relationship	verbiage, linkage, baggage, suffrage
reciprocal	empirical, superficial, matching, patching

In each line below, highlight or check off the two synonyms.

intended, corresponding, primal, correlative
contact, inspection, bombast, connection
fatuous, embryonic, attractive, delightful
conservation, eradication, notarization, safekeeping
enormity, significance, concern, relationship
surplus, pest, remainder, synthesis
purify, vilify, attract, libel
open, ambitious, obligated, prone
distracted, striking, protracted, outstanding
elegance, difference, softness, unlikeness
ancient, typical, traditional, experimental

In each line below, highlight or check off the two antonyms.

novel, horizontal, transient, antique
laxity, disparity, alacrity, conformity
suspect, obscure, well-known, uncertain

predisposed, unaffected, disinfected, opposed
pretend, excite, besmirch, defend
entire, habitat, piece, extremity
emphatic, revolting, mercurial, irresistible

If unsure about your comprehension choices, please see Appendix A.

Make your day—use a new word today!

New Word-Choices
From Ronald Steel, "The Domestic Core of Foreign Policy,"
<u>The Atlantic Monthly</u>, 275 (June, 1995) 6, p. 86.

By many measures of social well-being we fall <u>inexorably</u> behind our trading partners, just as each new generation of Americans trails its parents in income and opportunity. We put a higher <u>proportion</u> of our people in prison than does any other country except Russia. We murder one another at a rate that <u>astounds</u> the world. Whole sections of our cities resemble parts of the Third World. As in Latin American countries, an <u>affluent</u> elite hides behind walls, alarm systems, and <u>security</u> guards.

We hold our nation up as an example to the world, which in many ways it is. But <u>virtually</u> no country in Western Europe has a <u>multigenerational</u> <u>underclass</u>. None is <u>plagued</u> by the gun culture that has infected American cities and has now spread even to small towns. No other mass culture so <u>extols</u> violence. In no other Western nation is the civil society so much a <u>hostage</u> to <u>unrestrained</u> and seemingly unrestrainable violence. Indeed, that violence may be the major reason that Europe and Japan no longer look to the United States as a model and a leader.

Our <u>domestic</u> troubles are not in a <u>realm</u> separate from our foreign policy. They are an integral part, even a product of it. A nation that seeks not only to protect the world but also to <u>inspire</u> other countries with its values and achievements must be able to offer at least as much to its own people as to those it seeks to guard. Yet at home, even more than in our foreign policy, we have failed <u>abjectly</u>.

inexorably (in-EK-sur-uh-blee), relentlessly. From Latin negative
prefix *in* + *exorabilis*, moved by entreaty.

From same base: inexorable, inexorability.
Synonyms: unavoidably, certainly, irresistably, inescapably, inevitably, surely.
Antonyms: uncertainly, doubtfully, vaguely, casually, questionably, indefinitely.

proportion (pruh-P0R-shun), a part, share, or portion of. From Latin prefix *pro*, for, + *portio*, part, section.
From same base: proportional, proportionally,
Synonyms: ratio, percentage, quota, division, portion, part, share, segment, base, section, essence, unit.
Antonyms: completeness, entirety, totality, whole, aggregate.

astound (uh-STOWND), to amaze, astonish. From Middle English *astouned*, pp. of *astonien*, to astonish.
From same base: astounding, astounded, astoundingly.
Synonyms: amaze, astonish, dumfound, stun, surprise, awe, stupefy, shock, startle.

affluent (AF-loo-unt), wealthy, prosperous. From Latin *affluens*, prp. of *affluere*, to flow freely, to abound in.
From same base: affluence, affluently.
Synonyms: rich, wealthy, prosperous, opulent, moneyed, independent.
Antonyms: poor, impecunious, destitute, impoverished, humble, indigent, needy.

security (sih-KYUUR-ih-tee), something that assures protection from danger. Used here as adjective modifying guards in sense of "guards for security." From Latin *securitas* , freedom from care, and, in turn, from Latin *securus*, free from care (*cura*).
Synonyms: safety, protection, shelter, surety, certainty, ease, calm, assurance, asylum.
Antonyms: uncertainty, doubt, hesitation, suspense, timidity, unreliability, precariousness.

virtually (VUR-choo-uh-lee), in effect, for all practical purposes. Adverb from Middle Latin *virtualis,* being such practically but not in fact or name.
From same base: virtual, virtuality.

multigenerational (MUL-tih-<u>jen</u>-uh-RAY-shun-ul), extending over many generations of about thirty years each. From Latin *multi*, many, + *generatio*, the period of a generation.

underclass (UN-dur-klas), a group of people considered to be inferior socially, economically, etc. From German *unter*, under, + Latin *classis*, a class or division of the Roman people.

plague (playg), to afflict severely. From Latin *plaga*, a blow.
<u>From same base</u>: plaguing, plagued.
<u>Synonyms</u>: persecute, pursue, infest, molest, trouble, vex,irritate, harass, irk, fret, harry, badger.

extol (ik-STOHL), to praise highly. From Latin *extollere*, to raise up.
<u>From same base</u>: extolling, extolled.
<u>Synonyms</u>: praise, laud, commend, applaud, magnify, glorify, cheer, acclaim, exalt, admire, approve, eulogize.
<u>Antonyms</u>: censure, condemn, decry, disapprove, dislike, disfavor, disparage, ostracize, shun, blame, reproach, admonish, berate, upbraid, snub, defame, denounce, deprecate.

hostage (HOS-tij), the state of being held captive under certain conditions. From Old French *hoste*, a person taken prisoner until certain conditions are met, or someone turned over to others as a guarantee of certain action.

unrestrained (un-rih-STRAYND), not held back. From negative prefix un + Middle English *restreinen*, to hold back.
<u>From same base</u>: unrestrainedly, unrestrainable.
<u>Synonyms</u>: unchecked, unbridled, uncurbed, unrestricted, unconstrained, unconfined, unrepressed, unhindered.
<u>Antonyms</u>: checked, bridled, curbed, restricted, constrained, confined, repressed, hindered, suppressed, kept back.

domestic (duh-MES-tik), pertaining to one's home country. From Latin *domus*, home, household, estate.
<u>From same base</u>: domestically.
<u>Synonyms</u>: tame, domesticated, internal, home, native.
<u>Antonyms</u>: wild, untamed, savage, foreign.

realm (relm), an area or sphere of concern. From Old French *realme*, pertaining to royalty or lands held by royalty.

abjectly (AB-ject-lee), wretchedly, hopelessly. Adverb from Latin *abjectus*, pp. of *abjicere*, to throw away.
From same base; abject, abjectness.
Synonyms: despicably, wretchedly, hopelessly, worthlessly, basely, contemptibly, pitifully, absurdly.
Antonyms: nobly, exaltedly, proudly, magnificently, imposingly, excellently, worthily, commendably.

Language Uses and Abuses

More good advice, kind of

Kind, sort, and *type* are three easy-to-abuse words.

Those singular forms should not be used with the plural demonstrative adjectives *these* and *those*. Examples:

"These kind of houses are hard to sell" should be plurals with
plurals, as in
"These kinds of houses are hard to sell."

"Those type of bicycles make riding fun" should be
"Those types of bicycles make riding fun."

And with *kind, sort,* and *type*, the meddlesome article *a* should be dropped.

"I like that kind of a movie" should be
"I like that kind of movie."

"What sort of a cake is that?" should be
"What sort of cake is that?"

One way to solve the problems of *kind of, sort of,* and *type of* is to use them sparingly or not at all. For example,

"He was a strange sort of man" could be "He was a strange man."
"She's an intriguing type of girl" could be "She's an intriguing girl."

"The boy was kind of tall for his age" could be "The boy was tall for his age."

So *kind*, *sort*, and *type* have to be used with care in order to avoid falling into their special kinds of pitfalls.

Quick Checks on Comprehension

In each line below, highlight or check off the word or phrase that best matches the meaning of the word to the left.

inexorably	unaffectedly, unpardonably, unavoidably, unrealistically
proportion	notation, percentage, drayage, overfill
astound	shock, prorate, mock, perpetrate
affluent	insolent, opulent, somnolent, portentous
security	shelter, labor, integrity, empathy
plague	succor, honor, parade, badger
extol	pretend, transcend, commend, suspend
unrestrained	unhindered, unselected, unrealized, unsafe
domestic	natural, native, supportive, real
abjectly	hurriedly, endlessly, purportedly, basely

In each line below, highlight or check off the two synonyms.

separately, infamously, nobly, worthily
wild, curving, savage, proud
inspected, curbed, tempered, checked
applaud, approve, apprehend, appease
propagate, harass, encompass, irritate
realm, asylum, safety, accuracy
indigent, prominent, lucrative, poor
perceive, foretell, dumfound, amaze
quota, leverage, order, portion
certainly, rapidly, surely, unexpectedly

In each line below, highlight or check off the two antonyms.

questionably, functionally, peremptorily, inescapably
role, segment, whole, impediment
responsible, fastidious, destitute, prosperous
imagination, doubt, assurance, predicament

laud, dread, compensate, berate
unscathed, unbridled, confined, refined
domesticated, untamed, unlikable, sophisticated
preferably, exaltedly, crisply, pitifully

If unsure about your comprehension choices, please see Appendix A.

Every new word you say augurs a bonus coming your way.

New Word-Choices
From Albert Shanker, speech on "Restoring the Connection
Between Behavior and Consequences:
the Removal of Violent and Disruptive Youngsters,"
Vital Speeches of the Day, 61 (May 15, 1995) 15, p. 465 f.

There was a press conference on a <u>position</u> the convention [Texas Federation of Teachers] <u>adopted</u>, and they used the phrase "zero tolerance." They said that with respect to certain types of dangerous activities in schools, there might be <u>suspension</u>, there might be <u>expulsion</u>, or there might be something else but, nevertheless, consequences would be clear.

Schools should have codes of conduct. These codes can be developed through <u>collective</u> bargaining, or they can be <u>mandated</u> in legislation. We are all familiar with the fact that most of our labor contracts have a provision for <u>grievance</u> <u>procedures</u>. And part of that grievance procedure is <u>arbitration</u>.

Now why can't school districts establish a fair, inexpensive, <u>due-process</u> arbitration procedure for youngsters who are violent or <u>disruptive</u>? So that when the youngster goes to court, a district can say, "Hey, we've had this procedure. We've had witnesses on both sides, and here was the <u>determination</u>. And, really, you shouldn't get into this unless you can show that those school people are terribly <u>prejudiced</u> or totally incompetent or something else."

In other words, we could create a separate school <u>judicial</u> system that had <u>expertise</u> and knowledge about what the <u>impact</u> is on students and teachers and the whole system of these kinds of decisions. Arbitration is a much cheaper, much faster system.

position (puh-ZISH-un), a point of view, a stand. From Latin *positio*,
   a placing, a posture.
From same base: positional.
Synonyms: place, station, stand, state, condition, posture,
circumstance, attitude, situation, status, standing.

adopt (uh-DOPT), to put into effect. From Latin *adoptare*, to choose.
From same base: adopting, adopted, adoptable.
Synonyms: assume, appropriate, embrace, accept, approve, pass,
espouse, choose, utilize, employ, apply.
Antonyms: disapprove, deprecate, disfavor, dispraise, criticize,
condemn, denounce, censure, decry.

suspension (suh-SPEN-shun), the barring from an activity or function
   as punishment. From Middle Latin *suspensio*, a leaving undecided.
Synonyms: discontinuance, cessation, interruption, delay,
postponement, deferment.
Antonyms: continuance, maintenance, persistence, support,
perseverance.

expulsion (ik-SPUL-shun), a forcing out. From Latin *expulsio* with
   same meaning.
From same base: expulsive.
Synonyms: discharge, removal, eviction, elimination, ejection,
banishment, proscription, ouster, dispossession.

collective (kuh-LEK-tiv), relating to individuals in a group acting
   together, as in bargaining with another group or groups. From
   Latin *collectivus*, gathered into a whole.
From same base: collectively.
Synonyms: shared, common, joint, conjoint, mutual.

mandate (MAN-dayt), to authorize, order. From Latin *mandatus*, pp.
   of *mandare*, to put into one's hand (*manus*), entrust.
From same base: mandating, mandated, mandatory, mandatorily.
Synonyms: command, rule, direct, authorize, dictate, enjoin, demand,
instruct, decree, ordain, prescribe, impose.
Antonyms: petition, solicit, entreat, beseech, implore, seek, appeal,
beg.

grievance (GREE-vunse), a real or imaginary wrong regarded as a
cause for complaint. From Middle English *grevaunce* with same
meaning.
Synonyms: complaint, protest, remonstrance, expostulation,
representation, clamor, outcry.

procedure (pruh-SEE-jur), a particular course of action or way of
doing something. From Latin *procedere*, to move forward.
From same base: procedural, procedurally.
Synonyms: action, process, transaction, deed, performance, step,
course, undertaking, venture, operation, exercise, program, plan.
Antonyms: inactivity, inertness, passiveness, idleness, cessation.

arbitration (ahr-bih-TRAY-shun), the settlement of a dispute by a
person or persons chosen to hear both sides. From Latin *arbitratus*,
pp. of *arbitrari*, to hand down a decision.
From same base: arbitrate, arbitrating, arbitrated, arbitrative,
arbitrational.
Synonyms: judgment, conclusion, decision, opinion, determination,
finding, award, adjudication, prejudgment, review, notice, settlement,
ruling, resolution.

due-process (doo-PROS-ess) , the course of legal proceedings
designed to protect individual rights and liberties. From Old French
deu, owed, pp. of *devoir*, to owe, and from Latin *processus*, pp. of
procedere, to proceed.

disruptive (dis-RUPT-iv), causing a disturbance or interruption.
From Latin *disruptus*, pp. of *disrumpere*, to break apart.
From same base: disrupt, disrupting, disrupted, disruptively.
Synonyms: disturbing, interrupting, tumultuous, unsettling, turbulent,
uproarious, tempestuous, stormy, riotous, disorderly.

determination (dih-tur-muh-NAY-shun), a decision reached; in other
contexts, firmness in purpose or action. From Latin *determinatio*, an
end, a boundary.
Synonyms: (Same as for *arbitration* above.)

prejudiced (PREJ-uh-disd), inclined to disregard the facts or rule
against individuals or a group because of hatred or dislike. From
Latin *praeiudicare*, to decide beforehand or prematurely.

<u>Synonyms</u>: biased, prepossessed, bigoted, intolerant, unfair, jaundiced, discriminatory, slanted, subjective.

judicial (joo-DISH-ul), pertaining to the administering of justice.
From Latin *iudicialis*, relating to a court of justice.
<u>From same base</u>: judicially.
<u>Synonyms</u>: juridical, magisterial, arbitrative, critical, judgmental, forensic.

expertise (Ek-spur-<u>teez</u>), the special judgment, skill, or experience possessed by those in a system or by an individual. From Latin *expertus*, pp. of *experiri*, to know by experience.
<u>From same base</u>: expert, expertly, expertness.
<u>Synonyms</u>: knowledge, judgment, skill, experience, training, seasoning, background, sophistication, practicality.

impact (IM-pakt), a strong influence or effect. From Latin *impactus*, pp. of *impingere*, to strike forcefully.
<u>Synonyms</u>: collision, shock, concussion, brunt, clash, slam, contact.

Language Uses and Abuses

Some remarks on *some*

As the indefinite pronoun which it is, *some* may be either singular or plural, depending on whether or not the nouns or pronouns to which it refers are singular or plural. Examples:

"The greater part of the money was set aside in a bank account, but some was reserved for day-to-day expenses."
"Although many of the students went to the game, some preferred the beach and others the amusement park."

As an adjective which, strictly speaking, it is not, *some* has gained general acceptance, as in the phrase "Some remarks" in the subheading at the beginning of this section. Other examples:

"Some people fear flying; others are very nonchalant about it."
"For some workers, retirement seems too far off to worry about."

But the use of *some* in the sense of *outstanding* or *remarkable* should still be avoided in semiformal or formal speech or writing.

"Those are some brochures!" should be
"Those are outstanding brochures!"

As an adverb, the use of *some* is still not acceptable except in strictly colloquial speaking or writing.. Example:

"We'll have to hurry some to complete that presentation" should be
"We'll have to hurry to complete that presentation."

Quick Checks on Comprehension

In each line below, highlight or check off the word or phrase that best matches the meaning of the word to the left.

position	station, ration, proposition, dissension
adopt	presume, festoon, relinquish, assume
suspension	prosecution, delay, portray, inundation
expulsion	interdiction, prediction, eviction, conviction
collective	frugal, peripheral, ineffectual, mutual
mandate	dictate, alleviate, retaliate, isolate
grievance	instance, remonstrance, fruition, regard
procedure	plan, notion, project, change
arbitration	precision, incision, decision, recession
disruptive	unsettling, unsolicited, rapid, productive
prejudiced	recovered, trusted, embroiled, bigoted
expertise	duty, attitude, background, diction
impact	antagonism, collision, infraction, occupation
judicial	optional, conditional, arbitrative, elusive

In each line below, highlight or check off the two synonyms.

mettle, clash, slam, trash
fiction, experience, menace, seasoning
formal, judgmental, forensic, ecstatic
unfair, exhausted, slanted, generous
interrupting, castigating, disturbing, noting
decision, announcement, predicament, judgment
opinion, success, process, operation

insistence, protest, complaint, remark
qualification, exemption, stipulation, organization
imbibe, conjoin, prescribe, enjoin
stormy, common, joint, opaque
ouster, espousal, roister, removal
distribution, cessation, confusion, interruption
embrace, rescind, direct, approve,
enclosure, respite, posture, standing

In each line below, highlight or check off the two antonyms.

deferment, internment, nuance, continuance
incite, entreat, solicit, decree
suppleness, idleness, action, premonition

If unsure about your comprehension choices, please see Appendix A.

A new word and its sway? It pays its own way!

DAY 34

New Word-Choices

From James V. Schall, speech on "The Firefighters' Legacy: Duty and Sacrifice," <u>Vital Speeches of the Day</u>, 61 (April 15,1995) 13, p. 398.

In one sense, I should judge, if no fire actually threatened human life, we would not be here [Fifth Annual <u>Symposium</u> on Public Monuments]. It is precisely the awareness of the <u>intrinsic</u> dignity of human life caught in a <u>dire</u> and <u>incendiary</u> situation that draws the firefighter into his most dramatic and dangerous public position. He is to be there precisely as is his duty, as <u>commissioned</u> by his <u>polity</u> to meet a situation that no one wanted or <u>anticipated</u> but for which he is in some sense prepared. These are the dramatic stories and incidents that we finally see in the press and about which the highest <u>lore</u> of the firefighting profession is written. It is about these <u>poignant</u> scenes that monuments are built and firefighters <u>memorialized</u> before the citizenry.

That human beings can choose to spend their lives in these dangerous positions is the sign of the <u>nobility</u> of our kind, a sign that we are not merely people who spend our lives fearing death or avoiding any effort that might <u>jeopardize</u> ourselves. We seek to <u>routinize</u> such dangerous occupations so that we can <u>accumulate</u> a certain experience of what to do in emergencies. We think of the firefighter in his capacity of establishing and enforcing fire codes. We think also of the <u>enormous</u> <u>innovative</u> and technical effort that goes into improving materials and <u>devices</u> so that the dangers to property and life will be lessened.

symposium (sim-POH-zee-um), a meeting for the discussion of a
   particular subject. From Greek *synposion* (prefix *syn*, with, together,

+ *posis*, a drinking), a drinking together at which there was intellectual discussion.

intrinsic (in-TRIN-sik), inherent, essential; belonging to the real nature of a thing. From Latin *intrinsecus*, inside, inwardly.
From same base: intrinsical, intrinsically, intrinsicalness.
Synonyms: inherent, essential, inbred, inborn, inseparable, innate, natural, native, internal, ingrained.
Antonyms: superfluous, superficial, extrinsic, incidental, supplemental, supplementary, subsidiary, transient, casual, external, outward.

dire (dyr), fearful, dreadful. From Latin *dirus*, fearful, horrible.
From same base: direly, direness.
Synonyms: threatening, extreme, drastic, formidable, fierce, fearful, dreadful, alarming, shocking, frightening, appalling, calamitous, terrible.
Antonyms: unimportant, insignificant, trifling, commonplace, petty.

incendiary (in-SEN-dee-ayr-ee), capable of generating intense heat; also having to do with stirring up strife, riot (as in "an incendiary speech"). From Latin *incendiarius*, fire-raising.
From same base: incendiarism.
Synonyms: fiery, blazing, burning, flaming, combustible, flammable.

commissioned (kuh-MISH-und), authorized to act. From Latin *commissus*, pp. of *committere*, to entrust.
From same base: commission.
Synonyms: delegated, consigned, committed, assigned, charged, entrusted, authorized, empowered, appointed.

polity (POL-ih-tee), a sponsoring governmental agency at any level. From Middle French *politie*, an organized division of government.

anticipate (an-TIS-uh-payt), to look forward to, foresee. From Latin *anticipatus*, pp. of *anticipare*, to expect.
From same base: anticipating, anticipated.
Synonyms: expect, foresee, forecast, apprehend, hope, predict, bargain for.
Antonyms: fear, doubt, dread, despair, wonder.

lore (lor), all the knowledge about a particular group and its traditions. From German *lehre*, teaching.

poignant (POIN-yent), painfully and profoundly moving. From Middle French *poignant*, prp. of *poindre*, to affect keenly or painfully.
From same base: poignantly, poignancy.
Synonyms: keen, piercing, acute, pungent, biting, mordant, sharp, intense, bitter, painful.

memorialize (meh-MOR-ee-uh-lyz), to commemorate. From Latin *memorialis*, relating to memory (*memoria*).
From same base: memorial, memorially.
Synonyms: commemorate, celebrate, observe, honor, perpetuate.

jeopardize (JEP-ur-dyz), to place at risk, imperil, endanger. From Old French, *jeu parti*, a game with even chances.
From same base: jeopardy.
Synonyms: imperil, endanger, expose, hazard, risk.
Antonyms: protect, guard, safeguard, defend, secure.

routinize (roo-TEEN-yz), to establish a regular set of procedures. From Old French *route*, a regular route or course + verb-ending suffix *-ize*.
From same base: routinizing, routinized, routine, route.

accumulate (uh-KYOOM-yuh-layt), collect, pile up. From Latin *accumulatus*, pp. of *accumulare*, to heap up.
From same base: accumulating, accumulated.
Synonyms: amass, collect, heap up, pile up, gather, hoard, assemble, add to.
Antonyms: scatter, dissipate, disperse, divide, parcel, portion, spend, squander, waste.

enormous (ih-NOR-mus), far exceeding the usual amount, size, etc. From Latin *enormis* (*e*, out of, + *norma*, rule), out of the usual rule or standard.
From same base: enormously, enormousness.
Synonyms: gigantic, colossal, huge, vast, immense, monstrous, amazing, extraordinary, ponderous, great, mammoth, stupendous.

<u>Antonyms</u>: small, little, insignificant, microscopic, light, trivial, inconsiderable, petty, paltry, slight, trifling, imponderable, unimportant, inconsequential, slender, minute.

innovative (IN-uh-<u>vayt</u>-iv), pertaining to the introduction of new
    methods, procedures, etc. From Latin *innovatus*, pp. of *innovare*, to
    alter, renew.
<u>From same base</u>: innovatively, innovation.
<u>Synonyms</u>: original, fresh, novel, imaginative, inventive, creative,
enterprising, productive.

device (dih-VYS), a mechanical invention or contrivance designed
    for some specific purpose. From Old French *deviser*, to work out or
    create (something).
<u>Synonyms</u>: artifice, contrivance, machine, invention, design, scheme,
project, stratagem.

Language Uses and Abuses

Being sensitive to gender equity

As you read the paragraphs from "The Firefighters' Legacy," did you notice that the speaker used only *he* and *his* in references to the firefighter? It's true that most firefighters are male, but the number of women firefighters is growing steadily. In speaking or writing about firefighters or any other professional group, it is better practice to use *he* and *his* in one sentence and, in an alternating pattern, *she* and *hers* in the next. Or to use *he or she* and *his or hers* in every such sentence. Or to sidestep the problem entirely by using the plurals *they* and *their*.

Examples from the context-paragraphs:
"...that draws the firefighter into *his* most dramatic and dangerous
public position" could, instead, be
"...that draws the firefighter into *his or her* most dramatic and
dangerous public position" or could better be...
"...that draws firefighters into *their* most dramatic and dangerous
position."

Another series:

"*He* is to be there precisely as is *his* duty, as commissioned by *his* polity" could be

"*He or she* is to be there precisely as is *his or her* duty, as commissioned by *his or her* polity" or could better be

"*They* are to be there precisely as is *their* duty, as commissioned by *their* polity."

We should commend the speaker for his use of "firefighter" instead of the old male term, "fireman." We should also recognize that, until quite recently, it had been the custom to use *he* and *his* as impersonal words covering any and all references to both men and women. Without thinking about it or even being aware of it, many still use that approach. In language and actuality, sensitivity to the need for gender equity is expected of everyone in this progressive age.

Quick Checks on Comprehension

In each line below, highlight or check off the word or phrase that best matches the meaning of the word to the left.

intrinsic	forensic, fictional, inherent, insatiable
dire	soulful, material, farcical, dreadful
incendiary	fruitful, flammable, fanatical, fatal
commissioned	assigned, inclined, proclaimed, prohibited
anticipate	animate, predict, inspect, instruct
poignant	distant, lustrous, intense, pretense
nobility	diversity, proficiency, gentility, utility
memorialize	honor, belabor, maintain, flatter
jeopardize	dictate, frisk, insult, risk
accumulate	indemnify, hoard, retain, sustain
enormous	immense, impressive, oppressive, lively
innovative	successive, inventive, preventive, apt
device	hazard, incentive, appearance, contrivance

In each line below, highlight or check off the two synonyms.

ladder, machine, design, semblance
original, supportive, practical, creative
colossal, superior, endless, gigantic
emit, startle, collect, amass
endure, imperil, improvise, endanger
hauteur, grandeur, sublimity, sobriety

celebrate, commemorate, explicate, dilate
picayune, systematic, sharp, acute
expect, hope, respect, reveal
employed, entrusted, enraged, empowered
blazing, fierce, fiery, hazing
shocking, mocking, sprawling, appalling
inbred, instilled, untrained, inverted

In each line below, highlight or check off the two antonyms.

essential, intentional, accidental, incidental
submitting, alarming, trifling, permitting
perform, foresee, intervene, doubt
reprieve, guard, lead, expose
assemble, batter, inflate, scatter
feckless, paltry, great, reckless

If unsure about your comprehension choices, please see Appendix A.

Don't be shy—give a new word a try!

DAY 35

New Word-Choices
From Andrew Hacker, <u>Two Nations: Black and White,
Separate, Hostile, Unequal</u>
(New York, NY: Charles Scribner's Sons, 1992), p. 3 f.

Race has been an American obsession since the first Europeans sighted "savages" on these shores. In time, those original <u>inhabitants</u> would be <u>subdued</u> or slaughtered, and finally <u>sequestered</u> out of view. But race in America took on a deeper and more disturbing meaning with the <u>importation</u> of Africans as slaves. <u>Bondage</u> would later be condemned as an awful injustice and the nation's shame, even as we have come to acknowledge the <u>stamina</u> and skill it took to survive in a system where humans could be bought and sold and punished like animals. Nor are these <u>antecedents</u> buried away in the past. That Americans of African origin once wore the chains of <u>chattels</u> remains alive in the memory of both races and continues to separate them.

Other groups may remain outside the mainstream—some religious sects, for example—but they do so <u>voluntarily</u>. In contrast, blacks must endure a segregation that is far from freely chosen. So America may be seen as two separate nations. Of course, there are places where the races <u>mingle</u>. Yet in most significant respects, the separation is <u>pervasive</u> and <u>penetrating</u>. As a social and human division, it surpasses all others—even gender—in <u>intensity</u> and subordination. That racial <u>tensions</u> cast a <u>pall</u> upon this country can hardly be denied. People now <u>vent</u> feelings of hostility and anger that in the past they <u>repressed</u>. Indeed, race has become a national staple for private conversation and public <u>controversy</u>.

inhabitant (in-HAB-ih-tent), one who lives in a specified region.
   From Latin *inhabitans*, prp. of *inhabitare*, to inhabit.

<u>From same base</u>: inhabitancy.
<u>Synonyms</u>: resident, dweller, occupier, occupant, tenant, settler, squatter, colonist, cohabitant, native.

subdue (sub-DOO), to bring under control. From Latin *subdere* with same meaning.
<u>From same base</u>: subduing, subdued, subduable.
<u>Synonyms</u>: overcome, conquer, master, subjugate, vanquish, control, tame, surmount, beat, suppress. defeat.

sequester (sih-KWES-tur), to place apart, remove from others. From Late Latin *sequestrare*, to lay aside, separate.
<u>From same base</u>: sequestering, sequestered.
<u>Synonyms</u>: divide, separate, disjoin, disunite, disengage, sever, sunder, part, detach, disconnect, dislocate, disperse, scatter, isolate.
<u>Antonyms</u>: combine, collect, assemble, gather, mingle, blend, intermingle.

importation (<u>im</u>-por-TAY-shun), the act of bringing into from another country for commercial purposes. From Latin *importare* (*im*, in, + *portare*, to carry), to bring in, introduce.
<u>From same base</u>: importable.

bondage (BON-dij), subjection to enslavement. From Old Norse *bonde*, prp. of *bua*, to prepare, inhabit.
<u>Synonyms</u>: slavery, serfdom, servitude, subjection, subjugation, vassalage, servility.

stamina (STAM-ih-nuh), the capacity to withstand great hardship. From Latin plural of *stamen*, a thread, the warp.
<u>Synonyms</u>: endurance, vim, vigor, vitality, power, might, energy, intensity, concentration.

antecedent (<u>an</u>-tuh-SEED-nt), any happening prior to another. From *antecedens*, prp. of *antecedere*, to go before.
<u>From same base</u>: antecedently, antecedence, antecedency.

chattel (CHAT-ul), a movable piece of personal property, live or inanimate. From Old French *chatel*, cattle.

voluntarily (VOL-un-<u>tehr</u>-ih-lee), of one's own free choice. Adverb
  from Latin adjective :*voluntarius* with same meaning.
<u>From same base</u>: voluntary.
<u>Synonyms</u>: intentionally, spontaneously, deliberately, freely,
unconstrainedly.

mingle (MING-gul), to become mixed together or combined. From
  Middle English *mengelen*, to bring together, blend.
<u>Synonyms</u>: mix, blend, combine, fraternize, commingle, merge,
intermingle, join, conjoin, infiltrate, unite.

pervasive (pur-VAY-siv), that has spread throughout. From Latin
  pervadere (*per*, through, + *vadere*, to hasten), to pass through.
<u>From same base</u>: pervasively, pervasiveness.
<u>Synonyms</u>: spread, extensive, extended, widespread, prevalent,
current, common, potent, influential.

penetrating (PEN-ih-<u>trayt</u>-ing), that has pierced deeply. From Latin
  penetratus, pp. of *penetrare*, to pierce.
<u>From same base</u>: penetratingly, penetrate, penetrated.
<u>Synonyms</u>: sharp, keen, astute, acute, shrewd, sagacious, pointed,
piercing, incisive.
<u>Antonyms</u>: shallow, blunt, thick, heavy, obtuse, inept, confused.

intensity (in-TEN-sih-tee), the quality of existing in an extreme
  degree of strength, energy. From Middle Latin *intensitas* with same
  meaning.
<u>Synonyms</u>: energy, tension, concentration, force, strain, pressure,
vigor, strength.
<u>Antonyms</u>: inactivity, inaction, inertness, passivity, apathy,
moderation, indolence.

tension (TEN-shun), state of strained relations, racial or otherwise.
  From Latin *tensio*, a stretching.
<u>From same base</u>: tensional.
<u>Synonyms</u>: strain, stress, tensity, rigidity, tautness, constriction,
pressure.

pall (pawl), a dark and gloomy cover. From Latin *pallium*, a coverlet,
  mantle.

vent (vent), to give expression to. From Latin *ventus*, wind, rumor.
<u>Synonyms</u>: express, phrase, word, state, verbalize, describe, delineate, picture, speak, utter, frame, reveal, tell, convey, communicate, demonstrate.

repress (rih-PRES), to keep down or hold back. From Latin
  repressus, pp. of *reprimere*, to hold back.
<u>From same base</u>: repressing, repressed, repressible, repressive, repressively, repressiveness.
<u>Synonyms</u>: restrain, suppress, inhibit, check, curb, restrict, constrain, confine, withhold, hinder, prevent, coerce.
<u>Antonyms</u>: loosen, unchain, unbind, free, liberate, release, incite, arouse, aid, encourage, impel, disband, discharge.

controversy (KON-truh-<u>vur</u>-see), dispute, quarrel. From Latin prefix
  contra, against, + *versus*, pp. of *vertere*, to turn.
<u>Synonyms</u>: dispute, quarrel, argument, discussion, debate, wrangling.
<u>Antonyms</u>: peace, restraint, quiet, forbearance, patience.

Language Uses and Abuses

Regarding direct routes

"Regarding" is not the best way to get from here to there. The same is true of wordy phrases like "in regard to" and "with regard to."

  "She was evasive regarding her plans for the future" should be
  "She was evasive about her plans for the future."

  "He was uncertain in regard to his career goals" should be
  "He was uncertain about his career goals."

  "She spoke with regard to ways to write a prospectus" should be
  "She spoke on ways to write a prospectus" or
  "She spoke about ways to write a prospectus."

"Is when" and "is where" are two more double-word phrases to be avoided, especially in definitions. Examples:

  "A quiz is when you are tested on what you know" should be
  "A quiz is a test of what you know" or

"In a quiz you are tested on what you know."

"A wastebasket is where you put discarded papers" should be
"A wastebasket is a receptacle for discarded papers."

Then, there's that extra "of" when *inside* and *outside* are used as prepositions:

"If it's raining, stay inside of the house" should be
"If it's raining, stay inside the house."

"The decision is outside of his power to make" should be
"The decision is outside his power to make."

Quick Checks on Comprehension

In each line below, highlight or check off the word or phrase that best matches the meaning of the word to the left.

inhabitant	native, captive, fanatic, partner
subdue	respect, inspire, divest, overcome
sequester	contact, isolate, dispatch, unlatch
bondage	kingdom, solvency, potency, serfdom
stamina	perjury, injury, energy, synergy
voluntarily	initially, dourly, deliberately, separately
mingle	merge, splurge, forge, sprinkle
pervasive	suasive, widespread, seductive, massive
penetrating	marking, solving, yearning, piercing
intensity	maturity, proficiency, strength, demeanor
tension	stress, fortune, gratuity, chance
vent	repeal, repent, renew, reveal
repress	impress, coerce, submit, solicit
controversy	meeting, sentiment, consensus, dispute

In each line below, highlight or check off the two synonyms.

swindle, quarrel, argument, supplement
restrain, remain, correct, check
express, survey, impress, convey
complicity, rigidity, felicity, tautness
force, vigor, progress, approval
rude, shrewd, sagacious, mendacious

ambivalent, spread, prevalent, read
disgrace, combine, spend, blend
spontaneously, regretfully, joyfully, freely
bower, power, might, sight
penury, slavery, subsection, subjection
scatter, borrow, encompass, disperse
languish, vanquish, defeat, repeat
dweller, reveler, cohabitant, penitent

In each line below, highlight or check off the two antonyms.

divide, provide, combine, recline
passive, astute, infused, confused
concentration, manipulation, empathy, apathy
withhold, release, impeach, exhibit

If unsure about your comprehension choices, please see Appendix A.

Don't be overly tremulous; trying a new word is fabulous!

New Word-Choices
From Mortimer B. Zuckerman, editorial on
"Beware the Adversary Culture,"
U.S. News & Word Report, 118 (June 12, 1995) 23, p. 94.

The adversary culture—a <u>contemporary</u> culture whose <u>predominant</u> style is in-your-face aggression—provides a certain <u>spurious</u> <u>drama</u> that the media have been overly tempted to exploit. Too often, the only way to break into the realm of public attention is through controversy; declarations of values or beliefs in the American way are seen as boring or corny. Everything is the subject of ridicule. The media sense that <u>assaulting</u> social norms is good business.

It may be good for business, but it is bad for America. An adversary media attacking every person and every movement makes it difficult to build consensus or <u>coherence</u> in any society. America is particularly vulnerable because we have built our politics more on personalities. In the present environment, no hero or leader can emerge. Every mistake a public figure makes, every <u>idiosyncrasy</u> exposed, is <u>pounced</u> on. In such a <u>vindictive</u> culture it is virtually impossible to rally the nation or to bind its wounds. We are living in a time of <u>accelerating</u> social and economic <u>turmoil</u> that strains the <u>connective</u> tissues of many individuals to any sense of responsibility. That is why we have so many troubled individuals <u>prowling</u> the <u>margins</u> of society, their resentments on the verge of exploding into violence when <u>agitated</u> by hate speech.

contemporary (kun-TEM-puh-<u>rare</u>-ee), current, of the same time as
  the present. From Latin prefix *com*, with, + *temporarius*,
  temporary, seasonable.
<u>From same base</u>: contemporaneous, contemporaneously.

Synonyms: current, present, coexistent, topical.

predominant (prih-DOM-ih-nunt), most noticeable; superior in influence or degree. From Middle Latin *predominans*, prp. of *predominari*, to rule or control by superior power.
From same base: predominantly, predominance, predominancy.
Synonyms: supreme, prevailing, prevalent, ruling, reigning, controlling, ascendant, supervisory, directing, dominant, imperious, potent, influential, governing.
Antonyms: humble, lowly, unimportant, insignificant, slight, trivial, powerless, weak, submissive, obedient, subservient, servile, subordinate, dependent, restricted, restrained.

spurious (SPYUUR-ee-us), not genuine, false. From Latin *spurius*, not true.
From same base: spuriously, spuriousness.
Synonyms: false, counterfeit, fictitious, fraudulent, dishonest, erroneous, deceptive, faked, concocted, fabricated, misrepresented, pretended, deceiving, misleading.
Antonyms: genuine, real, true, proven, tested, actual, exact, accurate, authentic, valid, honest, excellent, sound, perfect, faultless, intact, accredited, worthy, positive.

drama (DRAH-muh), series of events resembling those of a play. From Greek *drama*, deed, act; a play.

assaulting (uh-SAWLT-ing), attacking violently. From Old French *assaut*, to leap against.
From same base: assault, assaulted.
Synonyms: attack, assail, besiege, beleaguer, storm, charge, invade, encroach, seize, violate.
Antonyms: protect, defend, shelter, support, uphold, sustain, resist, aid, befriend, shield, withstand.

coherence (koh-HEER-ense), the state of being united. From Latin *cohaerens*, prp. of *cohaerere*, to stick together.
From same base: coherent, coherently, coherency.
Synonyms: consolidation, cementing, integration, cohesion, adhesion, adherence, oneness, unity.

idiosyncrasy (ihd-ee-uh-SING-kruh-see), any habit, expression, or oddity peculiar to an individual. From Greek *idios* (idio), one's own, + *synkrasis* (*syn*, with, + *krasis*, a uniting), a mixing or blending together.
From same base: idiosyncratic, idiosyncratically.
Synonyms: distinction, peculiarity, feature, temperament, disposition, personality. character, nature.

pounce (pownse) on, to prey upon, seize upon. From Middle English *pownce*, the talon of a bird of prey and, by extension, to swoop down upon.
From same base: pouncing, pounced.
Synonyms: take, grasp, grip, clutch, catch, apprehend, seize.

vindictive (vin-DIK-tiv), revengeful or spiteful. From Latin *vindicta*, vengeance.
From same base: vindictively, vindictiveness.
Synonyms: vengeful, malevolent, rancorous, resentful, spiteful, unforgiving, malicious.

accelerating (ak-SEL-uh-rayt-ing), speeding up, increasing. From Latin *acceleratus*, pp. of *accelerare*, to hasten.
From same base: accelerate, accelerated.
Synonyms: hurrying, expediting, hastening, quickening, dispatching, pushing, forwarding, facilitating.
Antonyms: retarding, hindering, deferring, postponing, obstructing, impeding, blocking, resisting.

turmoil (TUR-moyl), confused motion, disturbance. From Latin *turba*, tumult, uproar, + *mollis*, yielding, pliable.
Synonyms: confusion, disturbance, chaos, tumult, turbulence, violence, disorder, commotion.

connective (kuh-NEK-tiv), serving to join. From Latin *conexus*, pp. of *conectere*, to fasten together.
From same base: connectively.
Synonyms: joining, uniting, associating, combining, binding, securing, compounding.

prowling (PROW-ling), roaming about in search of prey. From Middle English *prollen* with same meaning.

From same base: prowl, prowled, prowler.
Synonyms: roaming, strolling, tramping, roving, ranging, rambling.

margin (MAR-jin), border, edge. From Latin *margo* with same
  meaning.
From same base: marginal, marginally.
Synonyms: border, edge, brink, verge, brim, lip, brow, rim, bank,
shore.
Antonyms: interior, surface, area, background, hinterland, extension,
width, breadth, depth, thickness.

agitate (AJ-ih-tayt-id), aroused, disturbed. From Latin *agitatus*, pp.
  of *agitare*, to stir up.
From same base: agitate, agitating, agitatedly.
Synonyms: shaken, moved, perturbed, disturbed, aroused, provoked,
excited, driven, impelled, stirred, troubled, annoyed, flustered.

Language Uses and Abuses

Get lost, hopefully

Get is one of those heavily overworked words which crops up in
expressions like these: "Get lost!" "Get with it! "That really gets me!"
"Get on with it!" "It's getting better." "They got it done." Examples:

  "Relations with our in-laws are getting better" could be
  "Relations with our in-laws are improving."

  "We got it done in time" could be
  "We finished in time."

  Synonyms you might try for *get*: gain, obtain, receive, procure, earn,
  attain, achieve, acquire, secure, win.

Hopefully is also overworked and misused, especially in the senses of
"I hope," "Let's hope," or "It's to be hoped." Its actual meaning is
"*with* hope."

  An example of that preferred use: "His parents waited hopefully for
  his safe return."

An example of misuse followed by alternatives:

"Hopefully, we'll win the next game" should be
"I hope we'll win the next game" or
"Let's hope we win the next game."

Quick Checks on Comprehension

In each line below, highlight or check off the word or phrase that best matches the meaning of the word to the left.

contemporary   present, relevant, potent, nascent
predominant   prejudging, preparing, prepaying, prevailing
spurious   spooned, faked, swooned, raked
assaulting   encroaching, poaching, reaching, seeking
coherence   assistance, dominance, unity, prosperity
idiosyncrasy   creature, verdure, suture, feature
pounce   trounce, seize, appease, release
vindictive   spiteful, forceful, imposing, reversing
accelerating   surfacing, worsening, moderating, quickening
turmoil   neglect, confusion, separation, intrigue
connective   pursuing, joining, performing, renewing
prowling   ranging, paging, staging, failing
margin   triangle, brow, prow, circle
agitated   aroused, espoused, eradicated, eliminated

In each line below, highlight or check off the two synonyms.

perceived, disturbed, fashioned, annoyed
lintel, bank, stream, shore
roaming, rambling, cringing, foaming
uniting, surprising, sublimating, binding
insult, languor, chaos, tumult
constructing, obstructing, releasing, impeding
malevolent, malleable, malodorous, malicious
present, grasp, flush, clutch
temperament, disposition, incident, proposition
precision, cohesion, adherence, maintenance
enervate, trade, invade, violate
concocted, syncopated, enacted, fabricated
parlaying, directing, governing, signing
coexistent, topical, tropical, preexistent

In each line below, highlight or check off the two antonyms.

influential, inferential, powerless, effortless
prodigious, emblematic, valid, counterfeit
scorn, adorn, inspire, expire
pushing, postponing, proclaiming, preempting
path, atrium, border, area
acrimony, alacrity, alimony, amity

If unsure about your comprehension choices, please see Appendix A.

   With old words be penurious; with the new magnanimous.

New Word-Choices
From Juliet B. Schor, The Overworked American:
The Unexpected Decline of Leisure
(New York, NY: Basic Books, 1991), p. 1 f.

In the last twenty years the amount of time Americans have spent at their jobs has risen steadily. Each year the change is small, amounting to slightly more than one additional day of work. In any given year, such a small <u>increment</u> has probably been <u>imperceptible</u>. But the accumulated increase over two decades is <u>substantial</u>. When <u>surveyed</u>, Americans report that they have only sixteen and a half hours of leisure a week, after the obligations of job and household are taken care of.

When the decline in worktime hours abruptly ended in the late 1940s, it marked the beginning of an <u>era</u>. But the change was scarcely noticed. Equally surprising has been the <u>deviation</u> from Western Europe. After <u>progressing</u> in <u>tandem</u> for nearly a century, the United States <u>veered</u> off into a <u>trajectory</u> of declining leisure, while in Europe work has been disappearing.

How did this happen? Why has leisure been such a conspicuous <u>casualty</u> of prosperity? In part, the answer lies in the difference between the markets for consumer products and free time. Consider the <u>legendary</u> American market. It is a <u>veritable</u> consumer's paradise, offering a <u>dazzling</u> <u>array</u> of products varying in style, design, quality, price, and country of origin. [The author goes on to compare the U.S. market with those of the other industrialized countries.]

increment (IN-kruh-ment), a quantity added to another quantity.
From Latin *incrementum*, growth, increase.
<u>From same base</u>: incremental, incrementalism.

Synonyms: augmentation, increase, addition, extension, growth, development, gain, amplification.
Antonyms: decrease, contraction, shrinkage, lessening, reduction, subtraction, curtailment.

imperceptible (im-pur-SEP-tuh-bl), so slight as not to be easily
  noticed. From Middle Latin *imperceptibilis* with same meaning.
From same base: imperceptibility, imperceptibly.
Synonyms: inappreciable, inconsiderable, infinitesimal, insignificant, microscopic, minute, minimal, slight, insubstantial.

substantial (sub-STAN-shul), considerable, ample, great. From Late
  Latin *substantialis*, real, actual.
From same base: substantially, substantialness.
Synonyms: solid, durable, lasting, considerable, ample, great, real, actual, firm, compact.
Antonyms: insubstantial, immaterial, tenuous, intangible, unreal, inconsiderable.

survey (sur-VAY), to collect specific information about a population
  through questionnaires, etc. From Old French *surveoir*, to see over, beyond.
From same base: surveying, surveyed, surveyor.
Synonyms: look at, scrutinize, examine, observe, study, review.

era (EER-uh), a period of time measured from some fixed time or
  date. From Late Latin *aera*, a fixed date.

deviation (dee-vee-AY-shun), a moving away from. From Late Latin
  deviatio with same meaning.
From same base: deviationism, deviationist.
Synonyms: divergence, deflection, difference, variation, contrast, digression, turning, reversal.

progress (pruh-GRES), to move forward or onward. From Latin
  progressus, pp. of *progredi*, to go forward.
From same base: progressing, progressed, progressive, progressively.
Synonyms: advance, grow, develop, improve, increase, move, proceed, go, forge ahead,
Antonyms: decline, subside, slump, collapse, stagnate, pause, decrease, relapse, delay, check.

tandem (TAN-dem), one after the other, together, a team. A punning use of the Latin *tandem*, at length, at last.

veer (veer), to move off course, change direction. From French *virer*, to turn around.
From same base: veering, veered, veeringly.
Synonyms: skew, skid, swerve, turn, tack, deviate, swing.

trajectory (truh-JEK-tuh-ree), the curved path of something hurtling through space. From Middle Latin *traiectorius*, a passing over.

legendary (LEJ-unh-dehr-ee), storied, traditional, celebrated. From Middle Latin *legenda*, things read, stories told.
From same base: legend.
Synonyms: traditional, celebrated, fictitious, fanciful, fabulous, mythical.
Antonyms: historical, actual, real, true, genuine, certain, authentic, unquestionable.

veritable (VER-ih-tuh-bl), unquestionable, verifiable. From Latin *veritas*, truth.
From same base: veritably, verity.
Synonyms: tested, verifiable, verified, confirmed, certified, substantiated, corroborated, validated, authenticated.

dazzling (DAZ-ling), bewildering, brilliant. From Middle English *dasen*, to wear away, stupefy.
From same base: dazzle, dazzled, dazzlingly.
Synonyms: confounding, astonishing, blinding, overpowering, impressing, surprising, bewildering, brilliant, amazing, astounding, confusing.

array (uh-RAY), an imposing collection, an impressive display. From Old French *areer*, to put in order.
Synonyms: display, arrangement, disposition, assemblage, collection, gathering, muster, assembly.

Language Uses and Abuses

Fun impossible with a dictionary

terra firma = firm ground. terra incognita = ?
An alibi is an excuse. Why that meaning?
Has anyone ever delivered an ultimatum to you?
Have you ever taken umbrage for some reason?
Have you ever seen someone undulate?
Why is "Ubi" the name of a game posing questions about geography ?
If a somnambulist is a sleep-walker, what is a funambulist?
Do the words canopy and canape have anything in common?

And the dictionary happily answers:

incognita (in-kog-NEE-tah) is Latin for *unknown*. In a book on the
Vietnam war, Robert S. McNamara, U.S. Secretary of Defense at the
time, calls Vietnam "terra incognita." He is referring to our wartime
ignorance of Vietnamese history, language, culture, and values.

alibi (AL-ih-by), an excuse or defensive plea, is a combination of two
Latin words, *alius*, other, and *ibi*, over there. In other words, "I
didn't do it; it's that other person over there."

ultimatum (ul-tih-MAY-tum) is the Latin for *a final statement of
terms* with no further changes acceptable. One nation issues an
ultimatum to another and, unless that nation accepts its terms, the
first declares war or takes some other punitive action. Or a tenant
issues an ultimatum to a landlord: "Fix the plumbing or I'm moving
out."

umbrage (UM-brij), resentment, is based on the Latin *umbra*, shadow.
Being frightened by shadows is as old as humanity; being offended
by some slight (i.e., "taking umbrage") is the later and current usage.

undulate (UN-juh-<u>layt</u>), to move like a wave, to move sinuously.
Undula, little wave, is the Latin diminutive form of *unda*, wave. If
you saw someone undulating, she or he was dancing in a wavy way
like, for example, the flowing Hawaiian hula.

ubi (OO-bee) is Latin for "Where?" It makes a distinctive and
intriguing title for a geography game requiring the players to locate
cities, countries, rivers, etc.

somnambulist (som-NAM-byoo-list), sleep-walker, is made up of two
   Latin words, *somnus*, sleep, and *ambulare*, to walk.
funambulist (fyoo-NAM-byoo-list), tight-rope walker, comes from
   Latin *funis*, rope, and again, *ambulare*, to walk.

canopy (KAN-uh-pee), an overhead covering, comes from the Greek
   konopeion (Latin *conopeum*), a couch with protective curtains.
canape (KAN-uh-pay) is the same word adapted to mean an appetizer
   consisting of a thin cracker or piece of toast "covered" or "canopied"
   with cheese, caviar, fish, or spiced meat.

Quick Checks on Comprehension

In each line below, highlight or check off the word or phrase that best
matches the meaning of the word to the left.

increment   increase, surcease, element, supplement
imperceptible   unparalleled, susceptible, lethal, minimal
substantial   consequential, durable, formidable, lamentable
survey   preserve, conserve, observe, serve
deviation   observance, rotation, position, divergence
progress   advance, recede, impede, enhance
veer   unnerve, surprise, advise, swerve
legendary   logical, mythical, unethical, political
veritable   subsidized, certified, amplified, nullified
dazzling   astonishing, admonishing, implying, jarring
array   portrayal, cynosure, collection, infraction

In each line below, highlight or check off the two synonyms.

summons, display, appendage, assemblage
confusing, complaining, conducting, confounding
inundated, validated, corroborated, explicated
impervious, inebriated, fabulous, celebrated
swing, spring, deviate, permeate
envelop, grow, flow, develop
difference, reference, improvisation, variation
study, review, purview, preview
hardy, solid, stolid, compact
minute, insignificant, arrogant, destitute

In each line below, highlight or check off the two antonyms.

extension, supervision, amortization, contraction
fastidious, lasting, amorphous, tenuous
renounce, improve, move, pause
bountiful, fanciful, authentic, symptomatic

If unsure about your comprehension choices, please see Appendix A.

If at first a new word flops, your next try may well be tops!

New Word-Choices
From Michael Klare, <u>Rogue States and Nuclear Outlaws</u>:
<u>America's Search for a New Foreign Policy</u>
(New York, NY: Hill and Wang, 1995), p. 228 f.

As with every other <u>aspect</u> of foreign policy, U.S. military <u>doctrine</u> must be <u>reconfigured</u> in light of the emerging security <u>challenges</u> of the current era. Because the greatest threat the United States faces today arises from the worldwide proliferation of local conflicts and their potential <u>escalation</u> into regional <u>conflagrations</u>, it is essential that military strategy—like all other components of national policy— be <u>refocused</u> on efforts to prevent, contain, <u>abate</u>, and terminate violent conflicts. In essence, this means developing a military trained and equipped for a wide variety of peacemaking operations, enforcement of U.N. arms <u>embargoes</u>, and humanitarian aid and rescue--in addition to traditional military activities.

For the most part, such responsibilities <u>entail</u> small-unit operations in relatively <u>austere</u> environments with opposition (if any) coming from lightly armed <u>paramilitary</u> or militia-type forces. Such engagements pose challenges very different from those encountered in Operation Desert Storm, and require, in consequence, that American troops be trained and equipped in different fashion. Instead of relying on massive firepower as in the Persian Gulf conflict, they must learn to rely on <u>precision</u>, speed, <u>coordination</u>, knowledge of the <u>terrain</u> and the local population, and solid <u>negotiation</u> skills.

aspect (AS-pekt), a thing or detail as it appears to the viewer. From
   Latin *aspectus*, pp. of *aspicere*, to look at.
<u>Synonyms</u>: appearance, view, angle, facet, form, outlook.

doctrine (DOK-trin), a body of guiding principles or teachings. From Latin *doctrina*, that which is imparted by teaching.
From same base: doctrinal, doctrinally.
Synonyms: belief, dogma, precept, principle, teaching, opinion, theory, credence, persuasion, conviction.
Antonyms: unbelief, disbelief, error, falsehood, incredulity, skepticism.

reconfigure (ree-kon-FIG-yurh), to reform, realign, change. From Latin prefix *re*, again, + prefix *con*, together, + *figurare*, to shape.

challenge (CHAL-inj), a demand, claim. From Old French *chalenge*, an accusation, claim, dispute.
From same base: challenge, challenging, challenged, challenger, challengeable.
Synonyms: demand, claim, exaction, requirement, appeal, ultimatum, stipulation.

escalation (ES-kuh-lay-shun), a gradual increase, a step by step expansion. From Latin *scalae*, flight of stairs, ladder.
Synonyms: increase, expansion, magnification, addition, increment, growth, surge, spread, enlargement, inflation.

conflagration (kon-fluh-GRAY-shun), a great dispute; a raging fire. From Latin *conflagratus*, pp. of *conflagrare*, to burn intensively.
Synonyms: dissension, conflict, strife, friction, dispute, quarrel, contention, controversy, dissidence, factionalism.

refocus (ree-FOH-kus), to redirect attention, change emphasis. From Latin prefix *re*, again, + *focus*, hearth, flame (later *point of focus* in the modern sense).
From same base: refocusing, refocused.

abate (uh-BAYT), to lessen in intensity. From Old French *abattre*, to beat down.
From same base: abating, abated, abatable, abatement.
Synonyms: lower, lessen, moderate, mitigate, decrease, diminish, reduce, restrain, assuage, alleviate, allay.
Antonyms: enlarge, extend, increase, magnify, amplify, aggravate, foment, enhance, intensify, prolong.

embargo (em-BAHR-goh), an order prohibiting trade. From Latin
  prefix *in*, in or on, + Middle Latin *barra*, an obstacle or bar.
<u>Synonyms</u>: prohibition, ban, refusal, veto, rejection, bar, proscription,
interdiction, exclusion, deprivation.

entail (en-TAYL), to involve, necessitate. From Middle English
  prefix *en*, in, + *taile*, an agreement, decision.
<u>From same base</u>: entailing, entailed, entailment.
<u>Synonyms</u>: require, demand, cause, involve, necessitate, tangle,
entangle, compel, force, drive, constrain, oblige.

austere (aw-STEER), very plain, primitive. From Greek *austeros*,
  dry, harsh.
<u>From same base</u>: austerely.
<u>Synonyms</u>: plain, primitive, harsh, rigid, rigorous, severe, stern, cruel,
unrelenting, keen, sharp, strict, exacting.
<u>Antonyms</u>: mild, meek, gentle, kind, encouraging, placid, quiet,
peaceful, soothing, indulgent.

paramilitary (<u>pehr</u>-uh-MIL-ih-*tehr*-ee), designating a private or
  quasimilitary organization falling short of regular-military
  capability. From Greek prefix *para*, alongside of, + Latin *militaris*,
  of a soldier, military.

precision (prih-SIZH-un), the state or quality of being exact, accurate.
  From Latin *praecisio*, a cutting off.
<u>Synonyms</u>: accuracy, exactness, specificity, exactitude, nicety,
correctness.

coordination (koh-<u>or</u>-dn-AY-shun), the state of working well
  together. From Late Latin *coordinatio* with same meaning.
<u>Synonyms</u>: cooperation, teamwork, participation, collaboration,
concert, union, concurrence, coaction.

terrain (teh-RAYN), a tract of ground with reference to its fitness for
  some purpose. From Latin *terrenus*, belonging to the earth (*terra*).
<u>Synonyms</u>: territory, land, earth, ground, landscape, area, expanse,
region.

negotiation (nih-GOH-shee-<u>ay</u>-shun), the act of conferring to reach agreement. From Latin *negotiatio* with same meaning and, in turn, from *negotium*, business.

<u>Synonyms</u>: bargaining, conferring, consulting, contracting, arranging, treating, compromising.

Language Uses and Abuses

In a family way

Here are some of the Latin "family words" you often find as combining forms in our language: *familia* (fami), family; *filia* (fili), daughter; *filius* (fili), son; *mater* (matri, matr, mater), mother; *pater* (patri, patr, pater), father; *frater* (frater), brother; and *soror* (soror), sister. For typical word formations...

familiar (fuh-MIL-yur), the informal atmosphere associated with family life.
familiarity (fuh-<u>mil</u>-ee-AIR-ih-tee), friendly closeness, typical of most families.

filial (FIL-ih-ul), of, suitable to, or due from a daughter or son, as in "filial concern for their parents."

matriarch (MAY-tree-ahrk), a woman who exercises control over her immediate or extended family.
matron (MAY-trun), a woman having a mature appearance and manner.
maternal (muh-TER-nl), of, like, or characteristic of a mother or motherhood.

patriarch (PAY-tree-arch), a man who holds control over his immediate or extended family.
patron (PAY-trun), a person corresponding in some respects to a father; a protector, benefactor, sponsor.
paternal (puh-TER-nl), of, like, or characteristic of a father or fatherhood.

fraternal (fruh-TUR-nl), of, like, or characteristic of brothers as members of a society or brotherhood.

fraternize (FRAT-ur-nize), to associate with others in a brotherly way.

sorority (suh-ROR-ih-tee), a women's association or organization, especially at a college or university.

Quick Checks on Comprehension

In each line below, highlight or check off the word or phrase that best matches the meaning of the word to the left.

aspect	periodical, view, interview, peril
doctrine	dignity, perplexity, neglect, belief
challenge	fame, claim, manner, exposure
escalation	remission, expansion, motion, premonition
conflagration	removal, transformation, motion, premonition
abate	reduce, renew, renege, refocus
embargo	van, ban, fan, pan
entail	embroil, roil, require, perspire
austere	berm, stern, career, peer
precision	infraction, exactness, solidity, brevity
coordination	fusion, precision, union, escalation
terrain	moraine, disdain, dedication, region
negotiation	arranging, spacing, creating, berating

In each line below, highlight or check off the two synonyms.

narrating, bargaining, prohibiting, consulting
territory, area, laboratory, lariat
homework, teamwork, elaboration, cooperation
primacy, accuracy, correctness, aloofness
meritorious, rigorous, severe, riparian
compel, deprive, drive, revel
proliferation, component, exclusion, rejection
allocate, alleviate, allure, allay
premise, strife, mainstay, dispute
increase, unease, restraint, growth
sound, embodiment, demand, requirement
percept, precept, principle, mandible
vista, credenza, influenza, prospect

In each line below, highlight or check off the two antonyms.

conviction, patriotism, skepticism, configuration
remedy, purify, assuage, intensify
direct, harsh, respectful, soothing

If unsure about your comprehension choices, please see Appendix A.

Now pray hear this with equanimity—new words do spell opportunity!

DAY 39

New Word-Choices
From Jean-François Revel, <u>The Flight from Truth</u>,
translated by Curtis Cate
(New York, NY: Random House, 1991), p. 4.

Our century has witnessed a <u>notable</u> increase of knowledge along with a similar increase in the number of human beings who have <u>access</u> to that knowledge. To begin with, the educational <u>process</u> is being prolonged ever further. At the same time, the tools of mass communication have been <u>multiplying</u> and now shower us with words and images to a degree <u>inconceivable</u> in the past. Whether it is to <u>popularize</u> the news of a scientific discovery and the technical <u>prospects</u> it opens up, to announce a political event, or to publish figures enabling one to <u>analyze</u> an economic situation, the <u>universal</u> information machine is becoming more and more egalitarian and generous, ceaselessly reducing the old <u>discrimination</u> between the elite in power, who knew little, and the common run of the ruled, who knew nothing. Now both know—or can know—a great deal.

The <u>superiority</u> of our century seems to be due to the fact that those in <u>authority</u> have increasingly had at their disposal a far greater and more <u>abundant</u> fund of information and knowledge to back their decisions, while the public's receiving an <u>abundance</u> of information should enable it to judge the wisdom of those decisions. Such an <u>auspicious</u> <u>convergence</u> of favorable <u>factors</u> should logically have <u>engendered</u> a <u>prodigious</u> improvement in the human condition. But has this happened? To answer "yes" would be <u>frivolous</u>.

notable (NOH-tuh-bl), remarkable, outstanding. From Latin
  notabilis with same meaning.
<u>From same base</u>: notably, notability.

<u>Synonyms</u>: remarkable, outstanding, celebrated, significant, pronounced, striking, manifest, rare, apparent, evident.

<u>Antonyms</u>: obscure, false, abject, common, unimportant, insignificant, trivial, inconsequential, slight, ordinary.

access (AK-ses), a passage or path. From Latin *accessus*, pp. of *accedere*, to approach, come near.

<u>From same base</u>: accessory, accessible.

<u>Synonyms</u>: avenue, approach, path, passage, admission, entry.

process (PRAW-ces), a forward movement; a method of operating. From Latin *processus*, pp. of *procedere*, to move foward.

<u>From same base</u>: processor.

<u>Synonyms</u>: action, transaction, proceeding, performance, course, undertaking, venture, movement, operation, procedure.

<u>Antonyms</u>: inactivity, inertness, stagnation, passiveness, idleness, cessation, standstill, lethargy.

multiply (MUL-tih-ply), to increase in number. From Latin *multiplicare*, to increase many times.

<u>From same base</u>: multiplying, multiplied, multiplier, multiplicity.

<u>Synonyms</u>: increase, grow, redouble, magnify, surge, swell, rise, expand, extend, inflate, develop, amplify.

inconceivable (<u>in</u>-kun-SEE-vuh-bl), unbelievable. From negative prefix *in*, not, + Old French *conçeveir*, to conceive, to form in the mind.

<u>From same base</u>: inconceivably, inconceivableness, inconceivability.

<u>Synonyms</u>: incredible, unbelievable, strange, extraordinary, unlikely, rare, improbable, unimaginable, implausible, doubtful, questionable.

popularize (POP-yuh-luh-<u>ryz</u>), to cause to be liked. From Latin *popularis*, of a people (*populus*).

<u>From same base</u>: popularizing, popularized, popular, popularity, popularization.

<u>Synonyms</u>: restore, resurrect, revive, exploit, manipulate.

prospect (PROS-pekt), a chance for future success. From Latin *prospectus*, pp. of *prospicere*, to look ahead.

<u>From same base</u>: prospectus.

Synonyms: outlook, probability, expectation, expectancy, presumption, likelihood, view.

analyze (AN-ih-lyz), to determine the nature of, break into component parts. From Greek prefix *ana*, throughout, + *lysis*, a loosing.
From same base: analyzing, analyzed, analytic, analytical, analytically.
Synonyms: reason, conclude, deduce, reflect, deliberate, theorize, study, decide.

universal (yoo-nih-VUR-sul), pertaining to or typical of the whole under consideration. From Latin *universalis*, general, universal.
From same base: universalness.
Synonyms: general, entire, whole, complete, comprehensive, total, unlimited, boundless, exhaustive, widespread.
Antonyms: special, private, individual, distinctive, unique, limited, narrow, certain, partial, restricted, bounded, confined, small, abbreviated, curtailed.

discrimination (dih-SKRIM-ih-nay-shun), the act of distinguishing differences. From Latin *discriminatio*, a separating or dividing.
From same base: discriminatory, discriminator
Synonyms: acuteness, perception, caution, prudence, foresight, thoughtfulness, forethought, vigilance, care, heed, discernment, carefulness.
Antonyms: foolhardiness, rashness, temerity, haste, recklessness, imprudence, carelessness, negligence.

superiority (suh-peer-ee-OR-ih-tee), the state or quality of being higher, greater, better. From Latin comparative form *superior*, higher, of *superus*, over, above.
From same base: superior.
Synonyms: predominance, eminence, lead, excellence, rank, prevalence, advantage, power, influence, authority, prestige, position, supremacy, primacy, sovereignty, leadership.
Antonyms: inferiority, mediocrity, inadequacy, diffidence.

authority (uh-THOR-ih-tee), the state or right of being in command, in power. From Latin *auctoritas*, responsibility, power.
Synonyms: power, control, command, domination, mastery, supremacy, sovereignty, jurisdiction, sway, right, rule, prestige.

abundant (uh-BUN-dent), ample, abounding. From Latin *abundans*, prp. of *abundare* (prefix *ab*, away, + *undare*, to rise in waves), to overflow.
From same base: abundantly, abundance.
Synonyms: plentiful, ample, copious, profuse, opulent, flowing, lavish, full, rich, bountiful, bounteous, lavish.

abundance (uh-BUN-dense), a plentiful supply. (Same source as for abundant.)
Synonyms: affluence, flood, deluge, luxuriance, opulence, plenty, profusion, extravagance, bounty, lavishness.

auspicious (aw-SPISH-us), favorable, boding well for the future. From Latin *auspicium*, an omen, sign.
From same base: auspiciously, auspiciousness.
Synonyms: happy, lucky, promising, favorable, advantageous, timely, opportune, propitious.

convergence (kun-VUR-jense), the act, fact, or condition of coming together. From Latin *convergens*, prp. of *convergere*, to bend together.
From same base: convergent, convergency.
Synonyms: confluence, concourse, concurrence, concentration, meeting, encounter.

factor (FAK-tur), an element or cause contributing to a result. From *factus*, pp. of *facere*, to cause, bring about.
Synonyms: element, cause, instrument, means, aid, component, constituent.

engender (en-JEN-dur), to cause to exist, bring about, produce. From Latin *ingenerare*, to bring into being.
From same base: engendering, engendered.
Synonyms: produce, provide, yield, bear, cause, generate, bring about, result in, create, originate, devise, prepare.

prodigious (pruh-DIJ-us), enormous, extraordinary. From Latin *prodigiosus*, wonderful.
From same base: prodigiously, prodigiousness.

<u>Synonyms</u>: huge, enormous, extraordinary, strange, wonderful, immense, monstrous, vast, wonderful, great, amazing, marvelous, astonishing, miraculous, surprising, stupendous, indescribable, inconceivable, incredible, phenomenal, overwhelming, impressive.
<u>Antonyms</u>: common, commonplace, ordinary, small, meager, insignificant, petty, trivial, trifling, mean, poor, unimpressive, minor, slight, contracted.

frivolous (FRIV-uh-lus), lacking in importance, petty. From Latin, *frivolus*, trifling, worthless.
<u>From same base</u>: frivolously, frivolousness.
<u>Synonyms</u>: trifling, worthless, petty, unimportant, trivial, slight, silly, childish, inconsequential, inconclusive, small, paltry, insignificant, inconsiderable, futile, light, little, shallow, foolish, vain, idle.
<u>Antonyms</u>: serious, earnest, important, wise, witty, grave, solemn, weighty, formal, ceremonial, thoughtful, sound, deep, momentous, significant, relevant, dignified, essential, pertinent, applicable.

Language Uses and Abuses

Word-surfing with the Greek

Opposite the keys-to-meaning prefixes and c\forms below, write any words that come to mind. (If you have any problems, the Word Index shows the first page on which a particular term appears.)

ana	bio
syn, sym	anthrop
proto	tele
apo	arch
peri	phob, phobo
epi	astro
para	scope
eu	aut, auto

kata (cata)	pathy
hemi	ology
hetero	graph
mono	chron, chrono
pan	geo
dis, di	gram
deka (deca)	meter
anti	dem, demo

Quick Checks on Comprehension

In each line below, highlight or check off the word or phrase that best matches the meaning of the word to the left.

notable	unstable, rational, suitable, remarkable
access	passage, image, artifact, excess
process	ration, operation, infestation, subordination
multiply	mow, grow, flow, blow
inconceivable	unsightly, politely, unlikely, sprightly
popularize	inspect, suspect, elect, exploit
prospect	outlook, brook, opinion, proposal
analyze	synchronize, sympathize, conclude, preclude
universal	hostile, general, principal, agreeable
discrimination	foresight, oversight, refinement, defamation
superiority	destiny, infamy, efficacy, primacy
authority	tyranny, control, profligacy, endowment
abundant	ascendant, reticent, inspirational, bountiful
auspicious	opportune, immune, audacious, perspicacious
convergence	persiflage, confluence, consignment, vestige
factor	element, tenement, orator, mentor
engender	create, prosper, pretend, amend
prodigious	notorious, huge, staid, infectious
frivolous	monotonous, palatable, imminent, trivial

In each line below, highlight or check off the two synonyms.

futile, normal, painful, idle
amazing, great, protracted, subdued
induce, produce, field, yield
pause, lien, cause, means
encounter, escape, meeting, greeting
likely, lucky, happy, plucky
affluence, credence, effervescence, opulence
play, reality, sway, mastery
leadership, prestige, cohesion, leisure
prepare, heed, care, accede
original, haphazard, whole, entire
deduce, deny, decide, decry
asperity, inundation, probability, expectation
manipulate, exacerbate, probate, exploit
unassailable, doubtful, practical, improbable
release, increase, redouble, fumble
lethargy, idleness, suppleness, impropriety
pattern, edifice, entry, approach
apparent, shortened, evident, muddled

In each line below, highlight or check off the two antonyms.

striking, casting, ordinary, hereditary
settlement, movement, inactivity, complicity
curtailed, impaled, unlimited, unlearned
truculence, caution, unanimity, temerity
predominance, incidence, frequency, inadequacy
transient, volatile, wonderful, insignificant
silly, witty, kind, courageous

If unsure about your comprehension choices, please see Appendix A.

> In your vocabulary there'll be no detriment,
> if with new words you'll really experiment.

DAY 40

New Word-Choices
From Jeffrey R. Beir, speech on "Managing Creatives: Our Creative
Workers Will Excel—If We Let Them,"
Vital Speeches of the Day, 61 (June 1, 1995) 16, p. 502.

Many companies say "People are our most important asset," but
their actions don't live up to the claim. They act in ways that
minimize the contributions of their most productive employees. Even
from a cursory reading of the business press, we all know this
happens.

Many companies are also so obsessed with conformity that they
want to have rules for nonconformity. In contrast to this rigidity, the
leader of a creative team relies heavily on a knowledge of individuality
and diversity. The leader relies on an in-depth knowledge of each and
every member of the team, and of the dynamics and interaction of the
team. A richness of diversity on the team is a key ingredient of
innovation. And, if possible, a team should be contiguous—in one
physical location. And especially if it's a cross-functional team,
physical proximity is essential.

asset (AS-et), a useful or valuable person or thing. From Old French
assez, enough, sufficient.
Synonyms: possession, belonging, goods, stock, property, personnel,
riches, resources.

minimize (MIN-ih-myz), to lower the value or importance of. From
Latin *minimus*, least, + verb-forming suffix -ize.
From same base: minimizing, minimized, minimization.
Synonyms: depreciate, belittle, degrade, fault, detract, disparage,
derogate.

Antonyms: magnify, exalt, extol, praise, laud, applaud, acclaim.

cursory (KUR-suh-ree), rapid and superficial. From Late Latin *cursorius*, running.
From same base: cursorily, cursoriness.
Synonyms: hasty, rapid, superficial, slight, desultory, careless.
Antonyms: thorough, careful, meticulous, complete, perfect, thoroughgoing.

conformity (kun-FOR-mih-tee), action in accordance with rules, customs. From Middle Latin *conformitas* with same meaning.
Synonyms: accord, agreement, harmony, resemblance, likeness, decorum, observance, compliance, assent, submission, consent, obedience.
Antonyms: discord, disagreement, disobedience, divergence, conflict, dissension, dissidence, strife, friction.

rigidity (rih-JID-ih-tee), state of being inflexible, resistant to change. From Latin *rigidus*, stiff, unyielding.
From same base: rigidly, rigidness.
Synonyms: inflexibility, resistance, hardness, firmness, austerity, severity, strictness, harshness.
Antonyms: flexibility, mobility, tolerance, indulgence, clemency, mercy, leniency, kindness, suppleness.

individuality (in-dih-vij-oo-AL-ih-tee), a quality or trait that distinguishes one person from another. From Middle Latin *individualitas* with same meaning.

dynamics (dy-NAM-iks), the forces at work in any field. From Greek *dynamis*, power, authority (as distinguished from the Day 24 adjective *dynamic*, forceful, powerful).

interaction (in-tur-AK-shun), action between or on each other. From Latin prefix *inter*, between, among, + *actus*, pp. of *agere*, to act.
From same base: interactional.

ingredient (in-GREE-dee-ent), a component of anything; anything that enters into the composition of the whole. From Latin *ingrediens*, prp. of *ingredi*, to enter into.

Synonyms: part, component, element, base, basis, body, core, essence, nucleus, substance.
Antonyms: whole, aggregate, entirety, total, totality, unity.

contiguous (kun-TIG-yoo-us), close to one another or to another thing. From Latin *contiguus*, bordering upon.
From same base: contiguously, contiguousness.
Synonyms: near, close, immediate, near by, nigh, proximate, adjacent, bordering, next, adjoining.

functional (FUNGK-shuh-nul), designated for or suited to a particular duty or operation. (In combination with the word *cross*, cross-functional refers to a team responsible for a number of different functions.) From *functus*, pp. of *fungi*, to perform, discharge the duties of an office.
From same base: functionally.
Synonyms: practical, useful, utilitarian, serviceable, helpful, valuable, beneficial, worthy, advantageous, suitable, pragmatic, utilitarian.
Antonyms: wasteful, useless, worthless, futile, unavailing, inoperative, inadequate, inefficient, ineffectual, unproductive, unfruitful, fruitless.

proximity (prok-SIM-ih-tee), the state of being next or near. From Late Latin *proximatus*, pp. of *proximare*, to be near.
From same base: proximate.
Synonyms: nearness, vicinity, contiguity, adjacency, propinquity.
Antonyms: distance, remoteness, farness.

Language Uses and Abuses

Word-surfing with the Latin

Opposite the keys-to-meaning prefixes and c\forms below, write any words that come to mind. (If you have any problems, the Word Index shows the first page on which a particular term appears.)

circum	uni
ultra	mill, milli
contra	anni, enni

pre	semi
inter	corp, corpor
per	post
e, ex	ambi
super	magna, magni
con	extra
ab	scrib, scrip
sub	naut
intra	omni
ad	de
duo	cent

Quick Checks on Comprehension

In each line below, highlight or check off the word or phrase that best matches the meaning of the word to the left.

asset	obsession, possession, accession, impression
minimize	bewitch, belittle, bewail, bewilder
cursory	illusory, fearless, constrained, careless
conformity	accord, enormity, superiority, hoard
rigidity	complexity, austerity, firmness, fairness
ingredient	component, experiment, supplement, deterrent
functional	unusual, pragmatic, eccentric, experimental
proximity	emergency, utility, informality, adjacency
contiguous	performing, longing, consorting, adjoining

In each line below, highlight or check off the two synonyms.

practicability, nearness, plurality, contiguity
valuable, serviceable, impenetrable, unable
complacent, adjacent, hovering, bordering

case, spore, base, core
callousness, hardness, slowness, strictness
agreement, resolution, assent, persistence
bright, inescapable, superficial, slight
react, detract, depreciate, appreciate
attainments, riches, sources, resources

In each line below, highlight or check off the two antonyms.

laud, inspect, protect, fault
impartial, hasty, thorough, risky
harmony, patrimony, friction, apprehension
insistence, effervescence, resistance, tolerance
sobriety, part, cart, entirety
leading, weightless, worthy, useless
liquidity, vicinity, remoteness, timeliness

If unsure about your comprehension choices, please see Appendix A.

At a loss for words? That's frustration.
New words at the ready? That's elation!

Day 1—Comprehension Answers

Matching meanings:	Choosing synonyms:	Choosing antonyms:
explosive, resounding	bound, confined	hushed, deafening
prophesy, forecast	insult, attack	foretell, disappoint
outstrip, surmount	damage, injury	outdistance, retreat
detriment, drawback	eclipse, surpass	obstacle, advantage
epithet, invective	envision, predict	denunciation,
finite, fixed	eruptive, stunning	commendation
		limited, boundless

Day 2—Comprehension Answers

Matching meanings:	Choosing synonyms:	Choosing antonyms:
intriguing, fascinating	captivating, enchanting	uninteresting,
transformation,	calamitous, violent	attracting
modification	remarkable,	parted, consolidated
montage,	exceptional	separated,
composite of photos	conversion, change	desegregated
apocalyptic,	set apart, divided	
cataclysmic	merged, united	
unprecedented,		
extraordinary		
ethnically, racially		
segregated, separated		
integrated, unified		

Day 3—Comprehension Answers

Matching meanings:	Choosing synonyms:	Choosing antonyms:
deterrence, restraint	dissuasion, prevention	inducement,
alternative, option	selection, preference	discouragement
rehabilitation, renewal	revival renovation	constraint, choice
potential, possible	undeveloped,	restoration, demolition
dissuade, oppose	unrealized	latent, actual
disincentive, warning	hinder, deter	exhort, dishearten
severity, austerity	dissuasion, admonition	discouragement,
dramatic, exciting	gravity, austerity	inducement
courting, flattering	exciting, vivid	sternness, gentleness
fiscal, financial		uninteresting, striking
crisis, climax		

Day 4—Comprehension Answers

Matching meanings:	Choosing synonyms:	Choosing antonyms:

extrapolate, deduce
compose, write
comprehend,
  understand
emergence, issue
complexity, intricacy
enshrine, revere
inverse, opposite
expatriation,
  banishment
reversed, persisting
rejection, approval
	dismissal, expulsion
	overturned, reverted
	cherish, treasure
	involvement,
	  entanglement
	outbreak, eruption
	perceive, discern
	form, fashion
	conclude, decide
		arrange, scatter
		apprehend,
		  misinterpret
		exit, influx
		treasure, abhor

Day 5—Comprehension Answers

Matching meanings:	Choosing synonyms:	Choosing antonyms:

brilliantly
  intelligently
challenging,
  demanding
subversive, dissident
insightful, discerning
critic, analyst
trivial, frivolous
stunning, remarkable
inherent, characteristic
substance, essence
	indispensable,
	  inseparable
	impressive, astounding
	nonessential, trifling
	commentator, reviewer
	perceptive, intuitive
	seditious, perfidious
	requiring, exacting
	glowingly, brightly
		disruptive, supportive
		judicious, bewildered
		relevant, immaterial

Day 6—Comprehension Answers

Matching meanings:	Choosing synonyms:	Choosing antonyms:

intellectually,
  thoughtfully
acrimonious, bitter
priority, precedence
daunting, scaring
undiminished,
  extended
salience, prominence
	reflectively,
	  deliberately
	acerbic, severe
	antecedence,
	  precedence
	dismaying,
	  intimidating
	increased, prolonged
	noticeability,
	  emergence
		visibility, concealment
		lengthened, shortened
		assisting, frightening
		sharp, civil
		studiously, inanely

Day 7—Comprehension Answers

Matching meanings:	Choosing synonyms:	Choosing antonyms:
incremental, growing sophisticated, worldly expression, declaration obsolete, antique	time-worn, disused communication, designation polished, urbane developing, enhancing	artless, refined extending, eroding repression, utterance primitive, up-to-date

Day 8—Comprehension Answers

Matching meanings:	Choosing synonyms:	Choosing antonyms:
l extravagant, liberal aristocrat, socialite dominated, directed indulge, favor shrewd, cautious	prudent, guarded gratify, sustain controlled, supervised noble, blue blood extreme, excessive	stingy, lavish mastered, spirited nurture, thwart ignorant, cunnint

Day 9—Comprehension Answers

Matching meanings:	Choosing synonyms:	Choosing antonyms:
ineffable, inexpressible perceive, sense propitiate, placate component, part primordially, primitively secular, worldly manipulative, dominating	controlling, regulating mundane, earthly primevally, prehistorically segment, element conciliate, appease observe, discern unutterable, unspeakable	understand, misjudge traditionally, recently temporal, spiritual

Day 10—Comprehension Answers

Matching meanings:	Choosing synonyms:	Choosing antonyms:
litigator, claimant propitious, promising dichotomy, division egalitarian, democratic protestation, affirmation mandated, prescribed differentiation disparity infuse, instill	condition, requirement supporter, patron correction, revision inspire, inbue unlikeness, contrast enjoined, imposed objection, complaint friendly, considerate beneficial, providential	auspicious, discouraging commanded, petitioned variation, congruity

Day 10 (continued)

Matching meanings:	Choosing synonyms:	Choosing antonyms:
amendment, alteration guarantor, sponsor provision, stipulation		

Day 11—Comprehension Answers

Matching meanings:	Choosing synonyms:	Choosing antonyms:

commitment, pledge
commendably,
   laudably
philanthropy,
   compassion
adapting, conforming
genuine, tested
disparaging, belittling
indispensable,
   required
	essential, basic
	discrediting,
	   underrating
	harmonizing, fitting
	sympathy, charity
	approvingly,
	   praiseworthily
	promise, assignment
		kindness, greed
		dislocating,
		   accommodating
		questionable,
		   legitimate
		commending,
		   deprecating
		essential, uncalled for
		culpably, admirably

Day 12—Comprehension Answers

Matching meanings:	Choosing synonyms:	Choosing antonyms:

behavior, conduct
inflation, distention
generation, era
expansion, increase
implication,
   involvement
generalized, broad
	widespread, extensive
	inference, connection
	dilation, development
	creation, reproduction
	swelling, distention
	manners, deportment
		shrinking, dilation
		production, demolition
		decrease, enlargement
		entanglement,
		   separation

Day 13—Comprehension Answers

Matching meanings:	Choosing synonyms:	Choosing antonyms:

barrier, restraint
status, rank
perception, sensitivity
impression, feeling
dignitary, high official
utmost, greatest
mission, delegation
unanimously,
   harmoniously
arrogant, disdainful
	haughty, imperious
	conformably,
	   consistently
	deputation, legation
	conception, thought
	comprehension,
	   understanding
	standing, position
	obstacle, bulwark
		obstruction, passage
		sensation, apathy
		overbearing, servile

Day 14—Comprehension Answers

Matching meanings:	Choosing synonyms:	Choosing antonyms:
resolving, concluding	insupportable,	invasion, submission
aggression, attack	unrelievable	opposition, permission
tyranny, despotism	firmness, steadfastness	unsteadiness, firmness
intolerance, restraint	degeneracy, disgrace	needless, essential
stability, constancy	demoralization,	procreation,
vital, obligatory	discouragement	barrenness
proliferation,	required, imperative	dissuasion,
productivity	hindrance, censure	encouragement
terrorism, intimidation	autocracy, dictatorship	dismissal, admiration
degradation, dishonor	deciding, determining	favorable, unbearable
unsustainable,	fertility, creativity	
unendurable	offense, hostility	

Day 15—Comprehension Answers

Matching meanings:	Choosing synonyms:	Choosing antonyms:
cynicism, distrust	revocation, confutation	doubt, credence
passivity, docility	anger, corrode	compliance, defiance
unabashedly, boldly	embrace, comprise	fearlessly, timidly
committed, delegated	sweeping, common	desisted, assigned
wondrous, astonishing	joining, cooperating	astonishing, expected
participatory, sharing	surprising, amazing	sporadic, general
prevailing, general	promised, entrusted	
embody, contain	bravely, daringly	
fret, agitate	humility, submission	
negativism, denial	skepticism, suspicion	

Day 16—Comprehension Answers

Matching meanings:	Choosing synonyms:	Choosing antonyms:
vulnerable, helpless	polite, affable	unprotected, secure
inevitability, certainty	voluble, persuasive	surety, confusion
compromise,	detractor, adversary	strife, compromise
settlement	scorn, animosity	consensus, objection
consensus, agreement	rebuke, reprobation	commendation,
critical, crucial	debate, discussion	condemnation
discourse, conference	grave, serious	passion, humility
objurgation, criticism	compliance,	companion, competitor
indignation, acrimony	acquiescence	deterring, inciting
antagonist, rival	concession,	boorish, urbane
eloquent, inducing	accommodation	
civil, mannerly	sureness, definiteness	
	unguarded, exposed	

Day 17—Comprehension Answers

Matching meanings:	Choosing synonyms:	Choosing antonyms:
innate, natural	ingrained, inseparable	superficial, intrinsic
inspiration, sensation	endless, unremitting	understanding,
integral, necessary	preoccupied,	indifference
affinity, linkage	unobservant	essential, deficient
exclusively, entirely	hindrance, impediment	isolation, affiliation
obstacle, barrier	wholly, completely	obstruction, assistance
obsessed, absorbed	attachment, connection	occasional, ceaseless
incessant, unending	total, vital	extrinsic, inseparable
inherent, native	impulse, emotion	
	congenital, ingrained	

Day 18—Comprehension Answers

Matching meanings:	Choosing synonyms:	Choosing antonyms:
magnificent, stately	nullify, demolish	plain, majestic
vitality, vigor	wrest, compel	strength, lethargy
totter, falter	partition,	lurch, stroll
splinter, break	apportionment	crush, restore
disastrous, harmful	calamitous,	privileged, unfortunate
dismemberment,	catastrophic	wring, straighten
impairment	shatter, smash	restore, quash
wrench, twist	stagger, waver	
abolish, revoke	energy, stamina	
	brilliant, imposing	

Day 19—Comprehension Answers

Matching meanings:	Choosing synonyms:	Choosing antonyms:
infuriate, provoke	conclusion, outcome	soothe, agitate
advocate, champion	poor, indigent	thwart, favor
independent, separate	unbound, unleashed	alone, dependent
terminate, close	uncertainty, hesitation	conclude, initiate
incompetent, incapable	bold, firm	informed, inexpert
courageous, intrepid	bungling, inept	timid, determined
irresponsibility,	cease, desist	indecision,
unreliability	free, sovereign	responsibility
unfettered, unchecked	defend, recommend	unchained, restricted
impoverished, needy	anger, inflame	beggared, affluent
decision, judgment		deferment, disposal

Day 20—Comprehension Answers

Matching meanings:	Choosing synonyms:	Choosing antonyms:
sanction, approve	oversight, apathy	denounce, commend
intrusion, infringement	creed, persuasion	wariness,
ingenuity,	creative, inventive	inquisitiveness
inventiveness	laxity, instability	shrewdness, stupidity
creativity, originality	perplexed, confounded	invention, imitation
flexible, adaptable	impeded, thwarted	tractable, unyielding
accountability, liability	disability, incapacity	punishability,
inability, impotence	liability, responsibility	blamelessness
sustained, assisted	pliant, docile	futility, efficiency
distracted, diverted	imagination, enterprise	maintained, impaired
tenacity, persistence	cleverness, wisdom	pleased, puzzled
constructive,	shyness, caution	fragility, toughness
productive	allow, authorize	ingenious, unoriginal
conviction, assumption		opinion, doubt
tendency, bias		aim, negligence

Day 21—Comprehension Answers

Matching meanings:	Choosing synonyms:	Choosing antonyms:
ultimate, eventual	abolition, annihilation	decline, ascendancy
casualty, victim	void, vacant	exact, ambiguous
degeneration	expression, declaration	humble, enhance
degradation	indicate, mean	defile, cleanse
precise, definite	payment, stipend	allowance, emolument
debase, abase	way, approach	signal, nullify
oratory, discourse	improvement,	
adulterate,	embellishment	
contaminate	confuse, corrupt	
enhancement, increase	speech, eloquence	
technique, system	shame, impair	
compensation, gain	rigorous, austere	
signify, disclose	disgrace, decay	
utterance, assertion	sufferer, pawn	
vacuous, inane		
extraction, destruction		

Day 22—Comprehension Answers

Matching meanings:	Choosing synonyms:	Choosing antonyms:
lofty, eminent	sustain, train	arrogant, unassuming
lethal, mortal	rude, brutal	deathly, healthful
isolationism, seclusion	aptness, genius	unruly, tolerant
contentious, irritable	league, union	uniformity, conflict
harmony, accord	inability, inadequacy	efficiency, inadequacy

Day 22 (continued)

Matching meanings:	Choosing synonyms:	Choosing antonyms:
capability, skill	concord, unanimity	dispute, alliance
coalition, compact	fiery, impetuous	cruel, gentle
capacity, ability	insulation, segregation	
humanitarian,	deadly, destructive	
charitable	reserved, timid	
nurture, foster		

Day 23—Comprehension Answers

Matching meanings:	Choosing synonyms:	Choosing antonyms:
alleviate, lessen	power, impetus	mitigate, aggravate
disharmony, conflict	surpass, prevail	accord, contention
creed, belief	disciplinary, avenging	faith, doubt
moderate, temperate	connection, link	steady, intemperate
doctrinaire, unbending	illegal, prohibited	positive, indecisive
opposition,	habit, convention	support, counteraction
confrontation	hindrance, censure	variance, conformity
distinction, difference	severed, divergent	remotest, adjacent
ultimate, final	fate, chance	identical, distinct
initiative,	inauguration,	respect, restraint
commencement	beginning	unlawful, authorized
destiny, finality	terminal, extreme	separation, cohesion
mutual, common	feature, marking	revengeful, forgiving
tolerance, indulgence	checking, thwarting	vigor, weakness
tradition, custom	opinionated,	
legitimate, valid	domineering	
adherence, attachment	lenient, reasonable	
punitive, corrective	credence, trust	
transcend, exceed	disorder, strife	
momentum, force	abate, reduce	

Day 24—Comprehension Answers

Matching meanings:	Choosing synonyms:	Choosing antonyms:
receptive, interested	action, undertaking	strict, negligent
precise, exact	condense, constrict	destroy, compose
constitute, form	like, resembling	similarity, unlikeness
identity, oneness	mighty, energetic	superbly, defectively
peerlessly, uniquely	shift, turn	contemptible,
delicate, sensitive	gentle, refined	fastidious
transition, change	perfectly,	conversion, stability
dynamic, forceful	incomparably	impotent, vigorous
diverse, varied	unity, affinity	

Day 24 (continued)

Matching meanings:	Choosing synonyms:	Choosing antonyms:
compress, contract transaction, proceeding	formulate, draw up genuine, authentic acceptable, welcome	harmonious, discordant diminish, magnify

Day 25—Comprehension Answers

Matching meanings:	Choosing synonyms:	Choosing antonyms:

conclusively,
   decisively
controlling, guiding
materially, solidly
achievement, deed
delinquency, laxness
emotional, moving
adequate, satisfactory
alter, transform
objective, goal
experimentation,
   testing
formation, devising
acute, critical
escalating, growing
	increasing, expanding
	penetrating, sharp
	proving, verifying
	beginning, inception
	modify, reduce
	capable, qualified
	inflaming,
	   overpowering
	omission, neglect
	exploit, act
	substantially,
	   materially
	abandoning, forsaking
		giving up, directing
		tangibly, spiritually
		cessation, completion
		laxness, care
		temperamental,
		   apathetic
		suited, unqualified
		change, preserve
		severe, uncritical
		surging, diminishing

Day 26—Comprehension Answers

Matching meanings:	Choosing synonyms:	Choosing antonyms:

immigration, inflow
emerge, leave
passionately, intensely
taint, stain
systematically,
   uniformly
unquestioned,
   accepted
evolve, extend
fundamental, principal
obeisance, respect
observation,
   compliance
alien, strange
mutation, change
arbitrate, decide
	settle, conclude
	variation, deviation
	congenial, friendly
	observance, adherence
	homage, deference
	essential, intrinsic
	disclose, uncover
	obscure, vague
	normally, ordinarily
	tint, color
	fervently, ardently
	depart, withdraw
	entrance, incoming
		ingress, exit
		migrate, remain
		stolidly, vehemently
		habitually, casually
		doubtful, evident
		extend, curtail
		nonessential, basic
		reverence, disrespect
		acknowledgment,
		   evasion
		hostile, akin
		conversion, stability
		determine, waver

Day 27—Comprehension Answers

Matching meanings:	Choosing synonyms:	Choosing antonyms:
perennial, lasting	reality, fact	ephemeral, ceaseless
grotesquely, strangely	pious, self-righteous	unnaturally, normally
culture, education	substantially,	refinement,
variant, mutation	markedly	boorishness
imbued, inspired	boast, exult	deviation, uniformity
impetuous, headstrong	likeness, duplicate	inspired, unimpressed
exotic, entrancing	patrimony, birthright	violent, placid
tumult, uproar	estimate, measure	commotion,
assess, evaluate	restraint, patience	tranquillity
heritage, legacy	striking, enthralling	conformity, diversity
parallel, similarity	calm, placid	dream, event
trumpet, bluster	saturated, suffused	
incommensurably,	conformity, sameness	
immeasurably	learning, knowledge	
sanctimonious,	oddly, absurdly	
feigning	unfailing, endless	
illusion, apparition		

Day 28—Comprehension Answers

Matching meanings:	Choosing synonyms:	Choosing antonyms:
progressively,	creative, ingenious	cheat, validate
enterprisingly	equivalence,	seize, replace
betray, deceive	parallelism	abolish, establish
dispossess, deprive	conceal, screen	adverse, agreeable
eradicate, devastate	discontinue, desist	resistance, assistance
immigrant, foreigner	cooperation, support	compete, quit
fashion, fabricate	unfriendly, inimical	uncover, conceal
hostile, belligerent	form, mold	evenness, disparity
rivalry, opposition	settler, pioneer	fertile, unfruitful
contend, struggle	uproot, remove	
disguise, conceal	evict, dislodge	
equality ,parity	delude, mislead	
productive, inventive	forward, onward	

Day 29—Comprehension Answers

Matching meanings:	Choosing synonyms:	Choosing antonyms:
excellence, goodness	evidently, apparently	quality, mediocrity
appreciate, revere	deficit, shortage	enjoy, condemn
crass, coarse	clumsily, awkwardly	polished, crude
indictable,	depraved, immoral	censurable, excusable
blameworthy	obstruct, impede	regulation, disorder
compute, reckon	stride, step	

Day 29 (continued)

Matching meanings:	Choosing synonyms:	Choosing antonyms:
discipline, drill	snarl, shambles	secondary, fundamental
essential, vital	intrinsic, basic	
disrupt, derange	method, order	harmony, confusion
chaos, confusion	calculate, figure	promote, obstruct
pace, gait	culpable, blameful	firm, weak
abet, uphold	elegant, refined	cleverly, foolishly
lax, slack	reject, despise	shortcoming, adequacy
subtly, finely	superiority, merit	ambiguously, distinctly
deficiency, scarcity		
patently, manifestly		

Day 30—Comprehension Answers

Matching meanings:	Choosing synonyms:	Choosing antonyms:
translate, reword	standard, gauge	render, misread
outmoded, timeworn	combining, fusing	unfashionable, modern
inconsistent, unsteady	notion, opinion	contrary, constant
banish, dismiss	soulful, sentimental	exile, accept
professional, efficient	liable, susceptible	upshot, origin
translate, reword	standard, gauge	render, misread
outmoded, timeworn	combining, fusing	unfashionable, modern
inconsistent, unsteady	notion, opinion	contrary, constant
banish, dismiss	soulful, sentimental	exile, accept
professional, efficient	liable, susceptible	upshot, origin
consequence, outcome	helping, serving	
balanced, uniform	exploit, utilize	
capitalize, adopt	stable, poised	
instrumental, conducive	origin, source	
expressive, eloquent	practical, methodical	
sensitive, prone	expel, ostracize	
concept, idea	varying, inconstant	
blending, merging	outdated, obsolete	
norm, yardstick	change, convert	

Day 31—Comprehension Answers

Matching meanings:	Choosing synonyms:	Choosing antonyms:
primeval, prehistoric	corresponding, correlative	novel, antique
diversity, variety		disparity, conformity
conspicuous, prominent	contact, connection	obscure, well-known
	attractive, delightful	predisposed, unaffected
susceptible, predisposed	conservation, safekeeping	besmirch, defend

Day 31 (continued)

Matching meanings:	Choosing synonyms:	Choosing antonyms:
malign, revile	significance, concern	entire, piece
remnant, residue	surplus, remainder	revolting, irresistible
emphasis, importance	vilify, libel	
preservation,	open, prone	
protection	striking, outstanding	
charismatic, magnetic	difference, unlikeness	
relationship, linkage	ancient, traditional	
reciprocal, matching		

Day 32—Comprehension Answers

Matching meanings:	Choosing synonyms:	Choosing antonyms:
inexorably,	nobly, worthily	questionably,
unavoidably	wild, savage	inescapably
proportion, percentage	curbed, checked	segment, whole
astound, shock	applaud, approve	destitute, prosperous
affluent, opulent	harass, irritate	doubt, assurance
security, shelter	asylum, safety	laud, berate
plague, badger	indigent, poor	unbridled, confined
extol, commend	dumfound, amaze	domesticated, untamed
unrestrained,	quota, portion	exaltedly, pitifully
unhindered	certainty, surely	
domestic, native		
abjectly, basely		

Day 33—Comprehension Answers

Matching meanings:	Choosing synonyms:	Choosing antonyms:
position, station	clash, slam	deferment,
adopt, assume	experience, seasoning	continuance
suspension, delay	unfair, slanted	entreat, decree
expulsion, eviction	process, operation	idleness, action
collective, mutual	qualification,	
mandate, dictate	stipulation	
provision, condition	prescribe, enjoin	
procedure, plan	common, joint	
prejudiced, bigoted	ouster, removal	
expertise, background	cessation, interruption	
impact, collision	embrace, approve	
	posture, standing	

Day 34—Comprehension Answers

Matching meanings:	Choosing synonyms:	Choosing antonyms:
intrinsic, inherent	machine, design	essential, incidental
dignity, decency	original, creative	alarming, trifling
dire, dreadful	colossal, gigantic	foresee, doubt
incendiary, flammable	collect, amass	guard, expose
commissioned,	imperil, endanger	assemble, scatter
assigned	grandeur, sublimity	paltry, great
anticipate, predict	celebrate,	
poignant, intense	commemorate	
memorialize, honor	sharp, acute	
nobility, gentility	expect, hope	
jeopardize, risk	entrusted, empowered	
accumulate, hoard	blazing, fiery	
enormous, immense	shocking, appalling	
innovative, inventive	decorum, propriety	
device, contrivance	inbred, ingrained	

Day 35—Comprehension Answers

Matching meanings:	Choosing synonyms:	Choosing antonyms:
inhabitant, native	quarrel, argument	divide, combine
subdue, overcome	restrain, check	astute, confused
sequester, isolate	express, convey	concentration, apathy
bondage, serfdom	rigidity, tautness	withhold, release
stamina, energy	force, vigor	
voluntarily,	shrewd, sagacious	
deliberately	spread, prevalent	
mingle, merge	combine, blend	
pervasive, widespread	spontaneously, freely	
penetrating, piercing	power, might	
intensity, strength	slavery, subjection	
tension, stress	scatter, disperse	
vent, reveal	vanquish, defeat	
repress, coerce	dweller, cohabitant	
controversy, dispute		

Day 36—Comprehension Answers

Matching meanings:	Choosing synonyms:	Choosing antonyms:
contemporary, present	disturbed, annoyed	influential, powerless
predominant,	concord, harmony	valid, counterfeit
prevailing	bank, shore	scorn, inspire
spurious, faked	roaming, rambling	seize, defend
declaration,	uniting, binding	pushing, postponing
affirmation	chaos, tumult	border, area

Day 36 (continued)

Matching meanings:	Choosing synonyms:	Choosing antonyms:
ridicule, taunt	obstructing, impeding	acrimony, amity
assaulting, encroaching	refresh, revive	
coherence, unity	almost, well-nigh	
idiosyncrasy, feature	malevolent, malicious	
pounce (on), seize	grasp, clutch	
vindictive, spiteful	temperament, disposition	
virtually, nearly	cohesion, adherence	
rally, convene	invade, violate	
accelerating, quickening	mock, flout	
turmoil, confusion	presentation, proclamation	
connective, joining	concocted, fabricated	
prowling, ranging	directing, governing	
margin, brow	coexistent, topical	
resentment, vexation		
agitated, aroused		

Day 37—Comprehension Answers

Matching meanings:	Choosing synonyms:	Choosing antonyms:
increment, increase	display, assemblage	extension, contraction
imperceptible, minimal	confusing, confounding	lasting, tenuous
substantial, consequential	validated, corroborated	move, pause
survey, observe	fabulous, celebrated	fanciful, authentic
deviation, divergence	victim, pawn	
progress, advance	swing, deviate	
veer, swerve	grow, develop	
casualty, victim	difference, variation	
legendary, mythical	study, review	
veritable, certified	solid, compact	
dazzling, astonishing	minute, insignificant	
array, collection	gain, addition	

Day 38—Comprehension Answers

Matching meanings:	Choosing synonyms:	Choosing antonyms:
aspect, view	bargaining, consulting	conviction, skepticism
doctrine, belief	territory, area	assuage, intensify
challenge, claim	teamwork, cooperation	harsh, soothing
escalation, expansion	accuracy, correctness	
conflagration, conflict	rigorous, severe	

Day 38 (continued)

Matching meanings:	Choosing synonyms:	Choosing antonyms:
abate, reduce	compel, drive	
embargo, ban	exclusion, rejection	
entail, require	alleviate, allay	
austere, stern	strife, dispute	
precision, exactness	increase, growth	
coordination, union	demand, requirement	
terrain, region	precept, principle	
negotiation arranging	vista, prospect	

Day 39—Comprehension Answers

Matching meanings:	Choosing synonyms:	Choosing antonyms:
notable, remarkable	futile, idle	striking, ordinary
access, passage	amazing, great	movement, inactivity
process, operation	produce, yield	curtailed, unlimited
increase, redouble	cause, means	caution, temerity
inconceivable,	encounter, meeting	predominance,
unlikely	lucky, happy	inadequacy
popularize, exploit	affluence, opulence	wonderful,
prospect, outlook	sway, mastery	insignificant
analyze, conclude	leadership, prestige	silly, witty
universal, general	heed, care	
egalitarian, equitable	neutral, fair	
discrimination,	whole, entire	
foresight	deduce, decide	
superiority, primacy	probability,	
authority, control	expectation	
abundant, bountiful	manipulate, restore	
auspicious, opportune	doubtful, improbable	
convergence,	increase, redouble	
confluence	lethargy, idleness	
factor, element	entry, approach	
engender, create	apparent, evident	
prodigious, huge		
frivolous, trivial		

Day 40—Comprehension Answers

Matching meanings:	Choosing synonyms:	Choosing antonyms:
asset, possession	nearness, contiguity	laud, fault
minimize, belittle	valuable, serviceable	hasty, thorough
cursory, careless	adjacent, bordering	harmony, friction
conformity, accord	base, core	resistance, tolerance
rigidity, firmness	hardness, strictness	part, entirety

Day 40 (continued)

Matching meanings:	Choosing synonyms:	Choosing antonyms:
ingredient, component	agreement, assent	worthy, useless
contiguous, adjoining	superficial, slight	vicinity, remoteness
functional, pragmatic	detract, depreciate	
proximity, adjacency	riches, resources	

APPENDIX B

The Indo-European Family of Languages

English and the other "western languages" with which we are familiar go back to a common ancestor. We call that early source "Indo-European" because its descendants are found both in or near India (Sanscrit, Iranian) and in Europe (Greek, Latin, and the Germanic, Celtic, Slavic, and Baltic groups.) There are, of course, many languages lying outside the Indo-European family (e.g., Egyptian, Basque, the Semitic languages, Chinese, and the native languages of Africa and the Americas),

Developing from that Indo-European base, English owes both its structure and its basic vocabulary to the Germanic group of languages: German, Dutch, Danish, Swedish, and Norwegian. Over the centuries, however, that basic vocabulary has been augmented by thousands of Latin words, some of them directly from Latin and some of them through the Latin-based languages (French, Italian, Spanish, Portuguese, and Romanian). Hundreds of Greek words have also been added, many of them through Latin.

So it is that words of Germanic origin make up about 30% of our vocabulary, Latin and Latin-based 55%, and Greek 10%. The remaining 5% come from other languages, "coined words," etc. Beyond our basic Germanic vocabulary, then, our language is 65% Latin and Greek. Beginning with three English words as examples, the common ancestry of Indo-European languages is evident:

English	me	is	mother
Sanscrit	ma	asti	matar
Iranian	ma	asti	matar
Greek	me	esti	meter
Latin	me	est	mater
Old Irish	me	is	mathir
Lithuanian	mi	esti	mote
Russian	menya	jest	mat

The "parent languages" above are related, but none is derived directly from another in that list. Here are some examples of words derived from one of those languages, in this instance, Latin:

Latin parent	Italian	Spanish	French	English meaning
amicus	amico	amigo	ami	friend
liber	libro	libro	livre	book
tempus	tempo	tiempo	temps	time
manus	mano	mano	main	hand
bonus	buono	bueno	bon	good
dicere	dire	decir	dire	to speak
legere	leggere	leer	lire	to read
filius	figlio	hijo	fils	son

Examples in both lists above from Frederic M. Wheelock's <u>Latin: An Introductory Course Based on Ancient Authors</u>, 3rd ed. (New York, NY: Barnes and Noble Books, 1963), p. xx f.

Frederick Bodmer's <u>Loom of Language</u> is a comprehensive history of the development of Indo-Europoean languages and of the relationships existing among them. (For complete citation, please see Bibliography.)

BIBLIOGRAPHY

Dictionaries, general

Funk & Wagnalls Standard Dictionary. 2nd ed. New York, NY: Harper Paperbacks Div. of Harper Collins, 1993.

Merriam-Webster's Collegiate Dictionary. 10th ed. Springfield, MA: Merriam-Webster, Incorporated, 1993.

Webster's New World Dictionary of the American Language. 2nd College Ed. Editor-in-Chief, David B. Guralnik. New York, NY: The World Publishing Company, 1970.

Dictionaries, Greek and Latin

An Intermediate Greek-English Lexicon (based on Liddell and Scott's Greek-English Lexicon). Oxford, England: The Clarendon Press, 1983.

Cassell's Latin Dictionary. Editor D.P. Simpson. New York, NY: Macmillan Publishing, 1968.

Dictionaries, special

Devlin, Joseph. A Dictionary of Synonyms and Antonyms. Editor Jerome Fried. New York, NY: Warner Books, 1987 (2nd Warner Book printing).

Roget's II: The New Thesaurus. By the Editors of The American Heritage Dictionary. Boston, MA: Houghton Mifflin, 1988.

General interest

Bodmer, Frederick. The Loom of Language. Editor Lancelot Hogben. London, England: George Allen & Unwin, Ltd, 1945.

Fowler, H. Ramsey (with the editors of Little, Brown). The Little, Brown Handbook. 2nd ed. Boston, MA: Little, Brown and Company, 1983.

WORD INDEX

Note: c\form indicates a combining form.

E

F

About the author...

Ray Nadeau has taught vocabulary-building in continuing-education programs at Rollins College, Winter Park, Florida, and at Seminole Community College, Sanford, Florida.

His background includes a B.A. (English-Speech major, Latin-Greek minor) from Northern Michigan University, an M.A. (Latin major, Greek minor) from Catholic University of America, and a Ph.D. (Rhetoric and Public Address) from the University of Michigan.

After having taught speech communication at the University of Illinois for fourteen years, Nadeau was appointed head of the Department of Communication at Purdue University in 1964. He held that post for ten years and then continued to teach at Purdue for another four.

Besides writing a monograph and many journal articles, he has written three communication textbooks and is the primary author of a fourth. He has also written and produced business-industrial advertising which received six readership awards.

WITHDRAWN   6/02